ENGLISH IN USE

Randolph Quirk
University College London

Gabriele Stein
University of Heidelberg

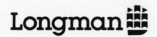

Longman Group UK Limited,
*Longman House, Burnt Mill, Harlow,
Essex CM20 2JE, England
and Associated Companies throughout the world.*

© Longman Group UK Limited 1990

First published 1990
Second impression 1990

Set in 10/12 point Palatino, Linotron

Printed in England by Clays Ltd, St Ives plc

ISBN 0 582 06613 1 paper
    0 582 06612 3 cased.

Preface

Given the great complexity of the English language, its multiplicity of roles, and its unparalleled extent of use worldwide as a medium of international communication, it is a formidable task to write a book on *English in Use*. Our aim has been to promote a mature and informed approach to the language, so that readers can understand something of the nature of English, be encouraged to use it more intelligently, respond to it more sensitively, and recognise more completely the implications of its international use today. We have sought to satisfy the natural curiosity about language that is there in every one of us, and to supply the kind of information that R G Latham — one of Britain's first professors of English, over a century and half ago — claimed should be the familiar equipment of every educated person.

We have written the book much in the spirit of *The Use of English*, though we have pursued the subject at somewhat greater depth and with rather more pronounced concern to help readers respond to the need for accurate and sensitively appropriate communication in an ever increasingly interdependent world. If, in the process, we have also encouraged readers to enjoy good English well used, and to take personal pride in the way they use it themselves, we shall be more than satisfied.

RQ
University College London

GS
University of Heidelberg   April 1990

Contents

C H A P T E R 1

Language at work and play

Language is so closely bound up with our everyday experience that we seldom stop to think of the roles it plays. In a well-known passage in his *Lives of the English Poets*, Dr Johnson says that 'Language is the dress of thought', and it has become commonplace to quote this in support of the view that conscious thought is behind all language, and that language is primarily used to 'dress up' thoughts and send them on their way: give *substance* to thoughts. 'Language', we are often told, 'exists for the expression of thoughts or ideas.'

There could be wide disagreement over what an idea or a thought exactly is, and therefore over the meaning of such a definition. But most of us would probably agree at any rate that the following quotation illustrates language being used 'for the expression of thoughts or ideas':

> The physicist Planck asserted that the energy of radiation is given out by a radiating body discontinuously, in definite fixed amounts or quanta, these being proportional to the frequency of the vibrations.

Most of us would equally agree that this statement of quantum theory represents a genuine, very important, and perhaps even very common use of language. We are not all physicists, but we all have to express serious 'thoughts or ideas' on this level from time to time, giving conscious thought to the language we are using:

> When the Grand Alliance had been formed, Louis recognised the impossibility of defeating his enemies on the Continent in any decisive fashion and ordered his Marshals to stand mainly on the defensive.

This novelist's concern is predominantly with the physical and mental growth of her characters, their subjection to accident, and to some extent their cyclic fluctuations of behaviour as circumstances come near to repeating themselves.

Some drugs, such as senega, act as stimulating expectorants because they increase the flow of blood which in turn increases the amount of the expectoration in the bronchial tubes and so aids its removal.

They must have known I had something on my mind, something I needed to talk about, but as we walked through the park that spring morning, they seemed determined to keep the conversation impersonal and give me no opening.

Genuine and even commonplace as these examples are, without doubt, we may well ask: are they what language is chiefly and primarily used for, what language 'exists for'? It may be illuminating at this point if we try to think back over a day's events and recall just how we have in fact been using our language. Calling someone to get up; singing to oneself in the bathroom; asking if breakfast is ready; grumbling about the weather or about where that other sock has disappeared to; teasing someone; appealing for help to open a sauce bottle. It would be stretching the meaning of 'thoughts or ideas' a very long way to make it cover all these language activities, yet we can be fairly confident that they bulk large in the daily use of language by any of us, whether we are company directors or school children.

We may get some confirmation that this is so by further reflecting that these uses of language seem 'easier', seem to come more naturally, than the examples dealing with careful 'thoughts or ideas' which were quoted earlier. We can surely agree that all of us find it easier to ask for more coffee or grumble about our work than to discourse on literary criticism, expectorants, or Louis XIV. And we should realise that this is not merely because some of these particular subjects are beyond our competence: it would still be true if for 'expectorants' we substituted the name of our favourite hobby.

It would be a big mistake to dismiss the 'easy' uses of language as trivial and unimportant merely because they seem so ordinary. Indeed, the more ordinary they seem, the more obvious it should be that we start from them in considering the use of English or any other language. If they seem ordinary, it is this very fact that makes the use of English seem difficult when we are writing an essay or describing some complicated electronic theory: difficult because unfamiliar and *extra*ordinary. And again, at the risk of being repetitive and obvious, we must stress that it is not that the *subject* is 'unfamiliar and extraordinary'. We may have a perfectly clear understanding of the experiment, and the essay may be on our favourite hobby. It is the use to which we are putting our language that is unfamiliar.

A bus driver, a ten-year-old, and a new graduate may be equally skilful in teasing, shouting instructions on the games-field, grumbling — or even swearing. They may be as skilful as each other or as Margaret Drabble or George Bush in any of these uses of language. But their skill will probably be unequal when it comes to drafting a letter, writing a report, or making a formal speech, because these last — for all their importance — are relatively rare and sophisticated uses of language. They might fairly be called 'exotic' — a term particularly apt for *written* language, in which we all need special training, which cannot be said to 'come naturally', and which has its own set of special rules and conventions.

However exotic or complicated the uses to which we have to put our language, we must all start from that common skill in the 'ordinary' and 'natural' uses of spoken language which we share with the bus driver and Margaret Drabble. Moreover, since all the uses — exotic or ordinary — require to some extent different kinds of English, we need to increase our consciousness of the quite distinct uses of English that we hear or read daily. Thereby we improve our sensitivity to occasion and improve also our command over the range of English.

'Language exists to express our thoughts.' We have seen some of the reasons for questioning this sweeping generalisation. There are several others. Voltaire is among those who have been cynical about language: People, he said, 'n'emploient les paroles que pour déguiser leurs pensées'. Goldsmith has a similar comment: 'The true use of speech is not so much to express our wants as to conceal them.' The Danish philosopher Kierkegaard went one better even than this: People use language not merely to conceal their thoughts, he said, but to conceal the fact that they have no thoughts.

Language functions

Among the many attempts at categorising language functions, let us look at the one suggested by the distinguished linguist Roman Jakobson (1896–1982). He postulated six 'factors' in human communication:

- the speaker
- the addressee
- the code — that is, the conventions (words, grammar, etc) of the language common to speaker and addressee
- the message — what the speaker says in the 'code'
- the context — the things, qualities, actions that the speaker wants to talk about
- the contact — the relations between speaker and addressee

Directly related to these 'factors' are Jakobson's six functions:

1 **Emotive** (*speaker*-related): The speaker seeks to express feeling, as in 'I'm terribly sorry about your father's illness' or 'How marvellous that your daughter has passed her law exam.'

2 **Conative** (*addressee*-related): The speaker seeks the achievement of a goal, as in 'Two tickets for this evening's performance, please.'

3 **Metalingual** (related to the form of the *code*): The speaker is talking, for example, in English about English, as in 'What's the plural of *syllabus*?' or 'That sounds unkind; let me rephrase it.'

4 **Poetic** (related to the form of the *message*): Though not necessarily in verse, the message is intended to catch the eye or ear with an aesthetic impact, as in 'Wash whiter with WHIZ!'

5 **Referential** (*context*-related): The primary concern of the message is with information, as in 'Hilda's plane was delayed in Houston' or 'I am staying at the Grafton Hotel' or 'What is the atomic weight of mercury?'

6 **Phatic** (*contact*-related): The speaker's focus is upon achieving a relationship with the addressee, as in 'Good morning, Bill' or 'Nice to see you' or 'Thank you very much indeed' or 'Not at all — you're welcome.' But we can also regard as phatic such formulaic uses of language as in testing an address system ('One, two, three . . .').

We shall have more to say about language functions as we consider English in use throughout this book, but for the moment let us just make clear that these functions are not necessarily divided off in separate watertight compartments. An utterance may readily involve several functions simultaneously; for example, phatic, referential, and implicitly conative functions in:

> Sorry to be a nuisance, Molly darling, but Jack has an awful headache and we don't seem to have any aspirins.

It may be helpful at this point to draw attention to the distinction between 'language' and '*a* language'. Language in the abstract is our capacity to talk to each other; it is the faculty of speech, which all human beings (except an unfortunate few) hold in common. On the other hand, *a* language is a particular code, a particular set of conventions which we operate through the possession of this faculty of speech; and *a* language is not held in common by all human beings but only by those who belong to a particular speech community.

'Mere' talk

It is important to notice how things have been put in making this distinction. Language is our capacity to talk to each other. The word 'talk' is used not merely to avoid a rather more technical and high-sounding word like 'communicate'; 'talk' is actually more precise and more relevant to the special nature of human language than 'communicate'. In the first place, all creatures — cat, sparrow, and bee — can be said to *communicate* with each other to some extent. They can attract each other's attention, warn of danger, woo their mates, and direct the way to food. We are still learning just how well animals can communicate with each other, but even so, there can be no doubt that animal communication is extremely rudimentary as compared with the complex and subtle control of language possessed by the most unskilled labourer or illiterate peasant. It is therefore appropriate to say that language involves 'talk' to emphasise that language is a peculiarly human activity.

In the second place, 'talk' is useful for the present purpose because it specifies the basic and dominant way in which human beings communicate. As we have already seen in this chapter, it is far from being the only way. We use language when we read a newspaper, write letters, draft notices, or send messages by morse code. But all these are *derivative* from talk, and — important as they are — they are for most of us relatively specialised functions as compared with 'mere talk'.

The use of language primarily and predominantly involves making noises with our speech organs and receiving other people's speech noises through our ears. It is not a necessary condition of a language's existence that it should have a written form or indeed any form other than talk. All natural languages had a very long history as solely speech before they were ever written down or became associated with rules of spelling and punctuation. Many languages exist in the world today which have still never been written down. Most of the changes that affect languages in time and space (the differences between Chaucer's English and our own, for instance, or the differences between British and American English) are to be explained in terms of language as *spoken* and *heard*. Most of the difficulties we experience in using language in what we have called here its more 'exotic' ways (writing an essay, for example) arise from the fact that our chief competence in the use of language lies in talking it.

In other words, it is vital to grasp that although we can transmit language by such 'unnatural' means as radio or telex, and can use language for highly sophisticated and intellectual purposes such as the statement of atomic theory, all languages are geared primarily to the quite ordinary needs of ordinary people and to the quite ordinary conditions of tongue and ear. It is easy for literate people with some education to forget this and to think of language primarily in terms of its *written* manifestations.

If all this makes it seem that language is a rather primitive activity, perhaps we ought to dwell on this for a moment, since we have here a word that is often used ill-advisedly in discussions of language. Many people think that 'primitive' is indeed a term to be applied to languages, though only to *some* languages, and not usually to the language they themselves speak. They might agree in calling 'primitive' those uses of language that concern greetings, grumbles, and commands, but they would probably believe that these were especially common in the so-called 'primitive languages'. These are misconceptions that we must quickly clear from our minds.

Languages compared

So far as we can tell, all human languages are equally perfect as instruments of communication: that is, every language appears to be as well equipped as any other for saying the things its speakers want to say. It may or may not be appropriate to talk about primitive peoples or cultures, but that is another matter. Certainly, not all groups of people are equally competent in nuclear physics or psychology or the cultivation of rice or the printing of batik cloth. But this is not the fault of their language. The Eskimos, it is said, can speak about snow with far more precision and subtlety than we can in English, but this is not because the Eskimo language (one of those sometimes mis-called 'primitive') is inherently more precise and subtle than English. This example does not illustrate a defect in English, a show of unexpected 'primitiveness'. The position is simply and obviously that the Eskimos and the people who speak English live in different environments and adapt their languages accordingly. The English language would be just as rich in terms for different kinds of snow, presumably, if the environments in which English was habitually used made such distinctions important.

Similarly, we have no reason to doubt that the Eskimo language could be as precise and subtle on the subject of horticulture or inner city social tension if these topics formed part of the Eskimos' life. For obvious historical reasons, Englishmen in the nineteenth century could not talk about motorcars with the minute discrimination which is possible today: cars were not a part of their culture. But they had a host of terms for horse-drawn vehicles which send us, puzzled, to a historical dictionary when we are reading Scott or Dickens. How many of us could describe the difference between a chaise, a barouche, a landau, a victoria, a brougham, a coupé, a gig, a diligence, a whisky, a calash, a tilbury, a carriole, a phaeton, and a clarence?

The discussion of 'primitiveness' provides us with a further reason for sharply and absolutely distinguishing human language from animal communication, because there is no sign of any intermediate stage between the two. Whether we examine the earliest records of any language, or the present-day language of some small tribe in a far-away place, we come no nearer to finding a stage of human language more resembling animal communication and more 'primitive' than our own. In general, as has been said, any language is as good as any other to express what its speakers want to say. An East African finds Swahili as convenient, natural, and complete as an East Londoner finds English. In general, the Australian outback dialect is neither more nor less primitive or ill-fitted to its speaker's wants than Cockney is to the Londoner's. We must always beware the temptation to adopt a naïve parochialism which makes us feel that someone else's language is less pleasant or less effective an instrument than our own.

This is not to say that individuals necessarily sound as pleasant or are as effective as they might, when using their language, but we must not confuse a language with an individual's ability to use it. Nor are we saying that one language has *no* 'deficiencies' as compared with another. The English words 'home' and 'gentleman' have no exact counterparts in French, for example. These are tiny details in which English may well be thought to have the advantage over French, but a large-scale comparison would not lead to the conclusion that English was the superior language, since it would reveal other details in which the converse was true. In 1947, it came as something of a shock that English had no exact word for translating the name that General de Gaulle had given to his party — *Rassemblement du Peuple Français*. The BBC for some time used the word 'rally', and although this scarcely answered the purpose, it was a rather better translation of *rassemblement* than some of the alternatives offered by French-English dictionaries, such as 'muster' and 'mob'.[1]

The more we consider the question, then, the less reasonable does it seem to call any language 'inferior', let alone 'primitive'. The Sanskrit of the Rig-Veda four thousand years ago was as perfect an instrument for what its users wanted to say as its modern descendant, Hindi.[2]

From what has been said, it will come as no surprise that we are totally ignorant about how language began. There is no material in any language today or in the earliest records of ancient languages that shows us language in a rudimentary and emerging

1 Some forty years later, when the policy of *glasnost* was proclaimed in the Soviet Union, again no English word (?candour, ?openness) quite fitted the bill and we settled for using the Russian word itself.
2 So too, Chaucer's English was different from but in no sense inferior to that of Ted Hughes or Saul Bellow.

state. It is often said, of course, that language originated in cries of anger, fear, pain, and pleasure, but there is absolutely no evidence of this. It is true that the absence of evidence does not *dis*prove the theory, but on other grounds too the theory is not very attractive. People of all races and languages (indeed, many animals too) make rather similar noises in reaction to pain or pleasure. The fact that such noises are similar on the lips of Frenchmen and Indonesians, whose languages are utterly different, serves to emphasise the fundamental difference between these noises and language proper. We may say that the cries of pain or chortles of amusement are largely reflex actions, instinctive to a large extent, whereas language proper does not consist of instinctive signs but of words which have to be learned and which are typically conventional.

This latter point, that the words in a language are *conventional*, is very important. There is no fixed or predictable relation between words and their meanings. From the word *dog*, no one could deduce that a spaniel was one kind of dog or that a tabby was not. Nor, of course, are there any grounds for believing that *dog* is a more appropriate designation for this animal than the corresponding words used in French, German, Russian, and Japanese (*chien*, *Hund*, *sobaka*, and *inu* respectively). The sequence of sounds that gives us the English verb *feel* is almost the same as what means 'many' (*viel*) in German, and the word *meal* in English sounds very similar to the word *mille* in French, which means 'thousand'. The word for 'rim' or 'edge' in Russian (*krai*) sounds like the word *cry* in English. So we must not expect the *words* in a language to be direct *symbols* of what they mean, in the way that '+' can symbolise a cross-roads or blue on a map can symbolise the sea.

Sound symbolism

There is no denying of course that all languages have some words which involve direct symbolism: these are the onomatopoeic, imitative or echoic words such as the English *cuckoo*, *splash*, and *whisper*. And even these are conventional to quite a large extent. The word *mutter* does not mean 'mutter' in German or French, even though these languages also have onomatopoeic words for 'muttering': *murmeln* and *marmotter*, respectively. If you throw a stone into the water, the sound you hear is by no means the sound made by the word 'splash'. In any case, words like these, which show some degree of direct symbolism, constitute only a small and untypical part of the vocabulary in any language. Nevertheless, their existence bears witness to a desire that seems to be present in every linguistic community: for a word to have as close and immediate a relation to its meaning as possible.

Such a desire is reflected in the manipulation of onomatopoeic effects by poets, who group words — which individually may be purely 'conventional' signs — in a way that makes them seem directly representational in their sound. Here indeed we can see language as a deliberately well tailored 'dress of thought'. In the following lines, only one or two of the words that Tennyson uses are themselves echoic in origin, but their grouping makes them onomatopoeic as a whole:

> The bare black cliff clang'd round him, as he based
> His feet on juts of slippery crag that rang
> Sharp-smitten with the dint of armed heels —
> And on a sudden, lo! the level lake,
> And the long glories of the winter moon.

The arrangement of sounds in these lines clearly contributes to the narrative: the sounds themselves tell us something about the journey to the lake-side and about the peaceful beauty of the lake itself. In so doing, they *also* give aesthetic pleasure as a sort of verbal music: in other words, they fulfil Jakobson's fourth ('poetic') function.

But verbal pleasure is not just a matter of onomatopoeia or any of the other devices that we associate with the great poets or with 'literary beauty'. No clearer examples of delight in sheer sound can be found than in the chants used by children at play. Here are some lines from a rhyme used when throwing a ball under one's leg at a wall; the words seem to have actual reference but of course this is not so:

> She sent for the *doctor*
> The doctor couldn't *come*
> Here comes the *ambulance*
> Rum, Tum, *Tum*.

The italicised words mark the points at which the ball passes under the leg. And note the word-play in the following:

> . . . Shirley Sevenple, Shirley Eightple, Shirley Nineple, Shirley Temple.

Delight in sound for its own sake ranges from Cockney rhyming slang to the use of puns and word-play which are carefully selected for the purposes of giving pleasure and at the same time adding punch to what is meant. In the time of President John F Kennedy, the process of legislation was laconically described by a Senator as follows:

> This is how Bills become law: delayed, frayed, re-made, okayed, J.F.K.'d, and obeyed.

And we find language for its own sweet sake also in ordinary, light conversation — though it is doubtful whether the conversation that follows can exactly be called 'ordinary', or whether all conversations that accompany bridge-playing are so good-tempered. The *referential* content is small: there is just the sequence 'Whose call?', 'My call — no bid', 'One club', One heart', 'Two diamonds', 'I double two diamonds', 'Two no trumps'. For the rest, we have the *phatic* function, much adorned by the *poetic* one.

> *The players examine their hands. When they talk, they do not look at each other, but concentrate entirely on their cards.*
>
> FIRST MAN (*humming softly as he sorts*): Pom-pom-pom-pom, pom-pom-pom, pom-pom-pom-pom, pom-pom-pom, pom-pom-pom-pom . . .
>
> SECOND MAN (*whistling through his teeth*): Ss, ss-ss-ss-ss. ss-ss-ss, ss-ss-ss, ss-ss-ss, ss-ss-ss-ss . . .
>
> FIRST LADY: Bub-bub-bub-bub, bub-bub-bub-bub, bub-bub-bub, bub-bub-bub-bub — whose call?
>
> SECOND LADY: Your callikins.
>
> FIRST LADY (*still engrossed in her cards*): My little callikins, well, well, well — *my* little callikins. Let me see, then, let me see — I think — I think — I think-a-pink-a-pink — no bid.
>
> SECOND LADY: Tch-tch-tch, tch-tch-tch, tch-tch, tch-tch, tch-tch-tch, tch-tch-tch — no bid.
>
> FIRST MAN: One cloob.

SECOND MAN (*dropping into Irish*): Did ye say one cloob?

FIRST MAN (*dropping into Irish*): I did that.

SECOND MAN: *Er hat ein cloob gesagen.* (*Singing*) *Er hat ein cloob gesagen, er hat ein cloob* . . . One hearty-party . . .

FIRST LADY: Two diminx.

SECOND LADY: No bid, no bid.

FIRST MAN: No bid-a-bid-bid.

SECOND MAN: Two diminx, is it? Two naughty leetle diminx. This, I think, demands a certain amount of *considération*. (*Drums fingers on table*) Yes, yes, my friends, *beaucoup de considération*.

SECOND, LADY (*after a pause*): Your *call*, partner.

SECOND MAN: I know it, I know it, I know it, I know it, I know it, indeed, indeed, I know it. (*Clacks tongue*) I know it, I know it, I double two diminx.

SECOND LADY: He doubles two diminx.

FIRST MAN: He doubles two diminx.

SECOND MAN: I double, I double, I double two diminx.

FIRST LADY: Very well, then, have at you. Two no trumpets.

FIRST MAN: Ha, ha!

SECOND MAN: Ho, ho!

FIRST LADY: He, he!

SECOND LADY: H'm. H'm!

They revert to their pet noises as they consider their hands.

Herbert Farjeon, *Nine Sharp*

SOME FOLLOW-UP WORK

1 Reflect on your own thoughts about something that has recently upset you. Discuss the extent to which such thoughts are in silent language or, on the contrary, beyond expression in language.

2 Collect from a daily newspaper (not forgetting sports reports, commercial and personal advertisements) examples that seem to represent as purely as possible each of Jakobson's functions 1–5. When you feel they fulfil another function in addition, say which and explain why you think so.

3 A dog can perhaps 'tell' us that it would like to go for a walk or believes there is an intruder in the garden — but not

that there was an intruder there yesterday or that it would like to go for a walk tomorrow. Consider examples of animal communication (including the 'speech' of parrots) and speculate on its limits.

4 'Every language appears to be as well equipped as any other for saying the things its speakers want to say.' From your own observation (e.g. your knowledge of another language):
a) support this claim, with examples;
b) attempt to refute the claim.

5 Find out as accurately as possible the difference between the various carriages listed on p. 7, and supply a similar list of different types of motor vehicle in use today.

6 The following are among the commonest exclamations used in writing and having a conventional written form: *Oh, ah, eh, aha, oho, ugh, oo.* Bearing in mind that each may have more than one use (*Oh, well; Oh!; Oh?*), try to give an account of how they are used and what they mean.

7 A '+' to denote a cross-roads was given as one example of a visual symbol which to some extent directly represents what it means. List as many others as you can, and explain in what respects they are representational.

8 'Croissant is the name we give to a kind of roll because it is crisp.'
'Soup is the sucking noise that is made when it is eaten.'
'Biscuits are so called because of the sound they make when you break them.'
Examine these reactions in the light of the discussion of onomatopoeia and of echoic words such as *splash* and *mutter*.

9 The popularity of scrabble and crossword puzzles shows our fondness for playing with words. Explain in full the solutions given for each of the following crossword clues and discuss the range of problems that they illustrate:
a) Is it the sun and wind that make you able to pass with credit in French and Latin? (*solvent*)
b) He struggles when summonsed. (*writhe*)
c) Take vain steps to provide support. (*strut*)
d) Develops and goes round topless! (*evolves*)

e) Does one pause expectantly or settle down?   (*colonist*)
f) An umpire's brusque verdict.   (*outspoken*)
g) In brief, an element that's all right with oxygen.   (*potassium*)
h) Honoured with a new sound track.   (*dubbed*)
i) You don't expect to find them in orchestras.   (*cart-horses*)

C H A P T E R 2

Speaker and speech: Which is in control?

We have seen something of what is involved in the *poetic* function of language, giving delight merely as 'sound'. We may now go back and look more closely at the rest of the list (page 4) which Jakobson gives of the functions of language. After what has been said about the primacy of 'ordinary' uses of language (as in greetings and grumbles), we can readily understand that *emotive* language often merely serves to get rid of *nervous energy*. We may feel such 'nervous energy' when we hit our thumb instead of a carpet-tack, and although we may not agree that the burst of language which releases and dissipates the energy is the mark of a civilised man, a linguistic reaction — however violent — is arguably more civilised than some such physical alternative as throwing the hammer at the china cabinet. It is conceivable, perhaps, that people may some day be able to dispute without slanging each other with the rudest names they can conjure; but for the present we may be content to admit that, if vicious words are regarded by both participants as a satisfactory substitute for vicious blows, language is performing a useful service.

But outbursts of anger are not the only kind of nervous energy to be considered here. One thinks of the thrill of emotion experienced as one turns a corner and sees a beautiful sunset. Even if alone, we may find it difficult to repress an involuntary exclamation, 'Oh, how absolutely lovely!' We may even add ('beneath our breath' or 'to ourselves', as we put it), 'What a violent contrast that glowing cloud makes with the sombre brow of the hill!' In fact, it is a common experience for many people to feel a special satisfaction according as they can release a flood of emotion by the means of *precise* language. By contrast, they have a vaguely uncomfortable, even painful, pent-up feeling if they cannot find adequate words. 'Words fail me!' The wider and more flexible our range of language, therefore, the more readily and completely can we relieve our feelings when we are overcome by a great spasm of 'nervous energy'.

But let us turn to Jakobson's fifth use of language — the *referential* function, related (we recall) to 'context': at its simplest, using language to talk about what we may call broadly 'facts'. These may be objective facts about the world outside us, as in 'The paper is on the floor', or subjective facts about our feelings, as in 'I'm tired' or 'I like chocolate mints'. These are not exactly statements of shattering importance, but they are good representatives of that important human characteristic of being able to express oneself through language. The non-linguistic alternatives to the three examples just given would be pointing to the paper; yawning (and perhaps going to sleep); and smacking one's lips or salivating freely at the mention (or memory) of chocolates.

From this basic and elementary type of referential language, it is worth distinguishing the communication of *ideas*, since ideas are rather rare — and ability to communicate them effectively still rarer. It is in this range of linguistic usage that we need most practice and special training, and it leads us to consider language as an instrument of *thought*. It is not always realised in how large a measure a language is tied to the thinking of its users, but this tie can be a source of further complication when we try to be precise and scientific in our 'exotic' uses of English.

Language and attitude

The word 'democracy', meaning 'rule by the people', means something of which in our particular culture we strongly approve, and we tend to ignore the possibility that 'democracy' could connote anything but what is noble and right. But in Nazi Germany and Stalinist Russia, where democracy was not an ideal, it meant something like 'rebellious lack of discipline' — and 'liberal' also had nasty connotations. Even in our own history, 'democracy' has not always been used approvingly. Lord Byron once wrote that democracy was 'an aristocracy of blackguards', and as recently as the middle of the last century, Sir Arthur Helps was able to speak — without implying a paradox — of having 'too affectionate a regard for the people to be a democrat'. There are unhappy signs that the 'permissive society' of the 1960s may have led to a reaction in which the word 'tolerance' may have a bad flavour, and 'liberalism' too. In the campaign which led to the election of George Bush as President, there was much talk of whether his opponent Michael Dukakis was a fit candidate because of allegations that he was 'liberal'.

In a country where there is a monarchy which is highly respected, the word corresponding to 'royal' will take on the meaning 'noble', 'splendid', as well as the literal sense of 'relating to the monarch'. But in another country, which has just become a republic after a bitter struggle against an unpopular, tyrannous king, the corresponding word will still have the meaning 'relating to the monarch', yet its additional connotations are more likely to be 'brutal' or even 'wicked' than 'noble' and 'splendid'. One would therefore have to be very careful in translating into the language of this second country something like 'They gave us a royal welcome'.

It has often been pointed out that discussion of racial conflict in the world today is not helped by the words we use, because *black* and *white* have in many communities powerful connotations in addition to the literal denotation of colours. The word *black* in many communities denotes sources of fear or even wickedness, and there is an equally widespread association of *white* with purity and goodness. Such connotations which accompany our words can dangerously affect our attitudes without our realising it. Would white people still feel superior about their colour if the more literally accurate term 'pink' were used of them? Consider what E M Forster had to say on this:

> The remark that did him most harm at the club was a silly aside to the effect that the so-called white races are really pinko-grey. He only said this to be cheery, he did not realise that 'white' has no more to do with a colour than *God Save the King* with a god, and that it is the height of impropriety to consider what it does connote. The pinko-grey male whom he addressed was subtly scandalized; his sense of insecurity was awoken, and he communicated it to the rest of the herd.
>
> *A Passage to India*, 1924, chap. 7

A hundred years before Forster wrote this, Jeremy Bentham

pointed out broader dangers which arise through the influence of language upon thought. Because many of our nouns refer to 'real things' like tables and shoes, having solid 'substance' (and classed grammatically as 'substantives'), we are in danger of thinking that nouns like *liberty, crime* and the like are equally 'real' and 'substantial'. Bentham's line of thinking was much developed in the twentieth century by men like C K Ogden and the American linguist B L Whorf. A favourite example in demonstrating the domination of language has been the spectrum, which, in spite of its being in reality a continuum, is divided up by language into discrete units like 'red', 'blue', 'yellow' which make it somewhat difficult for us to *see* (let alone talk about) intermediate shades for which our language does not provide us with names. And of course since a label like *red* in English does not correspond to a 'really' discrete unit, there is no guarantee that there is a colour-label in another language which exactly corresponds to our *red*. As Whorf pointed out:

> We dissect nature along lines laid down by our native
> languages. The categories and types that we isolate from the
> world of phenomena we do not find there because they stare
> every observer in the face; on the contrary, the world is
> presented in a kaleidoscopic flux of impressions which has to be
> organised by our minds — and this means largely by the
> linguistic systems in our minds. We cut nature up, organise it
> into concepts, and ascribe significance as we do, largely because
> we are parties to an agreement to organise it in this way — an
> agreement that holds throughout our speech community and is
> codified in the patterns of our language.

The Technology Review, vol. 42, 1939

One way in which we have traditionally been influenced by language is in referring to males as though they were truly representative of the species. 'The guests included a Norwegian and his wife,' we say — not 'a Norwegian and her husband'. 'No one should drive his car too fast,' we may say — ignoring the fact that the advice ought to apply to women equally. Because this orientation is believed to have disadvantaged women (in job applications, for instance), most organisations now have rules for 'inclusionary language' that will help us *think* of people as being both male and female.

A help to thought

But language does not only have a restrictive influence on thought: language also conditions our thinking in a positive and constructive way. In discussing a little earlier in this chapter how language released emotion, it was pointed out that people might have a pent-up feeling if they could not find the words to describe an experience. This is very largely because we feel that we have not thoroughly apprehended something if we are unable to put it into words.

Not all of us depend to the same extent on words when we are thinking to ourselves, but it is certain that, in general, thinking and decision-making are vastly supported and facilitated by language, even though we may be using the language *silently*. Most of us can grasp a distinction better when we have the linguistic apparatus to identify it amid the flux and chaos of raw experience around us. It may be rather arbitrary to divide up the minutely graded dwelling places that we see around us into huts, sheds, cottages, bungalows, houses, condominiums, mansions, and palaces: there is no hard and fast line between these in 'reality'. But even imposing this rough grid on what surrounds us is better than nothing: we are enabled to *see* the reality more clearly. Moreover, although it is not strictly to the present point, our cutting up of reality in this way helps us to *talk* about it to other people, 'because', as Whorf says, 'we are parties to an agreement' to organise reality in this particular way in our speech community.

It is not very easy to demonstrate conclusively that language helps thought, but we can usually recognise the truth of it from our personal inner experience. Most of us can remember passing through stages like the following. Let us suppose we have attained, in early childhood, the distinction between 'round' and 'square'. Later on, 'round' is further broken down into 'circular' and 'oval', and it becomes easier to see this 'obvious' difference between shapes when we have acquired the relevant labels. But then we come to metaphorical extensions of the terms. We grope towards a criticism of *arguments* and learn to follow a line of reasoning; we learn to exercise doubt or be convinced according to how the argument goes. Some arguments may strike us as unsatisfactory, yet they seem to have nothing in common except their tendency to give us a vague lack of conviction and some discomfort. Then we hear someone discussing a line of argument and we catch the word 'circular' being used. At once everything lights up, and we know exactly what kind of argument is meant; the idea 'clicks', as we say. There is of course nothing about an argument which resembles the shape of a circle, and we may never have thought of 'circle' except in terms of visual shapes. Yet in a flash we see the *analogy* that the *metaphor* presents, and thereafter we are able to spot this type of fallacious argument more speedily, now that we have this linguistic means of identifying it.

The importance of language in making distinctions is also seen in considering people who suffer from such conditions as 'nominal aphasia'. Here is an account of an experiment with a patient who had completely forgotten the names of colours but who had retained perfectly good colour vision:

> Asked to choose from among a number of coloured threads those belonging to the same category, he found the task impossible and even meaningless. To him all the threads were different in colour. And so they were in actual fact, as far as their purely visual appearance was concerned. By losing the names, the verbal labels, the patient had also lost the principle of classification, the faculty of subordinating individual differences to some higher unity, the habit of introducing some man-made lines of division into the unbroken continuity of the natural scale of colours. Thanks to language, the spectrum had been divided up and had become articulate; with the loss of the verbal signposts, it had relapsed into chaos.

> S Ullmann, *Words and their Use* (1951), p. 89

Leonard Bloomfield provided an everyday illustration of how indispensable the referential function of language is to us. After pointing out that a great deal of our thinking goes on by the use of words inaudibly, he continued:

> Our ability to estimate numbers without using speech is extremely limited, as anyone may see by glancing, say, at a row of books on a shelf. To say that two sets of objects 'have the same number' means that if we take one object from the first set and place it next to one object of the second set, and keep on doing this without using any object more than once, we shall

have no unpaired objects left over. Now, we cannot always do this. The objects may be too heavy to move, or they may be in different parts of the world, or they may exist at different times (as, say, a flock of sheep before and after a storm). Here language steps in. The numerals, *one, two, three, four* and so on, are simply a series of words which we have learned to say in a fixed order, as substitutes for the above-described process. Using them, we can 'count' any set of objects by placing them into one-to-one correspondence (as mathematicians call it) with the number-words, saying *one* for one of the objects, *two* for another, *three* for the next, and so on, taking care to use each object only once, until all the objects of the set are exhausted. Suppose that when we had said *nineteen*, there were no more objects left. Thereafter, at any time or place, we can decide whether any set of objects has the same number as this first set, by merely repeating the counting process with the new set. Mathematics, the ideal use of language, consists merely of elaborations of this process. The use of numbers is the simplest and clearest case of the usefulness of talking to oneself, but there are many others. We think before we act.

Language (1933), pp. 28–29

And, as Bloomfield's example shows, language plays a vital role in our ability to think.

Making contact

Let us turn now from Jakobson's referential function to the one that must seem its complete obverse, the *phatic*. It is a use of language that is easy to overlook by serious scholars in the serious business of studying language and it was indeed named only in the first quarter of the twentieth century: not by Jakobson, as it happens, but by the anthropologist Bronislaw Malinowski. In view of what we have been saying about the referential use of language enabling us to isolate something from a previously blurred continuum, it is worth quoting Malinowski himself at this point:

. . . *phatic communion* I am tempted to call it, actuated by the demon of terminological invention — a type of speech in which ties of union are created by a mere exchange of words.

Before hearing more from Malinowski on the subject, however, we might consider carefully the following fictive example from Josephine Tey's novel, *The Franchise Affair*:

> 'Have you had a busy day, dear?' Aunt Lin asked, opening her table napkin and arranging it across her plump lap.
> This was a sentence that made sense but had no meaning. It was as much an overture to dinner as the spreading of her napkin and the exploratory movement of her right foot as she located the footstool which compensated for her short legs. She expected no answer; or rather, being unaware that she had asked the question, she did not listen to his answer.

The comic insight here closely reflects Malinowski's observations:

> A mere phrase of politeness, in use as much among savage tribes as in a European drawing-room, fulfils a function to which the meaning of its words is almost completely irrelevant. Inquiries about health, comments on weather, affirmations of some supremely obvious state of things — all such are exchanged, not in order to inform, not in this case to connect people in action, certainly not in order to express any thought. It would be even incorrect, I think, to say that such words serve the purpose of establishing a common sentiment, for this is usually absent from such current phrases of intercourse; and where it purports to exist, as in expressions of sympathy, it is avowedly spurious on one side. What is the *raison d'être*, therefore, of such phrases as 'How do you do?' 'Ah, here you are', 'Where do you come from?' 'Nice day today!' — all of which serve in one society or another as formulae of greeting or approach?
> I think that, in discussing the function of Speech in mere sociabilities, we come to one of the bedrock aspects of man's nature in society. There is in all human beings the well-known tendency to congregate, to be together, to enjoy each other's company. Many instincts and innate trends, such as fear or pugnacity, all the types of social sentiments such as ambition, vanity, passion for power and wealth, are dependent upon and associated with the fundamental tendency which makes the mere presence of others a necessity for man.

> Malinowski's Supplement to Ogden and Richards, *The Meaning of Meaning* (1923), pp. 313–14

It is a matter of common experience that the person who does not speak (and who is on this account called 'unsociable') is liable to be somewhat distrusted, even feared or disliked. Walking along a country road at night, it is usual to break silence on passing someone, and the exchange of words is a mutual reassurance. People vary from place to place (and of course from individual to individual) in their habits and feelings over this aspect of behaviour, but all of us should realise that there are some of our fellows who feel a very unpleasant tension in the presence of a stranger (for example, sitting next to you on a flight) without some brief entry into 'phatic communion'.

If scholars had scarcely noticed phatic phenomena until the first quarter of the twentieth century, they made up for it in the last quarter when several book-length examinations of politeness phenomena appeared. In one of these, phatic communion is seen as 'fundamental in an evolutionary sense to social life and human intelligence', having 'a sociological significance altogether beyond the level of table manners'. This is because on the one hand such formulaic language disarms potential aggression and on the other it is directly related to 'the most fundamental cultural ideas about the nature of the social persona, honour and virtue, shame and redemption' (P Brown and S C Levinson, *Politeness — Some Universals in Language Usage*, 1987). Nor is it only a matter of discovering the relevance of linguistic formulae: it is the discovery of a whole range of pragmatic aspects in language use. As Geoffrey Leech has said, 'we cannot really understand the nature of language itself unless we understand pragmatics: how language is used in communication' (*Pragmatics*, 1983).

The value of vagueness

When we consider how vital and basic is the quite ordinary and unsophisticated use of language, it may be worth recalling what was said earlier (in Chapter One) about the primacy of speech. Here obviously is a use of language which relates chiefly to speech, to spoken more than to written language, and one ought in particular to recall the earlier statement that 'all languages are geared primarily to the quite ordinary needs of ordinary people'. It is from such 'ordinariness' in the use of language that we all start; it is in these uses of language that we are all fairly equally competent. However much we may wish to cultivate a more refined and delicate use of language for argument and for precise writing, our language has at the same time to be kept going for these relatively crude and elementary purposes, and most of our *practice* in the use of language is in these crude and elementary situations.

Our ability to use English subtly or precisely is continually being interfered with by a constant, unremitting need which pulls our language in the opposite direction: by our need to use language simply and *imprecisely* for everyday purposes — such as phatic communion. 'Nice day again,' we say cheerfully, and we would find it intolerable if such utterances had to be given meteorological precision, with reference to temperature, wind-speed, cloud-height, and barometric pressure.

We sometimes rather thoughtlessly criticise an announcement or a government form which refers to 'male persons over the age of eighteen years'. What ridiculous jargon, we think; why couldn't this pompous official have used the word 'man'! But officials may be forced into a jargon that they like no more than we do, by the imprecision of the ordinary words that we may prefer. In the present instance, *man* may sound perfectly obvious as the right gloss upon 'male persons over the age of eighteen years', but would the latter be equally our automatic interpretation if the word 'man' had been used? Many people would not apply the word *man* to someone as young as 18 or 19, while others apply it to lads of 16 or 17. Indeed, it can be applied to a schoolboy of 10 ('the team is a man short'). Further, it may simply mean 'brave person', as when we tell a little boy of four to 'stop crying and be a man'. Or it may mean 'human being', without regard to sex, as in a phrase like 'not fit for man or beast'. It may even mean a wooden disc — as in the game of draughts.

This is the *ordinary* use of language which makes the less ordinary uses of language (as in science, or official regulations) a constantly recurring difficulty, because — important as law and science may be — we cannot sacrifice the ordinary, everyday use of words merely in order to leave language permanently suitable for the 'loftier purposes'. And let us make no mistake: the imprecision of ordinary language is essential to the use and perpetuation of language of any kind. One simply must be able to make utterances of a general and imprecise kind: 'Quick — there's a man on the phone — long distance.' If one is not allowed a shorthand expression of this kind, it would cost the unfortunate 'person whose voice suggested that he was a male who had reached full maturity etc, etc' a fair amount of money merely to have his call announced.

We can see, therefore, that language is rooted in the ordinary events of everyday and in ordinary people's usage. We *need* language to be imprecise because a great part of its convenience lies in its very adaptability to the making of generalisations and abstractions. When we talk airily of improving our language ability, it must be perfectly clear that we mean improving our language's *range*. It does not mean abandoning the lowlier uses of language as heard loosely in greetings, grumbles and brief, sketchy observations. If we were to eradicate these, we should kill language itself in the process, since not only are these functions basic and essential but also language is kept alive and handed on by being used for these functions: they represent the basic, common uses of language. In other words, they give us most of our daily practice in language, and most of our motivation for using language.

For this double reason, we need to pay special attention to language in its most ordinary, everyday manifestations — the more so when we are trying to make our control of language suitable for more 'exotic' purposes. Our most elevated rhetoric and our most subtle dialectic are rooted in ordinary usage which alone gives life to language, and which in countless ways conditions, affects, stimulates, rejuvenates the finer language that we need to use for a minority of purposes on a minority of occasions. Even the finest language cannot be a perfect and logical medium, since it is so closely related to language in its underlying 'primitive' functions. But awareness of the latter should make it easier for us to make our language more careful and precise, when care and precision are called for, because they help us to see in what ways language is *not* normally careful and precise.

Just as learning about our friends' imperfections helps us to sympathise with them, to come to terms and co-operate with them, so awareness of the inherent imperfections of language will fit us to make more effective use of it. If we know that the steering of our car is in bad shape, we hold the wheel more carefully and avoid bumps in the road. So too, study of the points at which language is most liable to let us down can be a very useful safety precaution.

SOME FOLLOW-UP WORK

1 Whorf was quoted as saying, 'We dissect nature along lines laid down by our native languages.' Explain carefully and give examples. Where does the ankle end and the calf begin? Where does chest end and stomach begin? What distinguishes a branch from a twig? Consider the extent to which language makes arbitrary distinctions.

2 What do you think Bloomfield means by calling mathematics 'the ideal use of language'?

3 Try to recall experiences of your own in which your thinking has been (a) influenced, (b) assisted, (c) inhibited by your language.

4 'Language is called the garment of thought; however, it should rather be, language is the flesh-garment, the body, of thought' (Carlyle, *Sartor Resartus*).
'He gave men speech, and speech created thought,/ Which is the measure of the universe' (Shelley, *Prometheus Unbound*). Which of these now represents your view more nearly? Are the two quotations incompatible?

5 Outline the aspects of a person's behaviour which would qualify it in your view to be called 'sociable'.

6 We have noted that language is valuable in enabling us to make 'generalisations and abstractions'. Explore this idea further and discuss some of the different kinds of generalisation and abstraction that we find ourselves making habitually by means of English vocabulary.

7 Having studied Chapters One and Two, are there ways in which you would wish to expand, refine, or revise Jakobson's analysis of language functions?

CHAPTER 3

Language, identity, and nation

Countries have symbols of identity such as a flag or a national anthem. A country may also have a national language, as when we say that the language of Italy is Italian, the language of Iraq is Arabic. But just as no country is a simple, unchanging monolith comprising people all with the same background and habits, so equally no language is a simple, unchanging monolith. Convenient as they are, names like 'Italian', 'Arabic', and 'English' embrace in each case a wide range of language differences.

These differences arise for a number of reasons, but we may concentrate on two major ones: time and space. We do not hesitate to say that Shakespeare wrote in English, but in the 400 years between his time and ours, there arose many differences between his English and ours. We still understand when Rosalind and Celia converse in *As You Like It*, but our own conversation is now very different:

> 'Alas the day! What shall I do with my doublet and hose? —
> What did he when thou saw'st him? What said he? How look'd
> he? Wherein went he? What makes he here? . . .'
>
> 'Cry, holla! to thy tongue, I pr'ythee; it curvets unseasonably.
> He was furnished like a hunter.'
>
> Act III, scene 2

And just as there are differences when we are separated by time, so there are differences when we are separated by space. We do not hesitate to say that Americans, Britons, and Australians all speak English, and of course people from Leeds and London and Los Angeles understand each other, as do people from Vancouver, Sydney, and Wellington: but they all sound different and often recognisably so.

But there are limits to such understanding across time and space. The 600 years separating us from Chaucer give us some difficulty in reading *The Canterbury Tales*, and the further 500 separating him from King Alfred who died in 899 force us to cross a threshold where we seem to confront a different language — and (in the view of many) appropriately designated with a different name, 'Anglo-Saxon'. Consider, for example, some of the King's words from a famous preface:

> Gode ælmiehtegum si ðonc ðætte we nu ænigne onstal habbað lareowa.

('Thanks be to almighty God that we now have any supply of teachers.')

And of course separate languages emerge even more readily when the passage of time is compounded by spatial separation — even if the space concerned is only the distance between Dover and Ostend, Harwich and the Hook of Holland. Thus present-day English and present-day Dutch are clearly similar, but just as clearly they are different languages. The following is from another preface, this time to a recent book on the Dutch language:

> Het spreekt vanzelf dat met dit boek niet 'de' spraakkunst van het Nederlands geschreven is.

('It is self-evident that, with this book, *the* grammar of Dutch has not been written.')

But without any separation in time at all, and with only very minor separation in space, language differences readily emerge: in the English of two neighbouring villages in Lancashire, in the German of two neighbouring villages in Bavaria, an observer with a keen ear can spot differences — and these differences function as audible identity-cards to the villagers themselves. Nor is it a matter only of physical space; social space has the same effect. Some years ago, a British writer described growing up in a middle-class household where the children of neighbours belonged to a different socio-economic group, with language habits to match: 'I think it worried my parents more than anything else that our speech would be corrupted by the aitchless community at our doorstep. We were constantly being pulled up for some real or fancied coarseness of enunciation or vulgar phrase.'

Different identities

The kind of language that we ourselves speak usually sounds just right to us; the variant that others speak usually seems undesirable — 'low' perhaps, or 'affected', or just 'alien', the talk of 'strangers'. We feel a special loyalty towards (and security among) our own family and social set, and we take pride in there being linguistic markers of such kinship. Among these markers, we develop even more personal ones: particular words we like, particular turns of phrase that our friends recognise as our personal idiom; and a personal style of handwriting which again any of our acquaintances can at once recognise when they see it on an envelope. (See pp. 100f.)

Such a sense of personal identity is essential in every individual's development, and the educational processes must be careful to encourage and protect it. It is widely recognised that it is in the development of a personal sense of language that we shape our personality and learn to explore ourselves. So nothing must be done to diminish our regard for this local and most intimately known language or our self-respect that goes with it. As Polonius enjoined his son Laertes (*Hamlet*, Act I, scene 3):

> This above all: to thine own self be true,
> And it must follow, as the night the day,
> Thou canst not then be false to any man.

But if this were all and if it were followed to its logical conclusion, we would build linguistic barriers around ourselves and our immediate circle so that the separation we have discussed as triggering separate mutually incomprehensible languages would be given disastrously free reign. It is a convenience, as we have seen, to speak across time and space in what we can regard as the 'same' language, and it is a convenience that we can achieve through developing a second kind of identity. Besides (and without rejecting) a uniquely personal or local identity, we learn to acquire a sense of identity with a wider group — such as the nation. This does not come as naturally or as easily as the more personal identity — any more than it comes easily to learn to play as part of a team rather than regarding competitive sport as a matter of purely personal achievement. But the two senses of identity can readily exist simultaneously in any of us, as we see indeed in team sports such as soccer. The team plays as a disciplined co-operative unit, each member identifying with his own team to beat the opposing team on the field. Each goal is scored through the effectiveness of that co-operation, a player typically denying his personal ambitions by passing the ball to another player in the interest of the team as a whole. And it is the team that is rightly credited with each goal. But at the moment of scoring a particular goal, we see *individual* identity in personal appeal for personal applause from the fans as the player charges round with up-stretched arms. A brief glimpse of 'Me! Me! Me!' before subordination again into the team identity of 'Us! Us! Us!'

Acquiring a sense of wider group identity is a serious challenge which extends far beyond team sports. It is indeed precisely what John Donne was talking about in this deservedly oft-quoted passage from his *Devotions* (1624):

> No man is an island, entire of itself; every man is a piece of the continent, a part of the main. If a clod be washed away by the sea, Europe is the less, as well as if a promontory were, as well as if a manor of thy friends or thine own were. Any man's death diminishes me, because I am involved in mankind; and therefore never send to know for whom the bell tolls: it tolls for thee.

And of course for thee and thee and thee; for all of us. While Donne put this message in a moral and religious context, it is equally applicable in a social and linguistic one. Cultivating a sense of identity as wide as possible throughout humanity may be difficult, but it is plainly in our own interests to do so. It may be comforting to speak in your own way with your personal acquaintances and to recognise a typical and personal tone in a letter from your sister. But it is also comforting to know you can speak to a stranger from far away or to read with understanding *Tom Sawyer* and Donne's *Devotions*. In his *Reflections on the Revolution in France* (1790), Edmund Burke spoke of 'an enlightened self-interest' which is willing to 'identify with an interest more enlarged and publick'.

By satisfying just such a self-interest, we can have the best of both worlds, enjoying both kinds of identity: using the familiar language of our group for discourse within that group; and then, for communication with groups 'more enlarged and publick', ready to use at will the Standard English that we shall look at in some detail in Chapter Nine below. For the present, let us take a closer look at these 'more enlarged' groups who are beyond the family home and immediate circle. They may be social — the community of all fellow-anglers or stamp-collectors. They may be occupational — the community of dress-designers or electronic engineers or nurses or architects. They may be regional — the sense of identity a Texan feels with all other Texans.

National identity

But in extending our concept of identity and coming to understand the ways of others (in language as in anything else), we need access to *education*, and education is a process that is not generally organised on a social or professional basis, and not always on a regional basis either. Education usually relates to a further unit in this hierarchy, and that is the *nation*. We shall speak a little later of discourse with communities beyond the nation, but if one were to ask people, from whatever country or part of the world they came, to name the community with which they identified beyond their family and local acquaintance, most of them would probably say it was the nation. This would be heartily endorsed by anyone who had followed a world sporting event such as the Olympic Games.

So what we have, in fact, is less two discrete types of identity than an indefinitely widening range between two poles:

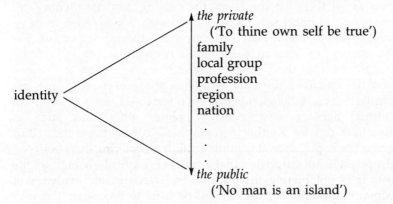

Yet in 'nation' we have a unit that is relatively new. Traditionally we had the kinship-based tribe, and beyond it power units such as kingdoms and empires whose bounds were determined by force, with more concern for strategic frontiers and material wealth than for homogeneity of population. In so far as the word *nation* was used during the Middle Ages, it essentially connoted race: 'the nation of England', we read in the *Cursor Mundi* of around 1300, 'is English'. This means roughly that the people occupying this territory are English by race, and not (for example) Celts or Walloons. But increasingly from the eighteenth century the word came to mean a *political* unit, and the formation of independent nation states (such as above all the USA in 1776) firmly indicated that people of many different races could unite under one flag and develop a sense of patriotic identity in respect of the 'nation'.

From 1776 onwards we have lived through two centuries in which nationalism has been one of the most potent political forces. The first parliament set up by the French revolutionaries in 1789 was called the 'national assembly', and in the decades that followed we saw over and over again the rejection of loyalty to a *person* (a duke, a prince, a margrave, a king, an emperor) and its replacement by loyalty to the *nation* — and the emergence of new independent nation-states. And the process that produced Romania and Finland in Europe went on with redoubled vigour in the second half of the twentieth century to produce Ghana and Bangladesh and scores of others.

But if the nation is 'relatively new' as an identity unit, it is not new in all respects: the bases for seeking national identity are often very old and very powerful. Though downgraded from its medieval supremacy, race is usually still extremely important. But the concept of 'nation' has enabled communities to extend the horizon of what they conceived of as identity, and other features held in common came to supplement or even supplant the primacy of race. Religion is one such feature; a sense of common cultural heritage is another; a political philosophy such as socialism can be another; geographical cohesion another. But, given the importance of communication in fostering links between people, it is not surprising that *language* is particularly high on the list. It is not merely the audible and recognisable evidence of common ground, but it can itself be used to propagate the very identity it demonstrates. This is well evidenced in Europe with the use of the Finnish language to arouse a sense of Finnish identity within Czarist Russia, the use of Hungarian to establish Hungarian identity within the Austrian empire, and perhaps most strikingly the use of German to call together the people in the myriad of separate principalities that constituted what we have recognised as 'Germany' for the past 100 years.

Nation and language

We call this example most striking but it is also of particular relevance to the theme of this chapter. The use of German caused Bavarians and Saxons and Württembergers to see themselves as Germans and to identify one with another at a higher level of identity. And bearing in mind the range of identities we have been discussing, we can see that they did this without giving up the more 'private' identity as Bavarians; as citizens of Regensburg where they are known by name; as members of a family where they are known by *first* name.

But in order to achieve the higher identity with the German nation through the German language, there had to be a consensus as to what constituted that German language. And in view of what we shall be saying about Standard English, it is interesting to note that in the case of German there are three aspects. First, the selection of one from among several competing dialects — the one likely to be least generally opposed. Second, the regularisation and promulgation of this by the institutions of authority — such as government, the education system, and the press. Third, making it more 'indigenous', especially by replacing recognisably foreign loan words (in this case chiefly French words) by recognisably German words with which therefore the members of this new community, the German nation, could the more enthusiastically and proudly identify.

In Romania, where a sense of identity was difficult to establish when Romanians were part of the vast Ottoman Empire, the story is similar. A sense of nationhood was established not just on ethnic and cultural and religious grounds, but on a *linguistic* basis made the firmer by standardising the Romanian language and promoting it by the institutions of power. Romanian is basically a Romance language like French or Italian, but sealed off from the other Romance languages as an 'island', with Hungarian to one side and with Slavic languages on the other three. As a result of history and location, the language had absorbed many Slavic, Turkish, and Greek words. Part therefore of the process of making the language a fit symbol for Romanian identity was 're-latinisation': the replacement of alien words by synonyms with Romance bases. There was even some modification of the grammar.

We may glance at another European example, where a similar course was followed but where the issues were rather different. Norwegians, Danes, and Swedes are racially cognate, and they speak Scandinavian languages that are for the most part mutually comprehensible. But in extracting itself from Danish and Swedish domination to become an independent country in 1905, Norway felt the need to assert Norwegian identity by developing a new Scandinavian language — clearly distinct from both Danish and Swedish. To this end, its leaders went to the farmers and away from cities like Oslo: they looked for language roots with which ordinary people could readily identify, appealing at the same time to the saga tradition of literature more than 500 years earlier to endow these roots with a cultural blessing. This became the Nynorsk ('New Norwegian') which co-exists with the older Bokmål ('Literary Language') in Norway today.

Let us turn briefly to a couple of analogous but far vaster language issues outside Europe. In promoting national languages in India and Pakistan after independence in 1947, a similar problem to that of Norway was encountered. From the language Hindustani that had been the common currency throughout the northern part of the sub-continent during the British raj, two new nations, Pakistan and India, felt the need to cultivate their separate national identities with separate national languages. So in Pakistan, Hindustani was reshaped as Urdu, with much deliberate replacement of words to incorporate the traditions of Islam; with a script (Arabic-based) to match. And in India, Hindustani was reshaped as Hindi, with many words replaced with help from the ancient Sanskrit in which the sacred Hindu texts were written; and with the Devanagari script to match. Here then we have the conscious dissimilation of languages to help create two national identities by appeal to precious cultural and religious heritages.

One brief mention of the largest nation-state in the world. The People's Republic of China has taken vigorous steps to establish a national language, taking the Peking-based Mandarin for this purpose but endorsing the nation's socialist identity with many new words, some script simplification, and an appropriate name: Pudong Hua — 'Language for the whole [Chinese] community'.

Sharing a language

Now, so far in this discussion of language and national identity, we have taken as examples the most obvious and perhaps the ideal model, which implies 'one nation — one language'. The language of Germany is German, of Finland Finnish, of Romania Romanian, each language matching a geographical, cultural, and ethnic unity. It is the model of which Japan with its language Japanese is the clearest and most unwavering example in the world.

But there are in fact three models:

one language	~	one nation (e.g. Japan)
several languages	~	one nation (e.g. Switzerland)
several nations	~	one language (e.g. Arabic)

Moreover, the first of these is far from being the norm. Switzerland has been a successful demonstration of the second model for 500 years: there is a Swiss nation but no Swiss language — instead it uses four (three of them shared with its neighbours Germany, France, and Italy, whose standards for these languages it accepts). Similarly, there is no Belgian language: Belgium uses Dutch and French, again observing the standards for these languages as they obtain beyond the Belgian frontier.

Belgium is not in some ways as cohesive a national unity as Switzerland, but the reason does not lie in seeking language standards abroad. Rather, it exemplifies a counter-tendency to what we have been discussing. While language can play a vital role in creating national identity, it can also operate (as in Belgium) to militate against national unity in favour of a sub-identity within the nation-state. Language is similarly used as a political as well as a social index by the Basques and Catalonians in Spain, and we see within the United States powerful demands for the right to use Spanish as a reactive claim to identity for the millions of ethnic Hispanics who are United States citizens. It would seem indeed that where it is available, language is the most potent force not only for national unity but also in separatist movements within nation-states: as it was in liberation movements within empires.

We turn now to the third model: several nations—one language. It will be noticed that with the first model (one nation—one language) there is two-way identity. If you are Japanese, then Japanese is almost certainly your native language; and equally, if you are a native speaker of Japanese, then you are almost certainly a citizen of Japan. By contrast, with the third model, nationality may predict the language but the language will not predict the nationality. In other words, the identity is only one way. There are many examples. If you are an Iraqi, you are likely to speak Arabic. But if you speak Arabic, it is unlikely that you are an Iraqi: there are for example more Egyptians than Iraqis in the world. If you are Portuguese, you are likely to speak Portuguese; but if you speak Portuguese, it is more likely that you are a Brazilian. If you are a native speaker of Spanish, your nation may be Ecuador or any one of twenty other countries — including (as we have just seen) the United States. If your language is Chinese, you are more likely than not a citizen of the People's Republic; but you may be among the many millions of Chinese speakers who are citizens of Taiwan or Malaysia or Singapore.

And then of course there is English, at least as striking as any of these examples. If you are a native speaker of English, there is a four-to-one chance that you are an American, but you might well be British or Australian or Canadian or South African or a citizen of one among a further half-dozen countries.

This third model can work against a sense of national identity, so powerful is the incentive to have one's unique *national* identity endorsed by a unique *linguistic* identity. It is for this reason that strong attempts were made to replace English by Irish in establishing the Republic of Ireland. Again, to many of those guiding the early steps of the young United States, it similarly seemed to the serious detriment of establishing a national identity that they should continue to use English, the language then chiefly associated with the country whose yoke they had just thrown off.

There are other examples of unease amounting to an identity

crisis where the language in daily use cannot by itself represent national identity, but on the whole they are exceptional. Rather, there seems to be a widespread sense of *gain* in sharing a language with other nations, whereby people can perceive — to quote Edmund Burke again — 'an enlightened self-interest' which is willing to 'identify with an interest more enlarged and publick'. In other words, just as we have seen language as the means of extending identity beyond the family, the locality, the region to the whole nation, so the 'one language—several nations' model of language use enables the speakers of that language to extend their sense of identity far beyond the confines of their particular nation-state. A well-known example is the special relation that has flourished for a century or more between the United States and Britain, each regarding the other as in some sense an extension of itself with a community of knowledge and sympathy far greater than between either and any neighbouring state speaking a different language. Another example is the sense of identity shared by the Arabic-speaking countries all the way from Morocco on the Atlantic to Oman, virtually on the Indian Ocean, 8,000 kilometres away. Yet a third most outstanding example of language as an instrument of identity, and one where this role has been resoundingly endorsed by powerful voices, is the case of Chinese. Thus, despite there being a sharply different socio-political ethos in the People's Republic from that in either Taiwan or Singapore, there is agreement on promoting a single Chinese for use in all three (though in Taiwan and Singapore it is called Mandarin, not Pudong Hua).

Sharing English

With this example of language as the instrument of a breathtakingly 'enlarged and publick' interest, we turn back finally to English. This is the language of perhaps greatest current interest among those of the 'one language—several nations' model. We have mentioned the sense of widened identity that is summarised as the 'special relation' between the USA and Britain. But of course this sense of identity extends to Australians and Canadians and many others as well. We read the same books, whether they are by the American Saul Bellow or the British Iris Murdoch or the Australian Patrick White. We watch the same television shows. We sing the same nursery rhymes to our children, crack the same jokes, share the same folklore, and our speech is interlarded with the same Shakespearian allusions. There is an international society called the English-Speaking Union whose very name proclaims the linguistic basis of its appeal.

But the English-Speaking Union has branches not only in London and Leeds and Los Angeles and Sydney. It has branches also in India and Ceylon and Hong Kong; it has branches too in Belgium, Germany, and Switzerland. This distribution draws attention to an aspect of English that marks it off sharply from the other 'one language—several nations' examples we have discussed. It has strong operational, instrumental, and even social roots well beyond the countries in which it is spoken natively. We saw a moment ago that, in the proposition 'If your mother tongue is English, you are a citizen of Y', it is by no means easy to predict the value of Y: it might be America, Britain, Australia, Ireland, Canada, and so on. Rephrasing the proposition to read 'If you make *daily use* of English in the course of *your work*, you are a citizen of Y', the difficulty of predicting the value of Y increases dramatically. It is probable that in every nation on earth, there are some of its citizens who use English every day. In consequence, the value of Y is more likely than not to be a country where English is not a native language. In other words, there are more speakers of English for whom it is not their native language than the worldwide total of native speakers.

Bringing these non-native users of English together with the native speakers gives us not just a very *large* community but obviously a very *heterogeneous* one. There is clearly no *ethnic* common bond nor a religious one nor a historical one, and the situation is very different from the sense of widened identity that we discussed with respect to Arabic or Chinese or indeed Spanish.

Rather, within the total community of English speakers, the language helps to articulate cross-national identities that would otherwise be difficult to sustain. The use of English at international conferences of doctors or engineers illustrates this. A Russian physicist and a Russian toxicologist adequately realise their Russian identity in Russian, but they feel an identity also with fellow scientists — be these Germans or Japanese or

Americans; and at the present time *this* identity is chiefly realised in English. So too, people who are engaged throughout the world in such fields as aid organisations like the Red Cross or Amnesty International need a common language to achieve their communicative goals and maintain their identity in these roles. And again, that common language is more usually English than any other. More generally and on a lighter note, we have a cross-national youth culture (manifest for example in pop music) where once more the identity is commonly realised in English.

It is because of its potentiality to establish identities that have nothing to do with the local self, the family self, the national self, that the 'one language — many nations' model of language use might be regarded as the most promising for mankind's future. Even in centuries past, it was recognised that for *some* people in *some* roles a widened identity must subsist and that this required more than a local language. Only consider the role of Chinese in linking scholars in the Far East, or the role of Latin in linking doctors and philosophers for a thousand years in the West. In the present era of fast travel, electronic communication, and a world network of multinational industries, such a common language is even more necessary — and for far greater numbers of people.

There are of course dangers of resentment in the use of a lingua franca. People who possess no mastery of it may be deeply suspicious of the identities assumed by those who do. Common people often feared the few around them who used Latin in medicine or law and who seemed thereby to cut themselves off in a higher and more privileged realm from their humbler fellow citizens who had no Latin. Such resentments are not unknown in some of the developing countries where English survives from the colonial era, useful in providing international links of course, useful often in being a relatively neutral *intra*-national link in a multilingual country such as Nigeria or the Philippines, but widely suspected and resented as well. Since the people so linked are inevitably the relatively well-educated and affluent, the use of English is sometimes attacked (by those without such advantages) as the language of privilege. English is therefore seen as intrusive, favourable to the powerful, and hence as far from neutral. Nor, obviously, can it be seen as neutral to people in France or Japan, Germany or Korea, countries well aware of the resources they

devote to the acquisition of English for those same external relations that are served by English in countries like the United States
or Britain who do not have to learn it.

SOME FOLLOW-UP WORK

1 How might a playwright express in modern English the
  fragment of dialogue from *As You Like It* (p. 27)? Why does
  the quotation from Donne (p. 30) present fewer difficulties?

2 The language of both King Alfred and of modern Dutch
  resembles modern English in some respects. Find examples
  of such resemblance in the two quotations (p. 28), bearing in
  mind that the Alfredian letter ð corresponds to the modern *th*.

3 Assess from your own experience the extent to which you
  value the sort of multiple identity discussed in this chapter
  and tabulated on p. 31.

4 a) What is the difference between 'nationality' and 'race'?
  Which has the closer connection with language? Consider the
  advantages and disadvantages of the 'one nation—one
  language' model.
  b) Write on cases in recent years where there have been
  troubles over matters of language in relation to nationality.

5 What are the principal languages used in (a) Luxembourg,
  (b) Malaysia, (c) South Africa, (d) the United States,
  (e) Singapore, (f) Nigeria, (g) the Philippines, (h) Tanzania,
  (i) India?

6 What languages besides English are used in the British Isles?
  Try to assess by whom they are spoken and on what
  occasions.

7 A cynic has said, 'A language is a dialect with an army.'
  Discuss.

C H A P T E R   4

Variation within English

We noted at the outset of Chapter Three that no language was a 'monolith', however much the name of a language (French, Italian, Japanese) might suggest that it was. This has long been recognised in the case of Chinese: one does not set out to learn 'Chinese' but a particular *kind* of Chinese — Mandarin or Cantonese, for example. And though the differences are less considerable in the case of Spanish or English, foreign learners can buy courses on Castillian Spanish or Latin-American Spanish, on American English or British English.

These last examples might be taken to imply that variation within a language arises from where you happen to live (and in Chapter Three we also saw the kind of variation arising from *when* you happen to live). But many other factors are involved. For example: what your purpose is in speaking; what you are speaking about; who your addressees are; how well you know them; whether you are addressing them orally or in writing. As well as 'British English' and 'American English', therefore, we are all familiar with other ways of being more specific: 'colloquial English', 'literary English', 'scientific English', 'religious English', 'dialectal English' are among the many expressions we freely use as we try to come to terms with the undoubted fact that English comes in many guises. Some labels we apply neutrally; some we apply in admiration and approval; some we apply in strong disapproval; some we apply with more or less precision, depending on the breadth of our experience. Much of our labelling, appropriate or otherwise, reflects the degree to which our sense of identity embraces or rejects the users of the English concerned.

Some samples of English

Let us examine a selection of passages and reflect on the extent to which we recognise features of the English in them which lead in turn to our recognising or guessing a suitable label for each:

1 'What's up with you, Miss?' Her father was still on the boil. 'Weeping for the sins of your father, is it? And for what,' he roared at Kathleen, 'did you want giving away my second-best boots? Nobody in this family thinks anything of property, only how to get rid of it hand over fist. Saint Francis of Assisi isn't in it with ye. Yez have him bet. He divested himself of what was his but ye're so charitable ye have to give handouts of what doesn't belong to ye at all. It's easy seen no one of ye ever worked for a day's wages in yeer lives. There's Eamonn off playing soldiers with a broom handle. God help us! Soldiers. Make a cat laugh. But work? Oh no. They've no respect for it or what it earns. Is it out drilling he is this minute?' he wanted to know. 'In the wet? It would be the price of him, and him with a weak chest.'

2 In Amsterdam, prices ended a thin day firmer on Wall Street gains; in Zurich the all-share index gained two points on low turnover; and in Frankfurt, a strong surge, said to stem from short-covering by London professionals, added 11.86 points to the DAX index, which closed at 1380.46.

3 He set the pace for the recital with a briskly rendered Pranamamayakam in Gowlai, a composition of Mysore Vasudevachar. One liked the manner in which he and his accompanying vidwan built up the Kriti embellishing it with little flourishes here and there . . . Then came Kamboji alapana for Pallavi . . . With Vedanayagam Pillai's Nane Unnie Nambinane in Hamsanandi, the recital came to a glorious end.

4 It is not in doubt that in determining the appeal by the developers and granting planning permission, the inspector was exercising powers under the 1971 Act, such that it was his duty to pay special attention to the matters specified by section 277(8).

   Nowhere in his decision letter, however, does he mention this subsection or his duty thereunder, either in terms or by the use of any language from which it might, in my judgment, reasonably be inferred that he was intending to refer to it. That omission nevertheless does not determine the issue raised by the applicants.

The obligation imposed by the statute is to pay special attention to the desirability of preserving or enhancing the character of the conservation area in exercising the power to determine the developers' appeal. For the due discharge of that duty the inspector did not, in my judgment, need to say that he was discharging or was conscious of that duty. What matters is that he does discharge that duty, and if he makes no reference to it in his decision it must, in my judgment, be apparent from his decision that he has discharged it or otherwise there will be error in law: either because the necessary inference must be that he has not discharged it, or because he has failed to give adequate reasons for a decision which he could not validly reach without discharging that duty.

5 I met ayont the cairney
A lass wi' tousie hair
Singin' till a bairnie
That was nae langer there.

Wunds and walds to swing
Dinna sing sae sweet.
The licht that bends owre a' thing
Is less ta'en up wi't.

6 'She is very upset. Her son is dying, and she knows that, and she don't know that . . . see . . . It's something she knows and something she don't want to know. You understand? And all this time, here she is, she's in trouble over a lot of parking tickets. She says to herself, "I have got to be with my son, and suppose they arrest me over a lot of parking tickets" . . . See?'
'Well, she — she don't have to worry about that,' said Kramer. In a room with three people who said *She don't* he couldn't get a *doesn't* out of his mouth. 'The district attorney is quashing the warrant. She's still gonna have to pay the tickets, but nobody's gonna arrest her.'

7 Calcavecchia began his round with '70 feet worth of putts' on the first two holes, birdies from a 30-footer followed by a 40-footer. For the rest of the day he missed only one green, and never came close to making a bogey. He eagled his 10th

hole, playing the 514-yard par five with a driver, then sinking the eight-foot eagle putt.

Sandy Lyle finished the first round nine shots back from Calcavecchia, with a two-over 74, a score that he was able to keep down only with good scrambling on the final holes. After a terrible approach to the 16th hole landed in a trap, he made a worse shot into the rough. With the flat 70 ft away he was on his way to a double bogey, but chipped it straight in for par.

8 When he hung up he told his colleagues: 'That na my brother. Just return from overseas.' . . .

'What department he de work?'

'Secretary to the Scholarship Board.'

'E go make plenty money there. Every student who wan' go England go de see am for house.'

'E no be like dat,' said Joseph. 'Him na gentleman. No fit take bribe.'

'Na so,' said the other in disbelief.

9 Passenger depend lah — good one also got, bad one also got. Some ah some taxi driver they want to go to this tourist area like hotel ah. They park there, y'know. Then if the tourist want to go and buy things, buy anything ah, they book the taxi say one hour I pay you how much. Then after that they brought the passenger go and buy thing already. Then the shop ah give commission to the taxi driver lah. Don't know how many per cen.

10 When this code is input, data in the print buffer is arranged so that the print position for following data is shifted left by one column (for current character mode) without actually moving the printer carriage. Therefore, in the Enlarged mode, a single BS [backspace] code causes the print position to be shifted to the left by two normal characters. The BS code is ignored when preceding data has been printed in bit image format.

11 So there I am in the outback, miles from anywhere, the sun red hot, stranded with a wheel to change. Half the nuts were rusted so I was as miserable as a bandicoot. Then up rolls this Sheila in a limo and we had a couple of beers together. Hers. She was no help with the wheel but.

12 The standard side lobe suppression receiver of an airborne

SSR [secondary surveillance radar] transponder is designed to
detect only the signals transmitted in the main beam of the
SSR ground station. This main beam would be three to six
degrees wide, which is equivalent to 1½ to 3 nautical miles
at 30 nautical miles from the radar head.

13

Mehr Chand Hostel,
D.A.V. College,
Jullundur.
12th July

Respected Father,
I felt very sad when you parted from me, after completing
the formalities of admission. I had misgivings about being
able to adjust myself to the new surroundings. But
fortunately I have been able to strike new friendships here.
The company of these friends has made life not only
bearable, but enjoyable for me. Sham was the one who
invited me to join their merry group, when he espied me
sitting morosely after your departure. . . . My new friends
are very good at studies and Sham is besides a member of
the college cricket eleven. That the seniors do not vex me is
entirely due to their good offices. On your next visit here I
will introduce you to my friends. I am sure you will like my
judicious selection.
Please give my regards to mother and love to Guddi.

Yours affectionately,
Suresh

14 Nah Jooab's middlin' thick like, bur 'e'd a 'ad to be a deeal
thicker net ta know ut ther wer summat wrang t'way ut shoo
wer preychin' on, an' so 'e late paper tummle ontut' flooar
an 'e sat theer an' gaped woll shoo stopped fer breeath, an'
then 'e sez. 'What the heck 'as ta agate on, lass? Is ther
summat up or summat?' An' that didnt mend matters one
iota. All it did wer ta start 'er off ageean.
'Just 'ark at 'im,' shoo sez. "Ere's me, as thrang as Throp's
wife when shoo 'ung 'ersen wit' dishcleyat, an' theer's 'im
cahrd uv 'is backside! Coint see a job ut ther is ta do! Wodnt
dreeam o' doin' it if 'e cud .. . .'
'Nay!' bust in Jooab. 'Ahm nooan takkin' that quitely.
Thers monny a one war ner me an' full weel tha knows it.'

The notion of 'institutionalisation'

One feature of these samples is so obvious that it need scarcely be mentioned: they are all in *writing*. The point is far from trivial, especially as we notice that some samples (notably (14)) draw attention to how they would have sounded if *spoken*. As soon as we pause over this fact, we reflect that our recognition of variation within English quite generally depends on hearing differences in pronunciation — without expecting such differences to be reflected in spelling. New Yorkers and Londoners say the words *dance, hot* and *bird* in ways that are recognisably American and British, but they make no attempt to reflect these differences when they write the words. And where British and American spellings differ (as in *humour/humor, travelled/traveled, centre/center*), these spelling differences do not capture pronunciation differences, nor are they meant to do so. In short, while pronunciation varies markedly from one group of English speakers to another, spelling for the most part does not; and when it does, it is without reference to pronunciation differences.

But spelling is a good point at which to introduce a major factor in language variation, and that is the extent to which a feature in language use is 'institutionalised'. With English (and apparently this is widespread among languages), there is a sense of orthodoxy about spelling. Whoever we are and wherever we are, we learn how to spell the word *thought* (it could hardly come naturally!) and we expect everyone else to spell it that way too. It is when we have such a consensus in society that we speak of 'institutionalisation', and of course it doesn't apply only to matters of language. The wearing of white trousers in the game of cricket, of a black tie at a funeral, of a ring on a certain finger after marriage: all these are institutionalised practices in many cultures.

So far as language is concerned, while spelling is the clearest example, institutionalisation applies to all aspects of language use. When someone writes *thought* in a sentence, we expect it not merely to be spelled in that way but to have the same meaning as we believe the rest of us understand from the word. That meaning is institutionalised; but the meaning of *bigalum* in what follows is not:

Their conversation was interrupted by the toddler on Mary's

knee: 'Bigalum!' Seeing her friend's puzzled look, Mary said, 'That means she wants a drink; don't know where she got the word from.'

The notion of institutionalisation is related to the concept of standard language which we shall examine in Chapter Nine, but for the moment we may note that to a very considerable degree we are influenced in our reactions to the specimens (1)–(14) by the evidence they present of being in a form of English that we recognise because it is institutionalised. Where such evidence seems to be notably lacking, as for example in sample (9), our reaction may well be, 'What interest is there in this? Surely the speaker is someone who has simply not learned English properly. As an English speaker, I would find it absurd to have a sample of my inadequate French being solemnly set alongside passages from Sartre and Camus and Mitterrand as an example of "variation within French".'

The objection is a good one, but we cannot always write off a sample of language variation as just a foreigner's poor attempt. The languages we now call Romanian and French cannot be regarded as merely 'bad Latin'. There is nothing to prevent a society from proclaiming its own variation from another language as its own new language. After all, what many people still call 'Pidgin English' was institutionalised and adopted a few years ago as the official language of Papua New Guinea: 'Tok Pisin', in which the sentence 'I can't fix the engine' might be translated as:

Mi no save mekin ensin i-gut gen.

Tok Pisin is an extreme example, but we must recognise that language variation is a lively political issue in many countries, with vigorous moves to adopt and institutionalise a local form of English specific to a particular region or country. This is less surprising, perhaps, in countries such as Scotland and Australia than in Nigeria or Sri Lanka where English is without deep roots and where its forms range widely both in their resemblance to the English of other countries and even in their adequacy to perform the local communicative functions required of them. Where in such circumstances variation in English is most obviously related simply to varying *command* of the language (varying, for example, as between the most educated and least educated of the population), the difficulties in achieving the kind of consensus that is a precondition of institutionalisation are profound. In consequence, we often find that Nigerian, Sri Lankan, and analogous authorities continue to recognise for official purposes only the institutionalised standard of a native-English-speaking country such as Britain or America, despite its remoteness from the English actually in local use. Meanwhile teachers may be permitted to promote local variation if they wish and face as best they may the consequent criticisms from their pupils' parents and employers.

Factors in language variation

Let us now consider the fourteen samples given above and set up a framework for analysing the ways in which language variation occurs. If we look at some of the examples that seem plainly to be motivated by the function which Jakobson (as we saw in Chapter One) called 'referential', for example (2) or (10), we realise that they might well proceed from one and the same person. A journalist might turn from reporting the financial news in (2) and proceed to instruct a colleague in the use of a new desk-top computer in the language of (10). This does not make the linguistic differences between (2) and (10) any the less remarkable but it shows that these differences are determined by the *use* to which the language is being put. By contrast, if we look at samples (5) and (14), the differences are not determined by the use of the language (to shape a poem in the one, to tell a story in the other) but by the backgrounds and personal histories of the users themselves, Scots in (5), Yorkshire in (14). Here we cannot plausibly imagine the same person being the source of both samples. Even a clever mimic or a well-trained actor giving a convincing performance of these would be *pretending* to be from Scotland or Yorkshire, since the samples in question are not related to a temporary use of language but to the habitual identity of the user.

So we begin with two opposing factors in language variation:

$$\text{variation} \longrightarrow \left[\begin{array}{l} \text{use-related: e.g. (2), (10)} \\ \text{user-related: e.g. (5), (14)} \end{array} \right.$$

But while we must see these as 'opposing' in the way already explained (an individual may operate several *use*-related varieties but only one *user*-related variety), they are also complementary. That is, any use-related variety must be expressed in terms of a particular user-related variety. The financial report of (2) may be uttered by a Scot or an American or someone from Yorkshire and must inevitably be coloured in pronunciation by the user-related variety in question.

Within use-related variation, we may apply the full range of Jakobsonian functions, but these may be simplified in the present discussion into a polar pair according as the form seems to be determined largely by the *content* or by the *tone*. Thus it is the content and subject matter that seems responsible for the choice and arrangements of words in (12), air traffic control, (10), computer operation, and (3), Indian music. By contrast, it is the tone in which the subject matter is communicated to the addressee that seems uppermost in the poetic form of (5) and the colloquial form of (11). Adjustments of tone enable us to evoke humour, irony, passion, personal involvement. But again the polarity must not be seen as mutually exclusive: content-marking and tone-marking are present in every utterance. Contrast, for example, the impersonal tone of (10) with the following more 'user-friendly' extract from another computer manual; a difference in tone, though concerned with the same type of content:

> To set up your RAM disk, copy the ramdisk.sys file from your utility floppy disk on to the disk you are using to boot the computer.

Our variation factors are thus now expanded as follows:

$$\text{variation} \left\{ \begin{array}{l} \text{use-related} \left\{ \begin{array}{l} \text{content-marked} \\ \text{tone-marked} \end{array} \right. \\ \text{user-related} \end{array} \right.$$

We turn now to the 'user-related' node on this diagram and we must begin by making clear that we are concerned here only with variation that is marked by differences of language form. This may seem a minor and indeed obvious point, but it is one that is necessary to make because an expression such as 'Indian English' is used with very different meanings. On the one hand, it refers to linguistic form — pronunciation, grammar, choice of lexical items that lead us to believe that the speaker is from the Indian subcontinent ('You are knowing my father, isn't it?'). On the other hand, it is used (for example by the Indian Academy of Literature in Delhi) to denote the ethno-political fact that Indian nationals may well use English in their work. A prize for an 'Indian English novel' means a prize for a novel written in English by a citizen of India — without reference to the form of the English itself.

The distinction in this case is very clear, in others it may be less so. When scholars speak of 'Taiwanese English' or 'Hong Kong English', they may well be thinking of the form of English as it is influenced by the native language background; but this is Chinese in each case. Alternatively, they may be claiming linguistic differences between the English used in Taiwan and Hong Kong. The term 'Black English' is likewise used ambiguously, sometimes to indicate common linguistic features, sometimes to refer only to the common ethno-political features of the speakers themselves.

Our diagram has now been further expanded as follows:

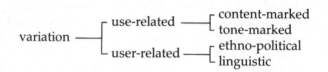

Native and non-native

Focusing on the *linguistic* node, we introduce a further distinction relating to the means by which speakers have acquired their command of the language. Again we can set up a polar contrast between learning the language unconsciously and 'naturally' on the one hand and learning it consciously through formal instruction on the other. In general, these nodes correspond to being a native speaker or a non-native speaker respectively (though in multilingual countries like Switzerland or Wales or India, people often acquire more than one language in childhood and might find it difficult to say whether they spoke one 'more natively' than another). We can say confidently that the English of most Britons and Australians is native, the English of most Malaysians and Ghanaians, Japanese and Pakistanis, is non-native. And although it will often be possible to judge whether a speaker of English is Australian or Japanese, in each case solely from the accent or other formal features of the English, the distinction between native and non-native is nonetheless of great significance. For example, broadly speaking, native speakers have an equally competent command of English, whether they are Americans or British or New Zealanders; by contrast, non-native speakers vary enormously in their command of the language and indeed a Nigerian or a Japanese sounds less identifiably Nigerian or Japanese the better that command is.

Then finally, we make a distinction at the native node between those native varieties of English that are fully institutionalised and those that are not. The clearest examples of the former are of course British English and American English, with well-established forms recognised not merely by social consensus within the territories concerned but worldwide, fully endorsed by the institutions of state, such as the education systems, and quite fully described in dictionaries and grammars. By contrast with British and American English, the other native varieties, whether regional (New York English, Yorkshire English) or national (Australian English, Irish English), are not fully institutionalised. Perhaps Scots comes closest, with a long literary tradition and sense of national identity, well represented in Scottish lexicography, and even an alternative (if rarely used) institutionalised system of spelling, exemplified in sample (5). There is also widespread consensus about Australian English, again represented in an indigenous lexicography. And in most of these native varieties a sense of institutionalised *pronunciation* exists, so as to make it beyond question that newsreaders and presenters on radio and television speak with a clearly identified Australian, New Zealand, Irish (etc) voice, as the case may be. But the fact remains that in general the language of the media and officialdom follows the institutionalised form of British English (in Canada more usually of American English), with little indication of any impending change of orientation.

Our diagram can now therefore be completed as follows:

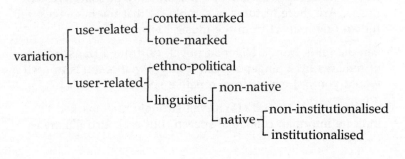

But in thus ending up with the institutionalised varieties, British English and American English, we need to remind ourselves that these are not monolithic either. As the full impact of the diagram entails, each of them is subject to the variation induced by the 'use-related' factors and also to 'user-related' variation, inasmuch as regional dialect colours the broad thrust of the overriding British variety of English. And there is plenty of scope too for the individual to realise his or her *personal* identity in language use.

SOME FOLLOW-UP WORK

1 Sample (2) is from the financial column of a daily newspaper. Identify the linguistic features that provide the relevant 'content-marking'. Provide a longer sample from a newspaper and extend the list of content-markers in consequence.

2 On p. 49 it was noted that the content of texts concerned with computers, such as sample (10), could be tone-marked with a greater or lesser degree of 'user-friendliness'. Look at one or two computer manuals and attempt to identify (a) the features peculiar to the content and (b) the features introduced to provide a specific tone.

3 Starting with sample (5), but adding further material by Hugh MacDiarmid and other modern Lallans poets, write a glossary of two dozen Scots words and an account of the spelling characteristics.

4 Compare sample (3) linguistically with a similar-sized extract from a newspaper review of a performance of some Western music. Are there features of sample (3) that might suggest an Indian origin apart from the musical terms?

5 Sample (8) is from a Nigerian novel, (9) from a transcription of remarks by a Singapore taxi driver. What features in each would you not expect from a native speaker of English?

6 Samples (1), (11), and (14) are all strongly tone-marked to indicate informal, colloquial speech. But each also illustrates

different non-institutionalised native dialects of English. Attempt a separation of these strands in each sample.

7 Examine the linguistic features in sample (4) which are consistent with its being part of a judicial pronouncement in court. Sample (6) also involves discussion of legal matters; point out the content-markers here too and discuss the vast differences in tone between (4) and (6).

8 What expressions in sample (7) are specific to golf? Match this extract with a newspaper report of another sport (such as football) and examine the differences and similarities.

9 Sample (13) is from a college text book for Indian students of English. How (and why) might you amend it if you were the author of the text book? If instead of addressing the book to Indian students, you had in mind students in your own country, in what ways would the model letter from a son to his father be different?

CHAPTER 5

The spread of English

In this chapter we shall look at 'spread' both in historical terms — how English has grown from being the language of a small community in a small European offshore island — and also in respect of the great spread of current responsibilities assumed by the language today. We glimpsed some of these responsibilities towards the end of Chapter Three: English in use not by a small island community but by a vast worldwide community, and in use for a comparably wide range of purposes. In use as a medium of uniquely international communication.

But in calling English uniquely international, we are by no means saying that English is unique in having an international role, still less that it is unique to find a language being used for international communication. As we have insisted in this book, communication is a permanent biological necessity and a precondition for our personal development as individuals and for our collective development as societies. This means that every language is uniquely important to those whose mother tongue it is. In this respect, all languages are equally important and precious. But as neighbouring societies have impinged on each other, whether for peaceful commerce or aggressive expansion, this has meant that — in addition to the need to know our own language — some people have always needed to learn the language of some other society. And a smaller number of people, engaged in more widely ranging trade or negotiation, have had to learn to communicate with quite a range of other societies.

This has meant that people have always come up against the *inequality* of languages. For speaking across frontiers, some languages have always thrust themselves forward as being apparently more important than others. The actual linguistic pecking order has changed from time to time, and we must expect it to go on changing. When Magna Carta was signed in 1215 not far from London, none of those present would ever have imagined English acquiring high value; at that time, many would have denied the possibility of English surviving even as the language of England. Nor were the prospects for English much better in Shakespeare's time. In 1582, Richard Mulcaster, who thought highly enough of the language to hope that there would one day be an English dictionary, nonetheless had to admit that 'our English tung is of small reatch, it stretcheth no further than this Iland of ours, naie not there over all'.

Linguistic 'reach'

The 'reach' of other languages was far greater, and over the centuries there have been several that have been used for the traffic across frontiers, whether for cultural, commercial, or military purposes. French is a familiar example, its aspirations well reflected in the title of a book by Antoine Rivarol in 1784: *Discours sur l'universalité de la langue française*. The 'universality' of French was represented by its spread to North America, though it was Spanish that developed an even more widespread role in the New World, matching the way in which some centuries earlier the Arabic language spread right across the middle of the Old World. In the Orient, the extensive adoption of Chinese charactery (for example in Japan) bears similar witness to the need for communication systems that transcend societal, tribal, regional, and of course temporal boundaries. At a somewhat more workaday level, we may note also the long-standing use of Malay as the lingua franca of trade in South East Asia, especially in the areas that are now Malaysia and Indonesia. In the Mediterranean and the Middle East, it was Greek that fulfilled the role of international language (and its mark is on the languages of the world in such words as *psychology*), but Greek was in due course succeeded by the heavily Greek-influenced Latin language. This survived the fall of imperial Rome by becoming the language of the Church and hence of virtually all education, culture, and the learned professions.

As such, the Latin language and the values it communicated

had a profound impact on Western development and on the vernacular languages of the West, not least on English. Indeed until the vernacular languages had absorbed — especially during the Renaissance of the sixteenth century — a vast number of Latin words, Latin replaced them for many purposes even within the countries whose native languages they were. Although we think of Francis Bacon as a great writer of English prose, it was in Latin that he chose to write when laying the foundations for modern science in such works as the *Novum Organum Scientiarum* (1620), with its emphasis on the need for the careful observation of natural phenomena. Many of his remarks have a continuing relevance, such as the following in relation to our concerns for the environment: 'Naturae enim non imperatur, nisi parendo' ('For we cannot command nature unless we obey it'). And he expressed such thoughts in Latin, partly so as to reach the intellectuals of other countries, and partly because — even after the triumphs in English of Shakespeare and his contemporaries — he had no faith in the stability or future 'reach' of English. Nor did the recourse to Latin die with Bacon. A couple of generations later, it was in Latin that Isaac Newton published his great work on gravitation and the laws of motion: *Philosophiae Naturalis Principia Mathematica* (1678). So too in other European countries. In Sweden we find Linnaeus choosing Latin for his numerous books on botanical description, such as *Genera Plantarum* of 1737. When the University of Ghent opened its doors for the first time in 1816, Latin was almost automatically adopted as the medium of instruction, Latin being quite normal as the language of European universities at that time and for decades later. The books by the German mathematician and physicist C F Gauss, who died in 1855, were regularly published in Latin — his influential *Theoria Motus Corporum Celestium*, for example, written soon after he had become director of the observatory at Göttingen.

Examples of such learned and academic uses of Latin could be far extended (even so prominent a scholar in the vernaculars as Jacob Grimm delivered his inaugural lecture of 1830 in Latin), but it must be noted that Latin was widely used in administration also, as late as the nineteenth century, in numerous contexts. It was still the state language of Transylvania in the first quarter of the nineteenth century; as late as the 1840s it was the language of parliamentary debate in Hungary and Croatia. It is still the language of the liturgy in some Roman Catholic services and was the language of the mass universally until a few years ago.

Now, the reason we have dwelt upon the role of Latin is that it has had this remarkable value over more than a millennium, without being the native language of those using it. There is a very different situation here from a German and a Pole agreeing to negotiate in German or Polish: in either case, it is the native language of one of them and is not functioning in what is generally understood to be the role of an international language. Contrast the situation in which a Czech and a Hungarian wish to communicate. Here it is very unlikely that either speaks the other's language, but both might very well know German and agree to discourse in that language. In this instance, German would be functioning as an international language.

The rise of English

It is in this sense that we have drawn attention to the role, at various times and in various places, of French, Spanish, Arabic, Malay, and Latin. Then, more recent in this role than any of these has been the rise of *English* as an international language.

More recent yet also vastly more widespread. Extensive as has been (and in many cases remains) the use of the other languages we have mentioned, there has never in recorded history been a language so widely used 'across frontiers' as English, never one so closely attaining the status of a universally accepted world language. Not long ago, two scholars at the East-West Center in Hawaii (Björn Jernudd and Willard Shaw) undertook a comparison of the current 'functional load' of some of the world's major languages. When it came to uses by non-native speakers, addressing other non-native speakers, English was by far the leading language. Here are some of the factors regarded as significant:

- as a medium of daily newspapers (for example, the *Times of India* or, in Japan, the *Asaki Evening News*)
- as a medium of instruction in higher education (in Nigerian universities, for example, this is English)
- as a medium for external broadcasting (English is used, for example, by the Soviet Union)

- named as one of the official languages in the constitutions of countries where it is not a native language (this, for example, is the position of English in Sri Lanka)

But there are many other measures that indicate the same result. Think of political protest. Whether a demonstration is taking place in Beirut or Berlin or Bogota, some of the slogans seen on television will be in English, reflecting the fact that there are more television broadcasts in English than in any other language: and the demonstrators know therefore that, as well as being more widely understood, the 'reach' of a slogan in English will be correspondingly greater. The story is the same in other areas of mass interest. English is more widely used in sport than any other language — soccer, tennis, golf, for example. More pop songs are written in English, more films are made in English. Even in judiciously plurilingual organisations like the United Nations and the European Community, English is used more frequently than any other language. And in international conferences, whether scientific, commercial, cultural, or philanthropic (such as world meetings of the great charities), it is usually taken for granted that English will be used more than any other language — and many such meetings agree on its exclusive use. Again, most of the specialised and learned journals established in recent years are in English, regardless of the discipline, though this is especially true of the sciences and medicine. But the trend has affected long-established journals also.

Two striking instances in West Europe are worth mentioning. Before 1960, the distinguished German journal *Physikalische Zeitung* only rarely contained articles in English; in more recent years, issues have often appeared in which more than half of the articles were in English. Around that same year, 1960, the Italian scientific periodical *Nuovo Cimento* relaxed its previous rule that all contributions had to be in Italian; within a decade, issues were appearing in which every single article was in English.

Let us pause to consider why people seize upon one language rather than another, one language after another, as the favoured international medium. It is often thought that there must be something special about the *quality* of the language concerned. We saw good reason in Chapter One to be sceptical about this. Whatever the language, native speakers will naturally revere it as something special. Alternatively, if we admire a people, its country, its civilisation, its architecture, its literature, we extend our admiration to its language and make extravagant claims for its quality. Witness the widely held views about the economy of Latin and on the elegance of French. Economical and elegant though they may be, these were not the qualities that gave these languages leadership. Nor, of course, was it the superiority of English in these respects that caused it to supersede these languages in world leadership. Shakespeare did not find it possible to endow *Hamlet* with literary greatness because English was thus and so. By the same token, the greatness of Racine, Goethe, or Tolstoy is not a function of the special qualities put at their disposal by French, German, and Russian respectively.

Cultural factors

We do not mean that cultural qualities are irrelevant: far from it. People are indeed attracted to learn another language because of the access it provides to cultural resources. Latin was the vehicle of the classical and silver age literature of Rome and it became the chief language of Western Christianity. Arabic was the language of the great Maghreb scientific culture which spanned the centuries between the science of Ancient Greece and that of modern Europe — a culture obliquely reflected in such words as *algebra*. And Arabic is the language of Islam, one of the few religions rivalling Christianity in its world spread. So, yes, undoubtedly the unsurpassed greatness of literature in English, from Chaucer to James Joyce and beyond, is among the powerful incentives to learn English in every country on earth.

But an even more powerful incentive to learn a foreign language is our perception of the power wielded by those who use it. Traditionally, languages have spread through conquest of lands and markets. We today may associate Ancient Greece with Aristotle, but the force which spread Greek influence, civilisation, and frontiers was the military might of his pupil, Alexander the Great. We today may associate Latin with the poetry of Vergil or the scholastic philosophy of St Thomas Aquinas, but the force which began the spread and influence of Latin was the military expansion which gave rise to the enormous Roman Empire more than two thousand years ago. So also we must relate the spread of Arabic to the Moorish expansion in the Mediterranean from the eighth century; the spread of Spanish and Portuguese to the imperial conquest of large parts of the world from the fifteenth century; the spread of French to powerful colonial expansion likewise — in North America, in Africa, and in the Far East.

And of course the web of English has a similar strand. In explaining the 'small reach' of English in 1582, Mulcaster said that 'our state is no Empire'. But in a very few years England was doing what Spain and Portugal had done, and France and the Netherlands were intent on doing likewise: establishing settlements in the New World. Jamestown in Virginia was settled in 1607 and the Plymouth Colony in Massachusetts was founded in 1620: small beginnings of what was to become the greatest single development in the historical spread of English. Between the time of Milton and that of Tennyson, the process went unbrokenly ahead, taking native English speakers, often in numbers and always with power, to the other continents of the globe: to large parts of Africa; to Asia (especially the Indian subcontinent); to Australia and New Zealand; to Hong Kong, Hawaii, the Philippines.

We have just mentioned numbers, a factor that is often exaggerated in assessing why a particular language is adopted for international communication. Undoubtedly, a certain critical mass would be a necessary condition: but it is by no means sufficient. Even with its world spread today, the number of native speakers of English (perhaps 350 million) is not all that impressive when we reflect that there are twice as many speakers of Hindi and at least three times as many speakers of Chinese. There are many millions more speakers of German in the world than there are of French, and there probably always have been; indeed there are more speakers of Portuguese than there are of French. But neither German nor Portuguese has ever had the international status enjoyed by French.

We have a mixture of determining factors, then: the language selected is the vehicle of a valued culture, is associated with power, has an existing large currency in respect of user numbers. Is it enough to say that the present — and unprecedented — world role of English results from just an appropriate mix of these factors? Perhaps; but we think not. These could have triggered the dominance of any among half a dozen languages, from Spanish to Chinese: and might still do so. But there were other factors favouring English. One was the hold its critical mass of native speakers exercised, not just numerically but in their strategic location in every part of the globe. Another can be seen as not much more than a historical accident.

International communication

The second half of the twentieth century saw the explosive growth of the *need* for an international language: need with an acuteness perhaps never previously experienced. And the need arose at just the time that the other factors we have considered had already given English a good deal of world currency. It arose through the dramatic developments in communications — the transport of both people and information — that have resulted in what is referred to in the cliché 'the global village'.

The concept of neighbouring societies has been radically changed by rapid transport systems which — very suddenly, even in terms of living memory, let alone in terms of recorded history — enable any of us to move in ten or twelve hours to the remotest point of the terrestrial globe: Wellington to Reykjavik; Manchester to Tokyo; Moscow to Buenos Aires. This is the time that would have been required in all periods of history until a few generations ago for anyone to travel only a mere 100 kilometres. And our use of *anyone* is significant too. In past ages only a very few — a very affluent or a very desperate few — would undertake journeys to communities 100 or 200 kilometres away. Now, very ordinary people for very ordinary purposes can in large numbers — four or five hundred at a time — undertake journeys of many thousands of kilometres. We can no longer be content with communication systems fitted to the needs of a tiny élite.

More dramatically still, information which once — with trivial exceptions — could move only at the speed of its human bearer (100 kilometres a day) can now be moved in effect instantaneously, not only to any individual remote location, but to *all* remote locations simultaneously: anywhere on earth, or indeed to and via satellites far beyond the earth. In other words, we can learn of an event on the other side of the world as quickly as we can learn of an event on the other side of the street. We can go and visit its location with a few hours' flight. These are the facts that lie behind hyperbolic images like 'the global village'. They are real: in many obvious respects, all human societies have been brought together in an interdependence analogous to that of the few hundred people comprising the traditional village community as we knew it in earlier generations.

But whereas this traditional isolated community depended for its coherence on every member knowing the language of every other member, there is no analogy here with the newly evolved global village: and not the remotest possibility of one emerging. Indeed, the position is rather that the technological revolution in the *means* of communication has highlighted and magnified a millionfold the urgency of our communication *needs*. Electronics and mass transport, along with the international commerce that they enjoin, make international communication on a massive and rapid scale a social and economic necessity.

In this sudden emergent need, the world has seized on the obvious language to hand and rapidly enhanced its roles in recent decades. And in part at least, what made English the obvious language was that it was the language of many of the great corporations devising the communications revolution itself: IBM, Plessey, Boeing, Cable and Wireless, for example. We see examples of the enhanced roles for English that we have just mentioned almost everywhere we look. In virtually every hotel in the world, instructions for using telephone or telex will be found not only in the local language but also in English. Passengers in virtually every aircraft in the world are given oral and written information not only in the language of the country where the aircraft is registered, but also in English.

English would thus seem to have developed a momentum of its own, independently of the numbers of native English speakers, independently of the cultural values associated with English-speaking countries, and — at least as striking — independently of their economic and military power. This indeed may well in aggregate be showing a relative decline during the very period in which the role of English has been most enhanced. The Czech and the Hungarian mentioned earlier as agreeing to discourse in German would today be at least as likely to agree on English, and a Polish government minister has told us of being present at a meeting of East European (Comecon) countries where the proceedings were in English, though of course no English-speaking country was represented. At any rate, the momentum is such that English is a vital curricular component in the education system of every country, taking pride of place with that other metalanguage, mathematics, as the keys to communication and science.

The future

How long that momentum can continue and sustain the present hegemony of English is a matter for speculation, in the face of shifts in economic and other indices of power, shifts too in world politics, in nationalist and religious movements, as well as in environmental and technological circumstances. We certainly cannot assume any parallel with the centuries of unchallenged Latin that we discussed earlier.

The choice of an international language must primarily be a matter of convenience for those using it. On neither side should participants feel they are making linguistic concessions that put them at a disadvantage with their interlocutors. But it may well be a significant part of this mutual convenience that the language is not unduly associated with allegiances such as national loyalties or political orientation. This was of course the case with Latin — at least until the Reformation caused its greater association with the Roman Church. Although little has been made of this factor in published discussion of international communication, it may already — during a period when in every country there is acute national consciousness — have exerted some influence in the increased reliance on English. Here we have a language whose *name* relates to one part of a small West European polity (the United Kingdom) but which is also the language of several other countries — notably the United States. One has only to reflect on the very different implications it would have for an international negotiation if we spoke of drawing up the agreement in the same language but called it 'the Australian language' or 'British' or 'American'. It would be difficult to avoid the impression that the form of the agreement must in some degree reflect the legal or moral or political mores of the nation concerned — if not actually promoting its national interests.

So it is, no doubt, that a Japanese firm can negotiate a deal in English with a Brazilian or a German or a Saudi-Arabian company with no fear of being seen as part of an American multinational, and equally with no fear of being thought to have a linguistic advantage. The use of English is a linguistic concession shared by both sides.

But of course English is used in international deals also by Americans, Britons, Australians, and many others for whom it is the native language, and then the position is very different. When an Australian is negotiating in English with a Brazilian, there can be no parity of linguistic sacrifice, and the advantage to the Australian in ease of expression may be heavily offset by the Brazilian's awareness of this. We have a problem here of which all too few Anglophones are aware. Indeed, there is a widespread belief that the general use of English worldwide gives Anglophones a head start: and this belief reinforces their reluctance to learn foreign languages themselves. But there are two dangers here — none the less potent in being largely hidden. One is the resistance that lurks in the inherent unfairness of a Brazilian or Korean struggling with an inevitably less competent command of English, as he or she negotiates with an Australian or American or Briton. The other is the unwarranted assumption on the part of Anglophones that since they understand the foreigner's English, the foreigner can equally understand theirs. This is in fact highly unlikely unless the Anglophones studiously restrict their lexicon, narrow their stylistic range, and adopt a carefully neutral variety of English which eschews grammatical ellipses and phonological slur that are natural in colloquial discourse between native speakers.

The discipline required is considerable and may be more burdensome on the largely monolingual Anglophones than it would be for people who are multilingual and who live in a multilingual country such as Belgium. But such a discipline is enjoined not only by the imperatives of multilingual communication: it is essential in human communication of any kind and in any language. We are constantly in the business of crossing frontiers.

SOME FOLLOW-UP WORK

1 Richard Mulcaster noted that in his time English was not spoken beyond 'this Iland of ours, naie not there overall'. What other languages were then spoken in 'this Iland'?

2 In Mulcaster's time, both French and Latin had roles in Britain among those whose ordinary language was English. Try to find out what those roles were and how long they persisted.

3 The English one-pound coin (in contrast to the Welsh one) bears a Latin inscription. Comment on this and such other continuing roles for Latin that you can determine.

4 Why did Latin not continue to have the major international roles illustrated on pp. 55–57?

5 In addition to the measures for assessing the international currency of English mentioned in this chapter, give additional ones arising from your own experience.

6 What are (a) the advantages and (b) the disadvantages to native speakers of English in the increased use of English as an international language?

7 Consider the replacement of English in its international functions by any other language that seems to you a plausible candidate. Devise a speculative scenario of how and why the replacement might take place.

8 In 1887, the Polish Dr L L Zamenhof presented the public with his invented Esperanto. It was to be the hope of the world (the Latin *spero* means 'I hope') in being a language fitted for international use through its simplicity of form and its fairness in requiring all users equally to undergo the discipline of learning it. Find out more about this and analogous proposals; discuss their potential and the validity of the claims made for them.

CHAPTER 6

Our ever-changing language

In Chapter Four we saw how separation in space — geographical or social — could cause a language to assume considerable variation. We have also noted that holding the location constant, we could see that the passing of time produces great changes likewise: between the English of Chaucer's London and Harold Pinter's London, let us say. In the present chapter we shall look at such changes over a much shorter time span: actual living memory. This has considerable interest for two reasons. First, it sharpens our awareness of the fact that language, even in the same place, among the same people, is constantly changing — though often the changes are so gradual and small that unless we train ourselves to pay attention, we do not notice them. Second, it helps to explain to some extent the wide range of choice we have in saying almost anything, since there co-exist at any one time expressions that have been current for hundreds of years and others which became current much more recently. Some started being used eighty years ago let us say (a convenient practical limit to 'within living memory'), some fifty years ago, some twenty years ago, and some have emerged in popular currency only in the past year or so.

Wherever you live and whatever your language, it is very rewarding to sit with grandparents or elderly neighbours and persuade them to talk. Can you remember (we ask coaxingly) the First World War or, even earlier, the sinking of the Titanic? Do you remember seeing pictures of Kaiser Wilhelm II, of Czar Nicholas II, of the accession of Emperor Hirohito in 1926? Tell me about dreadnoughts and zeppelins, Don Bradman, the 1936 Olympics, Lindbergh flying the Atlantic, Hilary and Tensing climbing Everest. Memory of the events is accompanied, often unconsciously, by the contemporary language that described them.

Among the present writers' elderly friends have been people who were present when Shaw's *Pygmalion* was first performed in 1912 and who remembered the titillating shock when Eliza Doolittle first said 'Not bloody likely!', using a word almost never heard in public and then believed to be chiefly used by men, and pretty rough men at that. Another of our octogenarian friends told us that when she was a girl the word *toilet* meant solely the activity of washing and dressing, and when we checked in *The Oxford English Dictionary* we found that when the relevant volume was published (1926) the sense 'WC' was noted as being an Americanism.

But even if we are unable to engage in actual talk with people in their eighties, we can easily get access through our local library to newspapers of eighty years ago; equally, of course, we regularly read books and poems that were written long before our own time. And we should get into the habit of noting just when any book we read was first published, because its language represents the period just as do the social and material allusions. Indeed the two often go together: *dreadnoughts* were not merely *things* — large and terrifying battleships — they were stimuli to the imagination for metaphor and hyperbole, rather in the way that the marvels of space exploration, microelectronics, and telecommunications are for the youth of today. Technological change has made the twentieth century particularly momentous, and so the language changes are also particularly momentous and interesting, as compared with most eighty-year periods in history. Wherever we live, Korea or Canada, Bolivia or Britain, there have been drastic changes in our environment and hence in our language.

Twentieth-century changes

But the impact of these years upon Britain has been more seismic than on most countries. Before the First World War, the British Empire was at its zenith, and Britain, as the undisputed leading world power, presided not only over the 'pax Britannica' but over an empire larger than any the world had ever known. As we saw in the previous chapter, this power and the sheer extent of imperial geography, as well as the fact that English was the language of the United States, had already caused English to become the leading world language, and had also already caused English to embody within itself many words and expressions culled from all over the world. Many of these have stayed in the language, as we shall see in the next chapter. But such exoticisms were far more numerous and far more familiar to ordinary people in 1910 than they are today; for example, words like *bint, cheroot, chokidar, dhobi, dungaree(s), gharry, kow-tow, pukka, punkah, sahib, tiffin*. And many English words were used with imperial meanings; for example, *bearer, bush, bungalow, native*: people who were born in India or West Africa were 'natives', but hardly people who were born in Kent or Scotland.

An imperial society is inevitably strict in its observation of hierarchy, not only within its dominions and colonies but also at home where those who would go out to govern received their education and training. This naturally conditioned attitudes of mind which — just as naturally — had their linguistic reflexes. What we now call 'racism' (the existence of the term is itself significantly recent) was freely expressed, and one example is the curious use and tone of the word *native* which we mentioned a moment ago. But an equally significant reflex was the necessity for linguistic *standards*. It is of considerable interest to see the impact of the boarding school (a necessity for the children of officials serving in Africa or the Asian subcontinent), of Oxford and Cambridge (where colonial officials were largely recruited), upon the status of that hieratic form of English known as 'Received Pronunciation' or 'RP'. It did not of course manifest itself only in pronunciation; the lexicon and grammar were also recognised as transcending both regional dialect and the usage of the uneducated alike. But it could be heard most immediately in the articulation of vowels and consonants. The significance of Shaw's *Pygmalion* (1912) was not the stereotype of the expert dedicated phonetician (like Henry Sweet), but of the current attitude to the one socially acceptable form of English. It was this pronunciation that Daniel Jones described in the first edition of his pronouncing dictionary (1917) and it was already the form of English being taught in the increasing number of schools in all countries that found the teaching of English essential. It is the English represented in the major British dictionaries and grammars, especially those written for foreign learners of English. It is the form of

English that is still most widely taught throughout the world. It remains the voice of the BBC — especially (it is also significant to add) in the BBC's World Service. But it no longer has unchallenged authority in the UK, and indeed the changing voice of the BBC in its home services mirrors with fair accuracy the changing and more variable linguistic scene in Britain as a whole.

Just as twentieth-century changes in Britain are not solely the result of technological development, so they do not solely result from the metamorphosis of a tightly organised Empire into a loosely associated Commonwealth. There have been two World Wars, resulting in the United States replacing Britain in world leadership and giving American English an entirely new power as the chief influence on the English of Britain — and of everywhere else. There were such events as the General Strike of 1926. There was the rise of democratic socialism enabling the Labour Party to replace the Liberals in competing with Conservatives as the alternative party of government. Such events have contributed to two social changes that have profoundly affected the language. One is a democratisation of British society and the other is a dramatic rise in the general standard of living: the two together making the mass of people — working-class and lower-middle-class — much more self-confident (and hence more linguistically assertive) and at the same time making them more highly valued by the powerful (and more assiduously wooed by commerce, increasingly the target of advertisers).

Standard of living

The greater affluence led to mass participation in the 'better life'. Folk aimed to live in a *semi-detached* (with a *lounge* as well as a *kitchenette*); they became *listeners*, owning a *wireless*, at first a *crystal set* with *earphones*, later a *valve* set with a *loud speaker*; they *tuned in* to different *stations* despite the frequent *atmospherics*. Their ambition was to have a *motor-car*, perhaps only a *tourer*, even if it was just a *two-seater* with a *dickie-seat* at the back. But far better, a *saloon*. Even without your own transport, you could afford now to travel abroad — usually on an organised *tour* as a *tourist*, but if you could afford it, you went on a *cruise*.

None of the words we have italicised was entirely new, but all acquired a new exciting meaning. And all this was new and exciting when Evelyn Waugh, at the age of 26, went travelling abroad on a Mediterranean cruise and wrote up his experiences in a book significantly called *Labels*, published in 1930. This little volume gives an excellent impression of what it was like to be born into the privileged classes and to witness the advance of both technological and social change:

> With the real travel-snobs I have shuddered at the mention of pleasure cruises or circular tours or personally conducted parties . . . Every Englishman abroad . . . likes to consider himself a traveller and not a tourist. As I watched my luggage being lifted on to the *Stella* I knew that it was no use keeping up the pretence any longer. My fellow passengers and I were tourists, without any compromise or extenuation . . .
>
> The word 'tourists' seems naturally to suggest haste and compulsion. One thinks of those pitiable droves . . . baffled, breathless, their heads singing with unfamiliar names, their bodies strained and bruised from scrambling in and out of motor charabancs, up and down staircases, and from trailing disconsolately through miles of gallery and museum . . . Are there still more cathedrals, more beauty spots, more sites of historical events, more works of art? . . . And as one sits at one's café table, playing listlessly with sketch book and apéritif, and sees them stumble by, one sheds not wholly derisive tears for these poor scraps of humanity thus trapped and mangled in the machinery of uplift.

The passage is of interest not merely as a linguistic document of 1930, with words like *charabanc* (not replaced till a decade later by *coach*, actually an older word but with a new meaning). It bears witness to the social tension of the time, and in the concluding sentence we have the grammar (*one . . . one's*) as well as the bored social graces of the outnumbered, outstripped past: the lone English gentleman with his sketch book, doing the Grand Tour, quite in the manner of A W Kinglake in his *Eothen*, a century earlier.

Then there is that concluding phrase, 'the machinery of uplift': social mobility, firmly associated with the advance of mechanisation. It was the upward social mobility that led gradually to the demotic voice being heard (and heard with a growing respect). In the English Middle Ages, 'Jack would be a gentleman, if he spoke

French'. Shaw's *Pygmalion* reflects a time when Eliza would be a lady, if she spoke the hieratic accents of Mayfair. Evelyn Waugh was entering a very different world from either, when people pretended that everyone was a 'lady' or a 'gentleman' and when it was thought rude to say 'This man is keen to meet you' or 'Our charwoman is off ill'.

The impact of youth

We recall another elderly friend, an Indian professor, G C Bannerjee, of Bombay. He was a student at Oxford in the twenties at about the same time as Evelyn Waugh. Around 1975 he told us of a return visit he had paid after more than forty years. He had been profoundly shocked to hear how differently the undergraduates spoke: all around him were young men and women speaking regional dialects and above all with a grammar, lexicon, and accent that he felt to be uneducated. Robert Graves noted a similar change in the 1960s when he returned to Oxford as Professor of Poetry. But Bannerjee's impression was more radical than that of Graves: Bannerjee was convinced that the language itself had changed, and it is doubtful whether we convinced him that — for the most part — what had changed was the linguistic *distribution*. When he was at Oxford in the 1920s, there was just as high a proportion of youngsters in England speaking these selfsame dialects and demotic accents: but they were not students at Oxford. This is not to say that Bannerjee now found Oxford full of working-class students (though there certainly were more than there had been half a century earlier). What we are saying is far more arresting: middle-class youth themselves by the mid 1960s had reacted against their parents' speech as well as the old upper-class English, and they affected to prefer the speech of the 'masses'. A reverse snobbery sneered at bourgeois expressions like 'a cleaning lady' and hesitated over using *lady* and *gentleman* at all.

Indeed the period between about 1950 and 1965 saw changes in the way of life, ways of thinking, ways of talking that were not unreasonably given the dramatic name of 'the social revolution'. The smarter dress that had come with nylons (*fully-fashioned*) was so much taken for granted as now to be rejected in favour of a *beatnik* look as youngsters thronged *coffee-bars* and were *turned on* by *skiffle groups*. *Hippie* appearance and mores were accompanied by hippie language, scorning traditional conventions in favour of a free-for-all as people *did their thing* and sought to be *with it*. One talked now about living in 'the permissive society', and newspapers of the time were full of comments upon it — comments of approval or dismay according to the writer's political views (or age). Contrasting schoolteachers of an earlier generation ('sadists in mortar-boards and often in dog-collars'), an observer in 1967 pointed out that 'some of today's jeans-and-gimmicks permissives may go too far the other way'.

There seem to be always two main forces at work in language development: one is an orientation to the fashionable, the other to the inescapable. The former makes us responsive to the springs of power: emulating the language of the socially dominant; quick to seize upon what is new and in some sense 'progressive', upon what will help us to keep in the swim of things. The latter restrains us to behaviour imitative of our everyday environment; it is difficult *not* to speak like those with whom we are in most regular and intimate contact, difficult *not* to learn what we daily hear and see. When these two forces happen to coincide, the influence is overwhelming. It was thus in the closed community of the English private boarding school or the ancient universities. It is somewhat thus today with the simultaneously magnetic and ambient influence of American English. On the one hand, this has come increasingly in the twentieth century to represent what is fashionable, exciting, innovative, creative (the dubious basis for such repute is beside the point). On the other hand, and again increasingly in the past few decades, its sheer statistical mass has made itself felt, so that even those who have no interest in trying to be 'trendy' — even those indeed who try *not* to be — absorb and adopt American English quite unconsciously and quite inevitably: wherever they live — in Canada, Australia, South Africa, or the British Isles.

The influence of America

The modes of infiltration are fairly obvious. Personal contact has increased exponentially: in 1910, the vast majority of Britons had never spoken to an American; by 1990, few had not. Even fewer, of course, had not *heard* an American by 1990; the overwhelming mass of the British population hear Americans every evening — now on television, but already from the early 1930s in the cinema. Oddly enough, however, American influence through the written word seems to be even more powerful. It is not that the British or the Australians read more than they listen, but the visual word disguises its origin. We must remember, after all, that there are many who stoutly resist overt American influence — and it is noteworthy that American *pronunciation* makes little or no inroad upon British speech. Perhaps also the visual word has greater impact and memorability. In any case, even though we all listen (and speak) far more than we read (and write), the extent of the written word should not be underestimated. A sizeable proportion of printed advertising and of popular escapist or thriller literature (perhaps the majority) to which the average Briton or Australian is exposed originates in the United States. And far more than we imagine of what appears in thoroughly local daily papers.

Let us just mention a very ordinary example. A British linguist happened to notice a headline in the *Daily Mirror* in the mid 1950s: 'Rocks thrown at French General'. The source was an American news agency but who was to be alerted to this by the two letters 'AP' (Associated Press)? The *Daily Mirror* had at that time a daily sale of five million and it is likely therefore that around ten million British readers absorbed that headline: ten million who were thus propelled along the road to learning that you no longer needed to be a fairy-tale giant to throw *rocks*. The linguist duly reported the headline to a class of British students the next day and they shared his interest. Ten years later, in the mid 1960s, he repeated the story to a similar group of 19-year-olds and they could not see the point of what he was saying. In other words, already to young people in 1965 the American sense of 'rocks' as small throwable stones was thoroughly familiar, the older British restriction forgotten or never known.

There are hundreds of such examples: unconscious adoptions into the lexicon of British English (*commuter* is another instance from the same period). They could be matched with British adoptions into American English, though these — such as the increased American use of *shop* for a small 'store' — have certainly been less numerous over the past twenty years. The adoption of

American grammar is not so common or so widespread. Nonetheless, the increased use of 'disjunct' adverbs such as *regrettably*, *thankfully*, *notoriously*, and — the most notorious of all — *hopefully*, shows that syntactic influence is also felt. Some of the new modal and aspectual forms in educated British English also owe a good deal to American influence:

I'm not about to do that (= I have no intention . . .)
You've got to be joking (= it must be the case that . . .)
She got to feel that she was a failure (= she came to the point of feeling . . .)
I'll get around to writing it (= I'll reach the point when I shall . . .)
Well, you could be right (= it is possible that you are . . .)
I never saw so much food (= I have never seen . . .)

It is possible, however, that these usages are surfacing from indigenous British dialects and city colloquial styles by reason of the sociolinguistic upheaval discussed earlier. Certainly, the forms cited are especially common in colloquial speech (though we should note 'I never kissed a girl before' in the libretto of Tippett's *The Knot Garden*). But at the opposite extreme it seems certain that it is to American influence that rather formal English is responding in the increased use of the old mandative and putative subjunctive, as in:

It is essential that he *acquire* a licence.

Here, British English would traditionally have used *should* or even the indicative:

$$\text{It is essential that he} \begin{cases} should\ acquire \\ \\ acquires \end{cases} \text{a licence.}$$

There are numerous other features of the English of Britain and other countries today that we can ascribe partly to American influence, partly to assertive defiance of traditional 'hieratic' norms. The latter is especially noticeable in the willingness to use in fairly formal print what would once have been heard only in the most casual informal speech among close friends. For example, the use of *data, media,* and occasionally even *criteria* with singular concord. Colloquial concord can be found even in *The Times* of London, once held to be a guardian of traditional language standards:

Neither of these are conclusive objections.
These sort of teachers . . .

Increasingly in speech, but infrequently in print, we find the use of 'hedges' that give many people the impression of a modest absence of dogmatism:

I sort of felt faint.
He kind of imagines things.

Then again, we have the spread of the pseudo-anaphoric use of *this*, as in:

Did you hear about Bill's adventure last night? Well, there was this girl he'd never seen before, and she . . .

And one may mention also the increased currency of verbs and other parts of speech with phrasal form: *lose out on, face up to, gang up on, far out, way out, a hand out, a teach-in.*

Moreover, the modern media (and the worldwide freemasonry of the young) can spread this informal style of language and even specific new expressions with extraordinary rapidity. In 1976, a British linguist was just about to visit New Zealand. The correspondence columns of the London press were at that time vibrant with caustic comment on the sudden popularity of the hyperbolic negative *no way*, as in:

There's *no way* I'm going to lend him my car.
'Have you finished the book?' '*No way*! I'm going to be weeks yet.'

On arrival in New Zealand, the British linguist went for a stroll in Auckland; he happened to ask a young man to direct him to a certain street, but to no avail. 'So I suppose', said the British visitor, 'that you're not an Aucklander.' 'No way,' was the reply, 'I'm from Wellington.'

New sensibilities

But perhaps the most noticeable and noteworthy effect of both democratic assertiveness and American influence is a manifestation in language of a shared concern throughout the English-speaking countries for what are perceived as the traditionally disadvantaged or even oppressed. Such increased sensibility is not of course new, nor is it confined to Anglo-Saxon societies: it is a world trend. Whatever may have entertained our forefathers, no civilised people in any country now take pleasure in the torment of animals (as in bear-baiting) or in laughing at people who are hunch-backed or who are mentally retarded or who have a speech defect such as a stammer. Even bar-room anecdotes now rarely make these unfortunates the butt of humour.

The politicised abstractions *discrimination, racism* and *sexism* represent a logical if rather extreme extension of this sensibility, and although again we are looking at a world movement, it is a movement that seems to have especially resourceful energy in the United States and Britain. So too, in the reverberations upon language, it is English that seems to be most affected. Two striking examples (both initially and still predominantly American English) are the affix *-person* and the titular *Ms*. Both of them concern sensitivity to discrimination within the area of 'sexism'. Despite historical attestation to the status of the element *man* as being sexually neutral (ie 'unmarked', with the meaning 'adult human', as in 'Man is mortal'), it has become acknowledged that there is always the strong inclination towards interpretation as 'adult *male* human'. We may contrast other generics like *cat* or *calf* which carry no such bias towards one or other sex. Even a social scientist can be unconsciously trapped by such a habitual linguistic orientation, as in the (attested) example:

Man's vital needs are food, shelter, and access to females.

Here the aim at the outset was clearly to make a statement about humanity as a whole, but it ends by showing both that the writer was influenced by the 'male' sense of *man* and that he (hardly she!) implicitly regarded humanity as being adequately represented by the male. So, it is claimed by those who set about 'consciousness raising' in these matters, if a body of people decide to elect a *chairman*, the very form of this word will inescapably if covertly direct our minds to the appropriate *men* that might be considered. Hence the insistence, especially in the 1980s, that we should use such forms as *chairperson*.

The emergence of *Ms* is directed at a different type of discriminatory problem. The goal here is not 'inclusionary' in the sense of 'unisex' language (both terms are current in the relevant sociological code), but it is still anti-discriminatory. In most Western languages, titular forms are asymmetrical as between men and women, the latter being subdivided into young (or unmarried) and mature (or married), the former not. Thus:

	Fräulein		Mademoiselle
Herr:		Monsieur:	
	Frau		Madame

In modern English, *Miss* firmly announces the unmarried status, *Mrs* the married, thus raising the objection not just to the absence of symmetry with *Mr* (used for both single and married men) but to the social and economic consequences. Why should women have to announce their 'sexual availability' on the one hand, or on the other hand disadvantage themselves on the job market through admitting possible domestic responsibilities? Theoretically, the polar system *Mr* : *Ms* resolves the difficulties. We need not pause to wonder whether these innovations have been successful (or whether people tend rather to associate the use of *-person* and *Ms* with a particular feminist stance or even political outlook). Our aim here has been merely to show the extent to which users of English are now prepared to adjust their language to accommodate social sensitivities.

Such accommodation is more widespread in response to guilt feelings about 'racism'. Though there are historical differences between the various English-speaking countries in the formation of racial stereotypes, the new sensibilities are similar in intensity, whether in trying to compensate for a history of slavery (in the United States), or of imperial domination (in Britain), or of earlier disregard for aboriginal peoples (as in Australia). This has meant that attitudinal redress has especially focused upon people who are non-European in colour. The redress has been strikingly rapid and thorough, so that we can now scarcely believe that even a writer as liberal and socially conscious as George Orwell used language that we reject today as intolerably 'racist'. In his *Burmese Days* (1934), where the publisher could not allow the word *buggers* to appear undisguised (it was printed as *b——s*), characters freely refer to *niggers* with nothing more critical than a question about whether the term could be appropriately applied to Indians and Burmese. In fact its application to brown and black people alike is confirmed by G B Shaw's play *On the Rocks* (1933) in which a British politician insults a prominent visitor from Ceylon by referring to him as 'a silly nigger'. The character's reaction shows how much Shaw was ahead of his time in racial and linguistic sensibility as well as in cultural relativism:

> I am called nigger by this . . . barbarian whose forefathers were naked savages worshipping acorns and mistletoe in the woods whilst my people were spreading the highest enlightenment from the temples of Brahma . . . You call me nigger, sneering at my colour . . .

In fact however, disparaging language was not reserved for people with brown or black faces. Racial stereotyping was applied to all 'foreigners' and was virtually always hostile, accompanied by hostile terms to match. The popular literature of the early twentieth century — especially in America but also in Britain — is peppered with racial terms that would now be regarded as obscene: *wop, boche, frog, chink, sheeny, ice-creamer, eye-tie, kraut, polak, yid, dago*; alongside these, the terms applied to black people were no worse in their grossness and contempt — *coon, nigger, nig-nog, munt, fuzzy-wuzzy, kaffir, wog*.

Such words were used without shame not only in the lowest pulp literature aimed at stirring blood lust, but by writers who would have regarded themselves as quite cultivated and cosmopolitan. Agatha Christie (*Poirot Investigates*, 1924), has a character displaying the usual mistrust of Orientals: 'That is what frightens me . . . it was from a Chink . . . that Gregory bought the stone.' Dorothy Sayers in 1931 wrote of someone 'ready enough to praise all . . . except dagos and niggers'. D H Lawrence in a letter of 1929 referred to an acquaintance as a 'Jew-boy' and made a jibe about his Jewish style of talking. Nancy Mitford's *Pigeon Pie* (1940) speaks of 'Chinks and Japs and Fuzzy Wuzzies, Ice Creamers and Dagos, and so on'. Even as recently as 1944, a writer as civilised and urbane as S J Perelman could coyly refer to 'little pickaninnies' and to 'a dusky handmaid . . . murmuring bitterly to herself in Gullah'.

Tolerance with frankness

Such language and — one hopes — the thinking behind it became intolerable in the second half of the twentieth century. Indeed the racial groups previously stigmatised became the focus of praise and admiration, with white Americans and Britons imitating the fashions of dress and hairstyle of blacks and adopting habits of speech which not merely eschewed racial slur but which actually replicated the speech forms of the racial minorities concerned: 'Dig this, man!' Note in this connection the replacement of *negro* (even more rigorously of *nigger*) not with the evasive *coloured*, but with the blacks' own *black*.

It will be seen that all of the trends we have been considering are broadly consistent with the emergence of the 'demotic' voice, including the voice of minority or previously disadvantaged groups, and responding to the obvious numerical preponderance of those who speak American English. Now, it is well known that the actual demotic voice is — and always has been — a great deal less mealy-mouthed about expletives than the hieratic voice of the old standard language (especially in print). The *Quarterly Review* in 1837 praised Dickens for his linguistic 'dilution' and for wrapping up the oaths of Bill Sykes in 'silver paper'. In 1937, David Jones (*In Parenthesis*) admits his avoidance of 'impious and impolite words'. Even as recently as 1951 a novelist felt it right to misrepresent, quite deliberately and as a matter of linguistic tact, 'the general obscenity and blasphemy of shipboard talk'. Thus Herman Wouk in *The Caine Mutiny* (1951); and he thereby earned the praise of the *Sunday Times* reviewer in London for abjuring 'conscientious obscenity'.

But in fact, the linguistic trends represent not so much a change in the language as such but, we have claimed, the admission, into contexts previously regarded as demanding formal language, of the style, idiom, and accent previously restricted to informal private talk. It would have been not merely inconsistent but hypocritical to continue making an exception of 'general obscenity and blasphemy'. We need not be surprised, therefore, that since the 1950s, first of all in speech and subsequently in print, the demotic tone has been supplemented in these directions also, with all the 'four-letter' words that go with it. But the taboos are not forgotten and rules are highly variable from social group to social group, as well as remaining basically unstable. There is still in most social circles a 'mixed company' constraint (upon men in the presence of women rather than the converse). It will still be normal to avoid obscenity-derived intensifiers in speaking to strangers or on programmed occasions (such as committee meetings). One notes too that language can be decidedly more 'frank' in novels and in the theatre than in newspapers or on television. But there is sufficient uncertainty about all of these to occasion a continuing hesitation about overstepping such ill-defined linguistic marks.

This brings us to note finally a steady pulse of linguistic *conservatism* about all the changes and trends we have been discussing — a conservatism that should not be underestimated. Just as, for all the inroads made upon its former supremacy, the minority 'RP' accent retains a good deal more prestige than any other, so there is a continuing respect for the traditional lexicon, the avoidance of neologism, the suspicion of Americanisms, and the observance of the style and grammar that continue to be associated with serious prose. The demotic voice is exciting, and loud, and it is brusque with challenge; but there is still the hieratic voice with its traditional tones and values, and these are the ones we respect and the ones to which we respond at 'moments of truth'.

SOME FOLLOW-UP WORK

1 Either from elderly relatives or by appeal to a local library, try to lay hands on documents such as letters, diaries or local papers of seventy or eighty years ago. Study these and make notes of expressions and allusions you would not expect to find in contemporary usage.

2 On p. 68 we listed words like *dhobi* which reflected the British imperial experience. Find out their meaning and the kinds of context in which they were used.

3 Study parts of *The Dubliners* or *Ulysses* and try to distinguish expressions used by James Joyce that relate to the *time* he wrote as distinct from his regional background.

4 Take some chapters of Scott Fitzgerald's novel *The Great Gatsby* and — as in (3) above — distinguish some expressions that are time-bound from those that reflect the American orientation of the author's English.

5 Reference was made on p. 72 half seriously to 'hippie' language. Find out as much as you can about youth culture in the 1960s and the linguistic expressions that went with it.

6 Many organisations today seek to avoid discrimination against women by prescribing various devices to establish 'inclusionary language' in documents. List and discuss some of the most outstanding of these devices.

7 Despite social and legal constraints, we still use expressions that may give offence by seeming to reflect racial or national prejudice ('He'll welsh on you', 'Full of Dutch courage'). With a group of friends, collect as many such expressions as you can and then discuss them.

8 Here is a quotation from *The Island of Terror* (1931) by the once widely read Sapper (H C McNeile), representing the speech of a fashionable young man in London, here called 'the village':

> Jim, my dear old friend and relative, you are the very bird I want. When did you return to the village? . . . We dine together, what? . . . And afterwards I shall take you to a gathering of the chaps . . . You'll love 'em, old fruit. We have one once a month . . . Just a rag, don't you know.

What features 'date' the piece? Attempt to rewrite it to represent the speech of a young man today.

9 In discussion with someone twenty years older than you are, try to establish that there are words and expressions familiar to you that he or she does not know.

10 There are language sensitivities in other areas than race and sex; for example, with reference to old age. Examine the extent to which we exercise linguistic constraint out of consideration for others.

C H A P T E R 7

English and other languages

In Chapter Three we recalled Donne's words 'No man is an island'. We can with equal truth claim that no language is an island. As visitors to Spain, we may be relieved to see familiar words: *teléfono*, perhaps, or *policía*. Recognising 'telephone' and 'police', we may even think that the Spanish are using English words, but they are not, of course. Both *teléfono* and *telephone* are equally formed from Greek words meaning 'remote' and 'voice'; both *policía* and *police* are derived from the Latin word *politia* meaning 'administration'. On the other hand, when we are relieved to see another familiar word in Spain, *camping* (usually meaning 'a camping site'), here indeed the Spanish are using an adopted English word, just as when we complain about *mosquitoes* or when we order a *paella* in a New York or London restaurant we are using words from Spanish.

It is as natural to pick up another country's words as it is to pick up another country's fashions of dress, ways of cooking, or technical innovations. In fact, adopting other people's words is so natural that we would not only find it difficult to speak English without using 'other people's words', but very often we would find it difficult to say which words are 'other people's' and which are 'our own'. In this last sentence, for example, the words *fact*, *adopt*, *people*, *natural*, *use*, *difficult* and even *very* have all been taken from French or Latin, though for the most part so long ago that they have been totally acclimatised and seem as English as such other words from the same sentence as *other*, *words*, *speak*, *without*, *find* and *say* which have been English since English began.

In fact, one of the reasons why the Old English (Anglo-Saxon) of King Alfred's time is harder for us to understand than the Middle English of Chaucer's time is, ironically, that many native

English words were replaced by French ones between these two periods, and it is just such originally French words that are familiar to us. For example, *adl* was replaced by *disease*, *andweard* by *present*, *andwlita* by *face*, *lof* by *praise*, *swigan* by (*to*) *be quiet*, *wilnian* by (*to*) *desire*. With the Renaissance a century or so after Chaucer, English took in thousands of words from the classics — especially Latin — and the works of Shakespeare are full of these rather learned words, most of which have never been so thoroughly absorbed into everyday English as the French words before them. For example *derogate*, *exigent*, *expiate*, *multiplicity*, *nutriment*, *obloquy*, *obsequious*, *obnoxious*, *paternal*, *prodigious*, *sequestered*, *sterile*, *subsidiary*, *uxorious*.

Contact with the classics came of course through books. But travel in the sixteenth and seventeenth centuries brought in many words from people meeting face to face. From French at that time, English adopted *alloy*, *chocolate*, *comrade*, *equip*, *moustache*, *probability*, *surpass*, *volunteer*, and a host of other words. From Italian, we learned *balcony*, *cartoon*, *cupola*, *portico*, *stanza*, and many musical words such as *trill* and *violin*. From Spanish and Portuguese, we adopted *alligator*, *banana*, *bravado*, *hurricane*, *mosquito*, *potato*, among others. All these examples are words that remained in the language: many more came, and disappeared again, such was the enthusiasm for foreign words, whether the language had a real need for them or not. Understandably, therefore, alongside the enthusiasm there was a good deal of hostile or satirical criticism, for example in Thomas Wilson's *Arte of Rhetorique* (1553):

> Some farre journeyed gentlemen at their returne home, like as they love to goe in forraine apparell, so thei wil pouder their talke with oversea language. He that commeth lately out of Fraunce will talke French English and never blush at the matter. An other chops in with English Italienated . . .

Indeed, the fashion for 'outlandish English' among the trendsetters was such, says Wilson with a flourish of dry exaggeration, that:

> I dare sweare this, if some of their mothers were alive, they were not able to tell what they say . . .

A century and a half later, Daniel Defoe similarly criticised English people for having their 'mouth full of borrow'd phrases', and 'always borrowing other men's language'. But this did not prevent us from adding further foreign words to our vocabulary in the eighteenth century, such as *brunette, dentist*, and *rouge*. Moreover, Britain's imperial expansion meant that we absorbed many words from far beyond Europe. From India, for example, came *calico, curry, dinghy, jungle, polo, verandah*. In any case, with the vast increase of rapid communication worldwide, there is now no language too remote to have impact on our own: we adopt *anorak* from Eskimo, *safari* from Swahili, and *karate* from Japanese with equal readiness.

The influence of English

The position is similar with speakers of other languages, of course; they too find it increasingly easy and inevitable to adopt foreign words. But with the growing importance of English worldwide for the past hundred years or more, it is from English that other languages are most strikingly acquiring new words. They may be disguised in spelling and by the orthographic type, or the phonological structure may find it difficult to accommodate an English word without adaptation. So we might not immediately recognise the Italian *giobba* as 'job', the Japanese *sutoppu* as 'stop', the Russian троллейбус as 'trolleybus', or the Hausa *sukurudireba* as 'screwdriver'. An item may even be disguised from those adopting it. On the back of the title page of books published in virtually any language, one finds the word *copyright*: 'Copyright by Max Niemeyer Verlag', 'Copyright by Neri Pozza', 'Copyright do autor'; but often this is abbreviated and so we get '© Presses Universitaires de France 1986' or '© 1988 by VEB Verlag Leipzig', or '© Katsuei Yamagishi 1984'. In such extreme disguise, the item shows little sign of its origin and so there is little reason for the French, German, or Japanese reader to regard the 'c' as English — any more than an American or Briton need know that 'e.g.' and 'i.e.' are Latin or still less know the Latin words here abbreviated: *exempli gratia, id est*.

But copyright is a legal technicality. Most of the words taken from English into other languages relate to ordinary everyday life — sports, clothes, entertainment, and youth culture. The surge of student demonstrations in Beijing and other cities during 1989 was said in a Chinese language broadcast to be the work of *rowdies*. Glancing through a randomly selected daily newspaper in Germany one day during 1989, we noticed a headline:

Designer mit tausend Tricks

The article was about 'TV-Designer Hans Donner mit seinem Team von sechs Designern und sechs Experten für Spezialeffekte'. In the same issue, a report on tennis talked about the 'Serve- und Volleyspiel' and of a player's 'phantastische Rückhand Returns' resulting in several 'Tiebreaks' before 'das Match' was finally won.

The Dutch language is similarly dense with words from English, as the following newspaper excerpt on naval armament strikingly illustrates:

> Kijk, de missiles zitten in roterende magazines, zij zijn daar in geladen via de strike down hatches. Zij liggen op een ready-service ring in ready-service trays, worden hydraulic omhoog gebracht, nadat de magazinedoors zijn opengeklapt, worden dan op de tilting rail gezet. De tilting rail kan ze naar achteren brengen naar de check-out room, waar de electronics worden nagekeken, maar hij kan ook omhoog klappen en dan gaan de blastdoors open en komen ze op de launcher.

Not surprisingly, perhaps, the Dutch reporter wonders mockingly whether this can really be about a *Dutch* ship, but has to answer in the affirmative, because (as he explains) if a Dutch sailor uses other than the English words, he would be reprimanded because of the danger of misunderstanding!

We have taken the Dutch anecdote from a 1986 book published in Budapest on *English in Contact with Other Languages*, edited by W Viereck and W-D Bald, where non-military influence on Dutch is equally well illustrated: *up to date, last not least, cocktail, computer* and (with Dutch spelling which suggests more complete absorption) *voetbal* 'football', *nek-aan-nek-race*. In Danish too, some Anglicisms retain their original form more than others: *fairplay* but *fodbold* 'football', *disc-jockey* but *ankermand, knowhow* but *saebeopera, computer* and *cocktail* but *kalde en spade for en spade*. As to other languages, here are some examples from this book:

Czech: *fotbal, ofsajd, gol; hokej; tenis, forhend, bekhend, volej, lobovat* 'to lob'

Polish: *futbol, drybler, drybling, stoper* 'fullback'; *tenis, singlista* 'a singles player'; *trener; spiker* 'announcer'; *globtroter; flircik* 'a flirt'; *chuligan* 'hooligan'; *biznes; autostop* 'hitchhiking'

Serbo-Croatian: *sport; ragbi; korner* 'area behind goal-line', *aut* 'area beyond touchline'; *bokser; bojkot; girla*

Russian: *futbol, lajnsmen; volejbol; trener; tennis; krossmen* 'a cross-country runner'; *koktejl; xobbi; uikend; kejs* 'briefcase'; *trenčkot; pop, xit, popgruppa, lejbl* 'label' (on records); *gerl; pablisiti; džemper* 'jumper'; *menedžer; džentlmen; dizajner; infajting; stepgelikopter* (figure in ice skating); *fen* (handdryer for hair)

Portuguese: *futebol, dribling, golo, match, offside, penalte, time* 'team'; *raguebi; oquei; tenis, tenista* 'tennis player'; *jogging; flirtar* 'to flirt'; *sexy; baby-sitter; freak; weekend; talkshow; playback; knowhow*

Romanian: *fotbal, ghem, ofsaid, penalti, meci* 'match'; *tenis, set, fault, volei; ferplay; blugi* 'blue jeans'; *flirt; discjockey; bestseller; boicot; playback; hardware, software; knowhow*

Italian: *baby; cocktail; jogging; night* 'a night club'; *slip* 'pants'; *clip* 'paper clip'; *lift* 'lift operator'; *sexy; flirtare* 'to flirt'; *scioccare* 'to shock'; *ghella* 'girl'; *pocket* 'pocketbook'; *sit in; in, out* (with reference to fashion); *hardware, software; mpai mpai* 'by and by'

Turkish: *futbol, penalti, forvet, korner, haftaim, maç* 'match'; *tenis, kort, set, avut* 'out'; *voleybol; hobi; centilmen* 'gentleman'; *viski, kokteyl, barmen; teyp* 'tape-recorder'; *dipfriz, mikser; tisort* 'T-shirt'

With Japanese, we turn to a language where the impact is relatively recent, but the story is all the more impressive given the depth of penetration, chiefly through the influence of the United States. Toshio Ishiwata estimates that no less than ten per cent of all words used today in Japanese are from English, though when written in Western script their origin is often deeply disguised, nor do they always *sound* familiar to English-speakers either. The word *maneejaa* 'manager' is accented on the second syllable, and *l*-sounds are replaced by *r*-sounds, as in *sarada* 'salad'. Consonant sequences such as *st* and *tr* are separated by vowels as in *sutoppu* 'stop', *saundo torakku* 'sound track'. Words are also abbreviated as with *terebi* 'televi(sion)'; both parts of the word for a general strike, *zeneraru sutoraiku*, are contracted as *zenesuto*, and the word just given for 'sound track' more usually has the form *santora*. Although many words are little changed in meaning (*geemu setto*, 'game and set' in tennis, *chenji rebaa* 'lever for gear-change'), others have specialised meanings in Japanese; *shea* has only the equity sense of 'share', *rejaa* 'leisure' again refers only to market stock (in leisure industries), *ooru uezaa* means 'an all weather garment', and *ranchi* 'lunch' means a set meal ('tabble d'hôte') as opposed to one selected 'à la carte'.

Influence and fashion

Unlike Japanese, German and French have naturally had contact with English for centuries (the word *gentleman* was recorded in German as early as 1575) and the number of English expressions absorbed in both languages is enormous. But since these two languages are spoken in several different countries, it is more accurate to talk of English words used in France or Belgium or Switzerland or Canada rather than 'in French'. The words are not always the same, nor are they equally numerous; for example, surrounded as they are by speakers of English, the French-speaking Canadians use many more English words than, say, the French-speaking Swiss. So too with German: we find rather fewer English words used by Austrians, East Germans, and the German-speaking Swiss than are used by Germans in the Federal Republic. And there are other idiosyncrasies. For example, the East German *Intershop* is an international shop accepting only hard currency, a *Miting* (taken from the Soviet Union) is a *political* meeting, and a *baby sitter* is a child's lavatory seat. In Austria, a casual jacket worn by young people in their twenties is called a *Twenjacke*. But all German speakers seem to know *Teenager, Shampoo,*

Knowhow, last not least, and *Hattrick,* just as they all seem to use *Kicker* for 'footballer', *Stopper* for 'fullback' or 'centre back' and *gefinished* in relation to the 'finish' of a manufactured product. Some English expressions are partly translated, as with *eine Party geben* 'to give a party', or wholly translated, as with *der Mann auf der Strasse, Körpersprache* 'body language', or the formula used by an assistant approaching a customer: *Was kann ich für Sie tun?* Examples of this sort may represent particularly deep influence but they may also suggest some hesitation over wholesale adoption of foreign expressions unadapted.[1]

Certainly, there have been numerous criticisms of the delight — especially among young people — in flaunting an acquaintance with Anglicisms. One does not need much knowledge of German to understand the following dialogue which amusingly satirises the eagerness with which expressions are being taken over into German from English and especially from American English:

> Kiki, sagt die eine, schau dir die Tinätscher-Dresses an, die würden gut zu unseren Släcks passen und unsern Sixapiel unterstreichen!
>
> O keh, sagt Kiki, ich würde mir gern Schorts kaufen, wenn ich Monneh hätte.
>
> Aber mit Schorts kannst du doch auf keine Paathie gehen, wirft die andere ein.
>
> Warum nicht? Der Nju Luck mit Schorts wird bestimmt ap tu deit mit dem richtigen Meik ap dazu, wenn ein paar smarte Mänätscher die Sache in die Finger kriegen. Last not liest ist auch bald Kämpingzeit! Das wär ein Gäg!
>
> Hm, ich kann mir jetst aber nix Neues leisten, ich will mir erst einen neuen Tschob suchen, in meinem Offis gefällt's mir nicht. Mit dem Tiemwörk klappt's nicht. Der Boss ist kein

---

1 Traditionally, after all, German has resisted wholesale adoptions, preferring to make new words from its own resources. Contrast the following English and German pairs:

foreign	ausländisch
fortunate	glücklich
exposure	Aussetzung
expression	Ausdruck
conceive	empfangen

Nor, of course, does English always look abroad when new words are required: compare the *spoiler* on cars or the use of *shuttle* in air transport.

Tschentelmänn, denk dir, sein Hobbi ist Schopäng. Wenn ich
dem was von der neuen Stardäst-Bänd in der Texasbar erzähle,
guckt er bloss doof. Von Bibop, Dixiländ, Bluhs, Bugie Wugie
und überhaupt von Tschäääs hat der altmodische Boy keine
Ahnung, obwohl er Televischen daheim hat. Er kaut keinen
Tschuing Gam, smaukt keine Kämmel, er kennt nicht mal die
Monru, trinkt keinen Wiski, liest keine Bestseller, kauft keine
Comik Bucks — und das will ein gebildeter Deutscher sein!

Kiki sieht auf die Uhr und sagt: Dämned, ich muss zum
Läntsch, sonst schimpft Päps. Also, bis morgen: bai-bai!

Die beiden Girls machen shakehands und flitzen davon.

Der Chronist sagt zu sich: Deutscher Michel, go home mit
deiner Muttersprache, sie ist nicht mehr up to date!

F U Gass, Des deutschen Bürgers Plunderhorn, 1959

Franglais

Writing not long after F U Gass and with a similar lightness of
touch, René Etiemble produced a book which became instantly
famous and which gave wide currency in French and English alike
to the word *franglais*, signifying a style of language that seems as
much *anglais* as *français*. The example on the cover of *Parlez-vous
franglais?* (1964) neatly exemplifies the way in which words,
idioms, and stereotyped exclamations can be imbibed through a
popular stereotyped literature: 'Humph! Ce shériff manque de
nerfs!' And as with the book by F U Gass, the examples and
themes reflect youth interests of around 1960:

> A peine sorti du teenage, l'ex-enfant-problème, l'ex-teenager
> français entre aux barracks . . . Lorsqu'il change son blue-jeans
> contre le (ou les) training slacks, et la tee shirt ou le pull contre
> le battle-dress . . . notre boy ne quitte son teen-gang que pour
> entrer dans un commando, s'il est un marine, ou bien un stick,
> pour peu qu'il se soit engagé dans les para-troops. Il reste donc
> fidèle à cette manière française de vivre que lui ont inculquée
> ses comics . . .
>
> (p. 93)

> Tous les jours il remerciera Dieu: *God save our gracious queen!*
> d'avoir si bien lu ses comics. Tout ce dont il a besoin pour vivre
> heureux (*life must be fun*), ses lectures l'en ont pourvu. Du
> chewing-gum aux chiclets, des digests aux dinky-toys, des

bobsleighs aux runabouts, des snow-cars aux scooter-balls, du suspense au happy end, des call-girls aux pull-overs, des starting-gates aux sleepings, tout lui fut prodigué à temps. Ainsi armé dans le struggle for life, il peut se dire comme un héros de Monty: 'Va, et n'aie pas peur: la victoire est dans nos pockets.'

(p. 98)

But in France, this is not a laughing matter, and quite strenuous efforts have been made to turn the linguistic clock back and to 'purify' the language — which in effect means to replace the Anglicisms by French expressions. Many of the words listed above as adopted into other languages (*football, cocktail, bestseller, weekend,* and the like) are now too deeply entrenched, but laws have been introduced since the early seventies which make the French media think twice about using foreign words, and lists of expressions have appeared from time to time giving explicit guidance. For example, a list was published in 1984 requiring that the use of *pacemaker, pay-tv* and *pile-up* be discontinued in favour of *stimulateur, télévision à péage,* and *empilement* respectively, and strongly discouraging the use of other words (for example *piggyback* and *payload* in favour of *ferroutage* and *charge utile*).

Resistance

Attitudes are very different across the border in French-speaking Belgium, where newspaper reports on a game of football are freely interlarded with words like *toss, corner, passes, linesmen, hand, stopper,* and of course *match.* The Belgians in fact, along with speakers of most of the languages we have been considering, are more like English speakers the world over in seeming to have little fear, indeed little consciousness, of foreign linguistic influence. There have of course always been *individuals* in Britain and the USA who feel very differently. We have already quoted Thomas Wilson and Daniel Defoe. We could have quoted Shakespeare, who was well aware of the fashionable excesses of his time. One has only to reread the speeches of Holofernes, Sir Nathaniel, and Armado in *Love's Labour's Lost,* or Mercutio's exasperation at 'the immortal passado, the punto reverso' of Tybalt in *Romeo and Juliet:*

> The pox of such antic, lisping, affecting fantasticoes; these new tuners of accents! . . . Why, is not this a lamentable thing . . .

that we should be afflicted with . . . these fashion-mongers, these *pardonnez-mois*, who stand so much on the new form that they cannot sit at ease on the old bench? Oh, their *bons*, their *bons*!

Act II, scene 4

Indeed, what the French seek to do by law today is paralleled by Joseph Addison in 1711:

I have often wished, that . . . certain men might be set apart as superintendants of our language, to hinder any words of a foreign coin, from passing among us; and in particular to prohibit any French phrases from becoming current in this Kingdom.

Spectator, No. 165

And later in the same century, George Campbell, the author of a two-volume *Philosophy of Rhetoric* (1776), spoke of English as in 'danger of being overwhelmed by an inundation of foreign words'. In 1919, the novelist George Moore protested that the teaching of French in schools:

amounts to no more than a sufficiency of French words for the corruption of the English language. To many people it sounds refined, even cultured, to drop stereotyped French into stereotyped English phrases. To use *badinage* for *banter* and to think that there is a shade of difference, or I suppose I should say, a *nuance* of meaning . . . I am looking forward to reading in the newspapers a *précis* of a *résumé* of a *communique*. You see I omit the accent on the last *e*, and I wish you would tell me if the people who speak and write this jargon think that *résumé* is more refined than summary, abridgement, compendium. In society every woman is *très raffinée*. I once met an author who had written *small and petite*, and when I asked him why he did it, he said: *Petite* means dainty as well as small; I said: No, it doesn't, but if you wanted to say *dainty*, why didn't you say dainty?

Avowals, p. 285

We should recall, moreover, that for some decades in the twentieth century there existed a Society for Pure English which attracted considerable support in Britain and America. And we have the Queen's English Society which is concerned in part with discouraging what members see as unnecessary and undesirable foreign influence.

Language purity?

But it is one thing to reprove people who 'powder their talk' with foreign words just to show off or be in fashion. It is quite another to cultivate an ideal of linguistic purity as a matter of principle. There are two objections to consider. The first is that the ideal, for all its emotive power in some societies at some periods, is both difficult to define and impossible to realise. So far as one can tell, there is no language on earth that is in such a pristine state that all of its words are formed from its own resources, still less are formed without influence from some other language. As we saw in discussing German, *Körpersprache* results from the influence of English though using neither of the parts, *body* and *language*, that occurred in the model. Moreover, though *Sprache* (cognate with the English word *speech*) has been in German throughout its recorded history, the *Körper* part has not, deriving ultimately from the Latin *corpus*. And we must also put a question mark over the phrase 'deriving ultimately'. Among the words that we have looked at as showing the influence of English on other languages were *gentleman* and *manager*. But the *gentle* part of *gentleman* came into English from French and derives from a Latin adjective that meant 'belonging to the same *gens* or family'. As for *manager*, we seem to have taken the verb *manage* from Italian, where it had to do with training horses. This is not however to say that the Latin *gens* is the 'ultimate' origin of *gentle*, still less that *manage* derives 'ultimately' from Italian and constitutes a 'pure' Italian word.

When we were illustrating influences upon English earlier in this chapter, we said that we had taken the word *safari* from Swahili: in other words, that speakers of English had learned the word from mixing with speakers of Swahili in East Africa. But if we trace the word farther back (we can rarely trace a word to its 'real' and ultimate origin), we find an Arabic source, *safariya*. Again, we noted that we learned the words *banana*, *hurricane* and *potato* from the Spanish and Portuguese; true, but *they* had learned the first from a language in Guinea, and the other two from Carib and Taino respectively, American Indian languages of central America. We adopted *algebra* from the Italians and they had adopted it from Arabic; the story of *assassin* is similar. The word *palaver* seems to have been passed on by sailors. Deriving from the Latin *parabola*, it was in use among Portuguese traders in West Africa before being taken up by English sailors in the eighteenth century, and from these in turn it was learned by German sailors in the early nineteenth century. In Polish, *džudowiec* is regarded as a word from English, but in English, of course, *judo* is a word from Japanese. In German, the word *Dschungel* has been adopted from English, but we took the word *jungle* from Hindi.

Welcoming foreign influence

The second objection can be inferred from the first. Even if we could, why should we want to stop this vigorous free-trade in language? In other words, linguistic purity is not merely an impossible goal, it is a highly undesirable one. Those who argue for it are frequently motivated — consciously or otherwise — by a dislike (or fear) of foreigners or at least of some particular aspect of a foreign culture. But if the objection is to teen-age morals or pop music or American advertisers, it is somewhat missing the point to take a stand against certain foreign words which are merely the *sign* of what is disliked.

On the other hand, if we welcome a particular cultural influence, can we effectively divorce this from the language in which it is couched? And if we can, what is achieved and is it worth the trouble? Let us take a simple example. In the sixteenth century, British people badly needed to know all that they could from Italy about music. Today, the influence of Italy is seen also in the language we use when we are talking about music: *pizzicato, cello, trill, cadenza*, for example. Of course, we could have used the violoncello in England without adopting the Italian word for it; we could have referred to it as 'a biggish fiddle'; or we could have invented a name for it: *faddle*, let us say. But the gain would have been dubious — to say the least — while the inconvenience would have been great. Everyone would then have had to learn the new term — even those cultured Britons who were effecting our musical education, who needed to refer to these things most frequently, and to whom the Italian terms (and those only) were perfectly familiar.

Over the past millennium, English has adopted many thousands of words and expressions from many languages. It can in fact be argued that being receptive to foreign linguistic influence does not mean that a language is decadent and impure, its speakers weak and unsure of their identity: but rather that the members of the speech community are keenly alive to what is going on in the world and eager to keep pace with cultural developments elsewhere.

And of course it is not just English. We began this chapter by noting the familiar words we find in Spanish like *teléfono* and *policía*. As travellers, we have a similar experience wherever we go: words like *hotel* and *taxi*, *passport* and *airport* are the same or at least recognisably similar in many languages, evidence not so much of the influence of one particular language on another as of a pervasive trend towards an international vocabulary in many areas of activity. It becomes increasingly irrelevant, in fact, to inquire from which language a particular word has been adopted.

The international trend

An international vocabulary is especially apparent (and valuable) in specialist fields such as medicine and science. Here as in so much else, we must probe beyond the level of linguistic influence from Britain or America and see the lexicon of learning as deriving from European culture as nurtured in Ancient Greece and Rome. Even though it would not have occurred to Aristotle to speak of an illness as *psychosomatic*, it was from the Greek words *psyche* and *soma* (roughly 'soul' and 'body') that the word was coined. This was in the nineteenth century though it came into general medical parlance only in the 1930s. So too, if the scientists who conceived of this had been Finnish or Russian or Dutch, they would probably have also looked to Greek elements to express it. In consequence, irrespective of their native language, physicists reading the first passage quoted in Chapter One about Planck, or pharmacologists reading the fourth, would understand many of the key words used. Similarly, when American or British scholars glance through a specialist article in German or Portuguese or (if they can read Cyrillic letters) Russian, they do not need a dictionary for the very words that seem hardest to the rest of us.

Some other fields of activity, equally specialised, do not rely on Greek and Latin to the same extent. In computer technology, specialised words are often (for native English speakers) decidedly more homely: *input, output, bit, diskdrive, floppydisk, chip, pack, software*. But the result is the same. These are now part of the international lexicon in information technology, as we have seen in the illustrations given early in this chapter: *hardware* and *software* occurred in the examples for Romanian and Italian, and of course the list of languages using these words could have been greatly extended.

Such a free market across linguistic frontiers is clearly to the benefit of us all, and its existence is of the essence in human communication. We cannot and should not live in sealed linguistic boxes. Nor should we think of linguistic internationalism just in terms of individual vocabulary items like *football* or *psychosomatic*. Though speaking different languages, we influence each other in the way we argue, formulate our thoughts, string our words together in sentences. This is most obvious and easy to illustrate, perhaps, among the communities who share the incomparably rich European heritage of philosophy and rhetoric. But happily, none of us is insulated from the great cultural influences of West or East: the Vedic writings of ancient India, the Analects of Confucius, the Bible, the Koran, the legacy of Plato and Aristotle. It is not merely *what* is said in such writing but the *way* it is said that has been influential, resulting in a good deal of common ground in educational curricula worldwide and in a sense of what constitutes good taste and good style in linguistic expression.

And, we need hardly add, such transnational models are not solely the great books of the remote past. Shakespeare, Milton, and Bunyan had a profound impact both within the English-speaking world and far beyond. More recent writers such as Goethe, Tolstoy, and Joyce are further examples of influences that have extended around the world, with ways of articulating experience picked up by multitudes who have never read *Faust* or *Ulysses*.

SOME FOLLOW-UP WORK

1 Reread the fourteen samples of English given at the beginning of Chapter Four, noting words that you suspect to have a fairly international currency. Discuss the extent to which some of the samples have more such words than others and form hypotheses about why this should be so.

2 Write out 100 English 'key words' and short phrases which you think would be most frequently required by someone (a) in the tourist industry, or (b) studying mathematics, or (c) interested in agriculture, or (d) visiting a trade fair.

3 Turn back to the German passage quoted from F U Gass and list the words that have been borrowed (sometimes in a strange disguise) from the English language. Which of them suggest that the speakers are young, adult and female?

4 If a cello might have been known in English as 'a biggish fiddle', suggest English terms which might similarly replace *piano, pizzicato, trill, cadenza, concerto, sonata, trio, oratorio, opera, scherzo*.

5 With the help of a good dictionary, find out from what languages we have adopted the words used in the last paragraph of this chapter. Rewrite the paragraph, trying to use as few originally foreign words as possible. Is your version an improvement? Consider our dependence on adopted words.

6 Suppose you were the author criticised at the end of the Moore quotation (p. 91); compose an argument, with examples, that you might use in reply.

7 Mention was made from time to time of the degree to which an adopted word is 'acclimatised'; spelling cropped up in this connection, and Moore in the passage referred to in (6) mentions accents. Discuss these and other indicators of 'acclimatisation'.

8 Go carefully through a recent daily newspaper in English, noting adopted words that you would regard as still foreign. What are their characteristics and in what fields do they occur?

9 Take a recent newspaper in a language other than English and make a list of the words and expressions that seem to have been adopted from English. Attempt to categorise them.

CHAPTER 8

Learning the language we know

The title of this chapter is deliberately paradoxical and draws attention to the anomalous position that the native language occupies in education. Planning a school course in mathematics or geography is difficult enough, but reasonably well-founded assumptions can be made about the pupils' knowledge at the outset and planners can reach agreement on content and goals using well-established criteria. The native language — a course of Danish in Denmark, German in Austria, English in Britain — presents very different issues. In the first place, the language is both a 'subject' and also the medium of instruction for this subject and virtually all other subjects. The mathematics teacher using words like *decimal* and *subtraction* is teaching not only the mathematical concepts but also the English words which express them. So too, the geography teacher with *latitude* and *altitude*, *plateaux* and *deltas*. Secondly, as this first point implies, pupils do not arrive at school like little empty buckets so far as the native language is concerned. In a New Zealand book on *The Teaching of English* many years ago, a youngster is quoted as saying:

> I speak English, don't I? My cobbers understand me. Why the heck should you have to teach me English at all?

It is not fanciful to detect a defensive ring here, and it compounds the difficulty in defining a policy for teaching the native language. What the pupils bring to school is *their* language and it is a very precious part of that identity which as we saw in Chapter Four is essential to their personal, family, and community pride. If the English teacher is going to challenge this, she or he had better look out.

Not surprisingly therefore, in many countries there is a lack of consensus over teaching the native language, and the issues have been rehearsed in monographs and governmental reports for a century or more. So far as Great Britain is concerned, they had a good deal of fresh attention in the 1970s and 1980s, and much of what we say in this chapter reflects the evidence and deliberations published by Her Majesty's Stationery Office in London from three government committees chaired respectively by Alan Bullock (1975), John Kingman (1988), and Brian Cox (1989). Their very existence points to public dissatisfaction with the teaching of English: *what* is taught, *how* it is taught, and *the results* of the teaching as manifest in the capabilities of school-leavers. And not just of school-leavers. A distinguished historian, Professor J R Pole, added to the 1989 debate by complaining of the 'galloping illiteracy' among university students at Oxford.

No question, we note, of agreeing with the New Zealand youngster who felt there was no need to teach him English at all. In part, the paradox lies in naming the native language as a subject. Children in Vienna certainly do not need to be 'taught German' in the sense that children in London or Wellington need to be 'taught German'. Equally, teaching English to children in London or Wellington means something very different from teaching English to children in Vienna. Indeed, the London children *start* with a better command of English than most of the Viennese children will have at the *end* of their schooling.

But that does not mean that the English teacher in London begins where the English teacher in Vienna leaves off. Our children arriving at school have a great deal to learn from the English teacher — and much of it they would not call 'English' at all: like learning to read and write. These skills are in fact two-thirds of the traditional requirements made of the whole education system, the alliteratively mnemonic 'three r's': reading, writing, and arithmetic.

The native language at school

So at the core of the native language as an educational subject — any native language, not just English — lies the requirement to achieve literacy. It is a tougher assignment in the Orient (where literacy involves learning thousands of different characters) than in any of the Western languages which are written in a system comprising only two or three dozen letters. But learning these characters or letters is a prerequisite for learning to read and write the words which are represented by stringing them together.

In this respect, the achievement of our first year or so in school is quite remarkable: a feat combining pattern recognition, memory, and reasoning. We learn the shapes *b* and *d*, distinguishing which side of the little circle the vertical comes. We learn to associate both of these with sounds so that we can read *bad* and *dab*, soon able to work out for ourselves *bab* or *dad*, even if we are encountering them for the first time. Again, once we have grasped *mad* and *bet*, we can work out how to read *met* and *bat*. We learn that although the processing is largely left to right in English orthography (Arabic is the other way round), we sometimes have to do a double take. For example, there is the 'silent' *e*, so that before we decide that the word is *mad* or *mat* or *bit*, we need to look at what comes after. In *made*, *mate*, *bite*, this final *e* not merely signals an entirely different word in each case but tells us to give a different sound value to the vowel letters *a* and *i*. In the same way, we have to observe when a *t* is followed by an *h*: this not merely signals a different consonant sound but often means that the preceding vowel letter may have a different value. For example, *slot* and *sloth*, *pat* and *path*. We learn that *y* as the only vowel at the end of a one-syllable word is sounded as in *my*, but otherwise is sounded like the *i* in *bid*: contrast *by cab* with *cabby*.

There will be many complications and irregularities to learn as well: that we write *moan* not *mone*, *height* not *hite*, *cupboard* not *cubbod*, for example. But we learn that English spelling is basically phonetic, letters corresponding to sounds, so that if we know how a word is pronounced, we can have a go at writing it; and if we see a word in writing, we can have a go at saying it aloud. This is by no means the only way of putting language into visual form, even in English. The numeral '7' gives no hint of the English word *seven* (or in Spanish the word *siete*). We read the sign ÷ in arithmetic as 'divided by'; and as we walk or drive around, we understand a red circle with a horizontal bar as meaning 'no entry'. A system somewhat similar to this occurs in the writing of Chinese and Japanese. The Japanese word for 'a person' is *hito* but the written character, an unusually simple one, rather like an inverted capital Y, is perfectly usual in one respect: it gives no hint as to how the word is pronounced. Since the Japanese took over so much of their writing system from China, it so happens that in Chinese the same symbol is used with the same meaning, though the Chinese word for 'person' (roughly transcribable as *ren*) is quite different. Contrast the way this same meaning is represented in English and German. In German, the corresponding word is *Mensch* which (like *person*) you can make an attempt at pronouncing just by applying what you guess is the value of the individual letters.

Writing and the individual

The feat of learning to read and write is further complicated by the fact that for most letters we have to learn several quite distinct forms. Even in print, the letter shapes for 'roman' and 'italic' can be very different, quite apart from the distinction between 'capital' and 'small'; compare the same word printed as GUARD, *GUARD*, guard, and *guard*. And when we turn to writing by *hand*, where the letters within a word are usually joined together, we face not only different letter shapes from those of print but differences from person to person. It is worth studying in careful detail the printed version of the following sentence and comparing the six individual handwritten versions by six British adults, three men and three women, all graduates around the age of 40:

> This time his play was absolutely trashy, and I am not going to go to another.

1   *This time, his play was absolutely trashy, and I'm not going to go to another.*

2 This time his play was absolutely
trashy, & I am not going to go to
another.

3 "This time his play was absolutely
trashy, and I'm not going to go to
another.

4 This time this play was absolutely trashy, and I'm
not going to go to another.

5 This time his play was absolutely trashy
and I'm not going to go to another.

6 This time his play
was absolutely trashy
and I'm not going to
go to another

Quite apart from a slip of the pen by one writer (*this* for *his*), there
is some variation over punctuation (some put a comma after

trashy, some do not), over abbreviation (some write *and* and *I am* in full, some do not), but above all in the shapes of individual letters. While none of the handwritten versions is as easy to read as the printed version, we can recognise and even admire the individual styles and we certainly find each version adequately legible. Now this obviously involves us in a sophisticated task of abstraction: consider only the degree of variation that is tolerated in the formation of a *y* or a *g* before the one could be misread as the other. But a good deal of the sophistication lies in our assessment of *probabilities* in relation to the particular context and our general knowledge of the language. For instance, in example (4) the word *trashy* is very carelessly written, and if we are to understand it correctly, we rely heavily on the context for clues. In isolation, if we found just this word on a scrap of paper, it would be virtually illegible because unintelligible. A better example: if we look at the six ways in which the *ing* part of *going* is written, we realise that each writer predicts its predictability and in consequence sees no need to form the distinct letters *i*, *n*, *g*.

The skills of reading

As we become expert in reading, we seem to take in whole chunks at a time, whole words or even sequences of words, using minimal graphic clues, provided what we read makes adequate sense. Consider our instantaneous understanding of the following, though in fact not a single one of the letters is complete:

THE ENGLISH
LANGUAGE

Or consider the following experiment. A group of students were confronted by a series of blank circles and were told that the whole corresponded to a written sentence, each group of circles consisting of a word:

o   oo   oooo   oooooooo   ooo   oooo

oooooooooo   ooooo

The students were asked to guess the letters in left to right sequence, and the following scores show the average number of guesses to achieve the correct answers:

1	11	9111	72111111	111	1111
I	am	very	grateful	for	your

3515321111	92921
improbable	roots

It is interesting that a one-letter word followed by a two-letter word seemed obviously 'I am'; that *very* needed only the initial *v*; that *for* was predictable in following *grateful*. But when the sentence became 'difficult' with the last two nonsensically unpredictable words, the students had to go laboriously letter by letter in a way unparalleled for the earlier words of the sentence: though even here, the last part of *improbable* and the plural ending of *roots* were easy to 'read'.

Respect for the addressee

There is a lesson for all of us here. However much we want our handwriting to reflect our personal style and individual identity, our first duty is to the reader. If this is someone we know well and whom we know to be thoroughly familiar with what we are writing about, we can reasonably relax the care we give to the actual handwriting. But when our writing is to be read by strangers, whose familiarity with the subject matter cannot be known to us for certain, we must make our handwriting clear, careful and consistent, not obliging the readers to rely on guesswork. The addresses on envelopes, for example. A precisely analogous lesson needs to be borne in mind when we are *speaking* — in many ways a more important lesson since we speak so much more than we write and speak far less consciously than we write. Again, of course, it is right to take pride in our own style of speech, our accent, our voice quality. But irrespective of our personal style or regional dialect, we must take care over our diction and take pride in our *clarity* of diction. We have all suffered from unseen bus or rail announcers whose only words we understand are the wholly predictable and formulaic expressions like a concluding 'thank you'. Because the announcers themselves understand exactly what they are saying, it seems to be all too easy for them to assume that their listeners are in a similar position: in fact, to the unfortunate passengers, the instruction to proceed to another platform or to transfer to another bus is as entirely unpredictable in detail as the 'improbable roots' in the experiment we have just discussed.

It will be clear that in teaching children to read and write — skills in their own language that they unquestionably need to learn on entering school — we are simultaneously teaching them a great deal more: namely, something about the nature of language itself. We engage them in the task of thinking consciously about this wonderful human faculty that hitherto they have taken almost totally for granted. Given that the teacher's goal is (as the Kingman Committee noted) 'to enable and encourage every child to use the English language to the fullest effect in speaking, writing, listening, and reading', knowledge *about* the language can scarcely come amiss. 'We believe that within English as a subject, pupils need to have their attention drawn to what they are doing and why they are doing it because this is helpful to the development of their language ability.' Of course, the committee conceded, it 'is arguable that such mastery might be achieved without explicit knowledge of the structure of the language or the ways it is used in society. But there is no positive advantage in such ignorance. It is just as important to teach about our language environment as about our physical environment, or about the structure of English as about the structure of the atom. And since we believe that knowledge about language, made explicit at that moment when the pupil is ready, can underpin and promote mastery as well, the argument is even stronger.'

Knowing about language

So what sort of 'knowledge about language' are we talking about? In teaching the skills of reading and writing, we noted that there must be constant cross-reference to the sounds we hear in listening and make in speaking. The written letters and spoken sounds can be usefully seen as our chief modes of *transmitting* 'messages' from one person to another. The 'messages' themselves can be seen as independent of the mode of transmission: we can telephone someone with a *spoken* message about a birth in the family; or we can drop a note through the letter-box giving the same message in *written* form. Indeed, we may construct a message in our minds and never transmit it at all.

Irrespective of transmission, messages consist of *words* arranged in accordance with the conventions of *grammar*. We shall consider each of these components more fully in later chapters, but let us pause long enough at this point to clarify them and explain how they work together.

The parts of messages that seem most obvious, even most important, are the words — also known as the *lexical items* or *vocabulary*. We may think of the word stock as our total collection of *names* for things: the names of actions, objects, qualities, and so on: items like *assume, taxation, box, finger, table, sharp, extraordinary*. The total vocabulary of English is immense and runs into hundreds of thousands. As individuals, of course, we are unlikely to know more than a modest number of these and we are likely to put into actual use an even smaller number. It is perfectly normal to have a 'recognition' knowledge far in excess of our 'active' knowledge: we recognise and understand (or we *think* we do) many words that it would not occur to us to say or write ourselves. But the more carefully we read and listen, the more words we come to understand, and the more words we therefore have a chance of putting to use ourselves as occasion arises. Indeed, often it is only when we venture to *use* a word that we complete or correct the learning process. We know of an otherwise very well informed man who was in his thirties before he was gently helped to understand that the verb *enervate* (which he had come across countless times and had probably even used on quite a number of occasions) actually meant the precise converse of what he thought it meant!

Words are so predominant in language, and a dictionary is so much regarded as the entire register of a language, that we are sometimes tempted to think that there is nothing else to consider. 'Man's word is God in man' — 'Your words, they rob the Hybla bees.' But a language cannot work with words alone. A group of words like *arrive, girl, man, say* cannot tell us much until we have added another component, grammar. Grammar contributes features like articles, prepositions, tense, number, and the conventions of arrangement — which word goes before which. With grammar added, the four words we mentioned can be made to tell us something: 'The *man said* that the *girls* had *arrived*.'

A glimpse at grammar

Grammar has done three things here. It has arranged the words in a particular order, making clear who did the saying and who did the arriving. It has contributed *tense* by the alteration of *say* to *said*, and *number* by the addition of *s* to *girl*. Thirdly, grammar has added some additional words: *the*, *that*, *the*, and *had*. This third point raises a difficulty. We have already described the first component of messages as 'vocabulary', the stock of *words*: now, it is being suggested that grammar also consists in part of words. At first sight, it may be confusing to find the same word, 'words', applied to part of grammar, as well as to the whole of the vocabulary. Like many another language, English has, in fact, two kinds of words, *lexical* words and *grammatical* words, and this basic distinction is important to learn — even if it is not very easy to apply in some cases. The distinction can perhaps best be seen (and the importance of the distinction for English most easily appreciated), if we contrast another language, Latin, in which 'grammatical words' are less numerous and play a much smaller part. The four words, *arrive, girl, man, say*, would be in Latin (devoid of grammatical endings) *adveni-, puell-, vir*, and *dic-*. If we now add grammar, we shall still have in this case just four words, since *inflexion* alone is able to achieve what in English requires both inflexion and grammatical words: *Vir dixit puellas advenisse*, 'The man said that the girls had arrived.

The grammatical words which play so large a part in English grammar are for the most part sharply and obviously different from the lexical words, as one can see by comparing the two sets in our present example: *the, that, the, had*, and *man, say, girl, arrive*. A rough and ready difference which may seem most obvious is that grammatical words have 'less meaning', and in fact some grammarians have called them the 'empty' words as opposed to the 'full' words of vocabulary. But this is a rather misleading way of expressing the distinction. Although a word like *the* is not the name of something as *man* is, it is very far from being meaningless; there is a sharp difference in meaning between 'man is vile' and 'the man is vile', yet *the* is the sole vehicle of this difference of meaning. Moreover, grammatical words differ considerably among themselves as to the amount of meaning they have, even in the lexical sense (as we may see by comparing *the* and *should*, for example). Another name for the grammatical words has been 'little words'. Elizabeth Barrett Browning told her husband, 'You sometimes make a dust, a dark dust, by sweeping away your little words' — perhaps having in mind lines such as:

> Still bidding crouch whom the rest bade aspire.

But size is by no means a good criterion for distinguishing the grammatical words of English, when we consider that we have lexical words like *go*, *man*, *say*, *car*. Apart from this, however, there is a good deal in what Mrs Browning says: we certainly do create a good deal of obscurity when we omit them. This is illustrated not only in the poetry of Robert Browning but in the prose of telegrams and newspaper headlines. 'General Flies Back to Front' is an example from war-time days which manages to be amusing without being confusing, but 'Liverpool Tea Breaks Strike Leader Under Fire' is clear only in a context of daily news about a strike in Liverpool over tea-breaks. Otherwise one might wonder what there was about Liverpool tea that could break a strike-leader — or even why tea-breaks in Liverpool should strike a leader already unfortunate enough to be under a fire.

Words and grammar

Grammatical words, then (or 'function' words, as they are called in some books), are vital signals telling us about the kind of relation that is being expressed between lexical words. It is not that they have no meaning, but that they have a special kind of meaning, sometimes called 'grammatical meaning' or 'structural meaning'. Another important characteristic is that they belong to a relatively small and permanent set of words as compared with the 'full words' of vocabulary. They do not come and go with changing fashions and changing ideas. In different occupations, in different places and at different periods, we tend to use very different nouns and verbs: *totalitarianism*, the *axis*, or *evacuee* may be very often on our lips for a while; we may create entirely new words like *vitaminise* or *penicillin* or *microchip* or *cosmonaut*; we may even adopt foreign words and bandy them about freely and familiarly — *blitz* in the forties, *sputnik* in the fifties, *ombudsman* in the early sixties, *kungfu* in the seventies, and *glasnost* in the eighties. Vocabulary consists of *open* lists of words. But we very rarely add to our stock of prepositions and pronouns, and it is equally rare for one to go out of fashion. Grammatical words are in (relatively) *closed* sets. They remain constantly (and unobtrusively) at their station whether we are saying, 'The man said that the girls had arrived,' or 'The dictator claimed that the democracies had deteriorated,' or 'The beatnik found that the coffee-bar had closed,' or 'The president argued that the short-range nuclear missiles had become obsolete.'

One may suggest an analogy in the goods and equipment of a store. On the one hand we have the articles for sale — dresses, hats, fur-coats; and on the other hand price-tickets, stands, coat-hangers, and measuring-tapes, which are used to handle the goods in which the shop deals. It is the stock that claims most of our attention: it changes from time to time; some parts of it are more in demand in one season, and other parts seem more important at another. But the things used by the shop-assistant — though often beneath our notice — are no less essential to handling the day-to-day business, and a hanger which supports a fur-coat one month may be used for a wedding-dress the next. So too, we may think of vocabulary as the word stock, and grammar as the set of devices for handling this word stock.

But classroom English does not, of course, stop at learning *about* these things. Pupils need to extend their grammatical repertoire so that they can manipulate words into just the right *structure* that will express what they want to say to the best possible effect. Again, pupils have to extend their vocabulary and learn how to find just the right *word* that best expresses what they have in mind — and they need to learn that such vocabulary extension will be a continuing necessity throughout their lives.

Language and convention

And there is much, much more. We have to learn at school (and go on learning after school) the vital importance of *co-operation* as the basis for successful communication: the need for give-and-take, for watchful sensitivity, for linguistic tact, for the respect of conventions.

To begin with this last, it is natural for young people to be impatient with traditional conventions and to subject them to questioning. Bit by bit, we come to recognise that a certain arbitrariness is in the nature of things and perhaps even beneficial as a sort of social discipline. We come to accept, for example, that it is a mark of respect to interrupt an opera to applaud the performance of an aria but that it is unacceptable to interrupt a concerto to applaud a movement or a particular cadenza. Logic does not enter into it; nor is the young New Zealander's logic in 'My cobbers understand me' a relevant criterion in the delicate matter of matching expression to occasion. You might just as well relate table-manners to the speed with which people can gulp their food.

The way we eat particular dishes is not determined primarily by desire to get the food into our mouths in the quickest and easiest way. If it were, the time-and-motion experts would very soon effect a revolution in our eating habits. No, our table-manners are part of our conforming to the social conventions of a community. So too, in our choice of clothes: we do not think merely of keeping warm or cool, but of doing so within the conventions of our society. With our language habits also, then, we must always be sensitive to our environment and use the 'accepted' forms of English, just as we eat and dress in the 'accepted' ways.

Now, all of us at some time have experienced a certain amount of doubt with food and dress: the sudden alarm as to how one manipulates asparagus or what to wear at that wretched garden-party today. Yet the total system of conventions for eating or dressing is triflingly simple as compared with the delicate complexity of the conventions in language. It is not to be wondered at, therefore, that doubts can arise much more frequently (and letters can appear in the press and questions be set in examinations) about the choice of linguistic forms. Of course, there is no problem while we are with our 'cobbers'. Even cabinet ministers need opportunities for linguistic collar-loosening and for speaking without having to consider what it will look like in Hansard.

Outside the circle of our intimates, however, we begin to feel restraints of many kinds, and the further our activities carry us from the people and the background that we are used to, the more careful we have to be in our use of English. We become aware that there is such a thing as linguistic etiquette and linguistic tact. There are 'right' things to say or write, just as there are 'right' things to wear. And this is not only a matter of avoiding embarrassment to ourselves by committing a linguistic *faux-pas*. Linguistic tact also induces us not to embarrass others. If someone looking at your garden admires the 'broad-end-rums' (and obviously means it seriously), can you refer to them in the next breath as 'rhododendrons' without seeming to correct him?

If we look back at Chapter Four, we see that in passage (6), a novelist (Tom Wolfe) depicts a lawyer hesitating over the use of a particular verb-form in the presence of speakers who use a different one. Where they and many other New Yorkers would say *she don't*, though doubtless well aware that (in educated speech and writing) only *she doesn't* is acceptable, the lawyer guesses that he would seem to be criticising the speech of the others if he did not use the demotic *don't* as well. This is a comic instance of linguistic tact and it is not to imply that we have to be taught when to use bad grammar! But at least it reminds us that however much we enlarge our linguistic horizons we still have to talk to our 'cobbers'.

SOME FOLLOW-UP WORK

1 The words *pass*, *sit*, and *piece* each consist of three sounds, one of which they have in common. From these and other examples, work out some general statements as to how the 's' sound is represented in English spelling.

2 As we saw in Chapter Seven, when English words are taken into another language, they are sometimes respelled according to that language's conventions, but often they retain the English spelling. In English, too, we have a mixture of spelling conventions according to the origin of the word: compare the value of 'ch' in *chin* and *machine*, or the spelling of the 'f' sound in *phenomenon*. Compile a list of

foreign spelling conventions that we seem to take in our stride.

3 Bearing in mind the mixture of conventions (*machine*) and irregularities (*height*), devise alternative spellings and argue the case for and against spelling reform.

4 The division sign ÷ was given as an example of visual language that is not 'phonetic'. Consider some areas of communication where non-phonetic symbols are used, giving examples in each area.

5 In a minority of cases in English, two different words may sound alike but be spelled differently (*homophones*), as with *meet* and *meat*; or two different words may be spelled alike but have different sounds (*homographs*), as with the verb *lead* and the name of the metal *lead*. Which type do you regard as the greater nuisance and why does neither cause severe problems in practice?

6 We noted that in handwriting the *ing* of *going* could be less distinctly written because of its predictability. In speech, too, we say things like 'I'm not *gonna* go'. Consider and discuss other sequences and items where, in both speech and writing, understanding proceeds despite gross unclarity.

7 Can you guess which of the handwriting samples on pp. 100–101 are by men and which by women? If so, on what grounds?

8 Given that *bread* is a lexical word, *of* a grammatical word, *girls* is the inflected plural of *girl*, and *said* the inflected past of *say*, study the last paragraph of this chapter and list (a) the lexical words, (b) the grammatical words, and (c) the inflexions found in it.

9 Reconsider the analogy of the shop (with its goods and ancillary equipment) and language (with its vocabulary and 'grammatical equipment'), and point out where the analogy breaks down.

10 Discuss instances of linguistic tact (and tactlessness) that you can recall from personal experience.

CHAPTER 9

What is Standard English?

We all know the little episode in Molière's play *Le Bourgeois Gentilhomme* where Monsieur Jourdain makes a comic discovery in conversing with a professor:

> What? When I say 'Nicole, fetch me my slippers' . . . that's *prose*?

And when the professor assures him that this is indeed prose, Monsieur Jourdain responds in wonderment:

> Good heavens! For more than forty years I have been speaking prose without knowing it!

Something of the sort can be said about Standard English. There is nothing esoteric, obscure, or special about it: whoever and wherever we are in the English-speaking world, we have been familiar with it all our lives. This is especially true if we recall the distinction made in the last chapter between 'active' knowledge and 'recognition' knowledge. Virtually all the English we respond to on television and radio is Standard English. All the announcements we hear as we await our plane's departure, the correspondence we read as it reels out of our fax machines at work, all we read in our morning papers: all this is in Standard English.

Nor do we have to pick and choose the morning paper concerned. It is equally true of the highest circulation tabloid press, addressed deliberately to those who want their news in short simple sentences enlivened by vigorous hyperbole: 'The grief-stricken father was stunned by the news,' 'Youngsters jammed the terraces howling for the referee's blood.' Indeed, the tacit acknowledgement of Standard English as the ubiquitous norm means that popular broadcasting or the tabloid press can depend on our awareness of when a *non*-standard usage is deliberately introduced: 'And who gets the ultimate accolade for social graces? Why, her nibs, of course.' The effectiveness of this (from the entertainments column of a mass daily) depends on the ironic juxtaposition of the slang 'her nibs' with the formality of 'accolade' and 'social graces' — and the writer was confident that readers would recognise the contrast.

When a sandwich bar was boycotted because the proprietor had put up the price of cheese rolls, not one but three popular London papers reported the incident with a pun involving the phrase 'cheesed off' (roughly meaning 'annoyed'), the readers' supposed pleasure arising not only from the pun but from the surprise at finding this non-standard expression in a news item. Again, the British Rail advertisement of low prices for family travel ('A kid a quid') is not so worded for the benefit of those who habitually use *kid* for 'child' and *quid* for 'pound', as though they would be unable to understand the more formal alternatives: rather, the wording is a deliberate counterpoint to the normal language of public communication, Standard English.

Taking the standard for granted

The same point can be made from the present book itself. It is of course written in Standard English, as are the short samples of writing on various subjects given at the beginning of Chapter One. The samples of English that have stood out as unfamiliar and esoteric are some of those given in Chapter Four: the ones that are *not* in Standard English. If you are not familiar with the colloquial English of Ireland, you may be momentarily puzzled by the sentence 'Yez have him bet' in sample (1), where the corresponding Standard English 'You have him beaten' would give no difficulty. Here we contrast standard and non-standard *grammar*. In Irish English, the pronoun *you* can have a plural form (here written *yez*), and the past participle of the verb *beat* can be *bet*. In sample (14), there are items of *vocabulary* that do not belong to Standard English, and if we are unfamiliar with Yorkshire dialect, we are unlikely to understand, for example, the word *thrang* (meaning roughly 'harassed'). But of course, any of us could read the *Irish Times* as easily as Irish people do, the *Yorkshire*

Post as easily as Yorkshire folk do, because these papers are written in Standard English, just as are the London *Times* or the Washington *Post*. The most remarkable thing about Standard English is in fact its unobtrusiveness: we tend to notice someone's use of English only when it is *not* standard.

But if Standard English is as general and commonplace as we have been claiming, it may come as something of a surprise that the Kingman Report of 1988 (see page 98 above) felt it necessary to insist that it be taught: that 'one of the schools' duties is to enable children to acquire Standard English, which is their right'. There are two reasons for such insistence. One is the widespread concern that teachers, in very properly reassuring children against feeling ashamed of their local language habits, may fail to stress sufficiently the value for wider communication of the *standard* language and that pupils may not be adequately taught how to express themselves in it — 'which is their *right*'. The other reason takes us back to the distinction between a 'recognition' knowledge and an 'active' knowledge. Through television, radio, and the press, pupils may well pick up an effective *recognition* knowledge of Standard English and come to understand quite naturally most of what they hear and read in it (though careful teaching in school makes this learning process much speedier and more efficient). Acquiring an *active* control of Standard English is quite another matter. Long after we have come to understand that *you* means 'yez', *worse* means 'war', *beaten* means 'bet', *only* means 'nobbut', it takes a good deal of disciplined learning to remember that (when we are talking beyond our local environment) we should say *you* when we mean 'yez', *worse* when we mean 'war', *beaten* when we mean 'bet', and *only* when we mean 'nobbut'. Long after we have learned to *understand* sentences in a newspaper like:

A young couple were killed last night when their car hit a lamppost.

we have the greatest difficulty in *writing* such sentences ourselves.

Well, as we saw in the last chapter, a good deal of our schooling is concerned with acquiring the skills of reading and writing. What we now add is the obvious fact that the material we learn to read is mostly in Standard English and that when we speak of learning to write, we really have in mind learning to write Standard English.

What we mean by 'standard'

Let us now look in more analytic detail at what we mean by Standard English. The term is somewhat figurative and suggests the analogy of standard measures. Consider the following pairs

1a Pour two cupfuls of water on to the mixture.
 b Pour a quarter of a litre of water on to the mixture.
2a I measured the path and it is twelve paces long.
 b I measured the path and it is 9 metres long.
3a The temperature is terribly high outside.
 b The temperature is 29°C outside.

The (*a*) sentences are comprehensible enough, but they very much depend upon private knowledge or the willingness to accept vague approximations. The first is all right in a family where we know the size of cups meant; (2a) is all right if we have some idea of how long the speaker's pace is; (3a), if we know what the speaker regards as very hot weather. But the (*b*) sentences are fully comprehensible by anyone, anywhere, because the statements are geared to standard measures; you not merely know exactly what 29°C means, but in the last resort you can have the thermometer itself checked for accuracy — right or wrong.

Now, in the figurative application of 'standard' to English, the analogy has only limited validity. It is closest with spelling. The right spelling of *right* is *r-i-g-h-t*, not *r-i-t-e* (which is however the right spelling of the different word *rite*). The right spelling of *centre* in most parts of the world is *c-e-n-t-r-e*, but in American English the right spelling is *c-e-n-t-e-r*; and the spellings 'senter', 'cenntre', 'centor' are wrong anywhere. And, as with 29°C, we can check the correctness of a spelling: we can look it up in a dictionary.

But even in spelling, rightness or wrongness is not always so absolute and has to be related to a more subjective scale of style, judgment, even personal preference. As we saw in Chapter Four, there must be scope in our use of English to vary the style and tone according to the particular occasion (the subject matter, the addressee, etc). So, for example, we can have two spellings, like the following:

I do not know.
I don't know.

Both are correct and standard, differing only in degree of formality, the latter relatively colloquial and more likely to be found in a personal letter or in the dialogue of a novel than in a legal deposition or in the preface of a book. But as our use of 'more likely' suggests, these judgments are not absolute and the two authors of the present book themselves differ on whether contracted forms like *don't* are appropriate in serious writing. On the other hand, when Alison Lurie in her novel *The Truth about Lorin Jones* uses from time to time two further spellings for this same expression:

I dunno.
I d'know.

we can be confident that she is aware (and aware that her *readers* are aware) that these are *non-standard* spellings seeking to capture the sound of very casual conversation.

The position is somewhat similar with grammar. There are vast areas where the distinction between Standard English and non-standard is absolute:

They didn't know anything about it.
He was terribly frightened as he walked home.

The grammar here is unquestionably standard, and in the following it is just as unquestionably not:

They didn't know nothing about it.
They didn't know nowt about it.
He was right frit as he walked home.
I asked her who done it.
Him and her are getting married next week.

On the other hand, grammar sometimes confronts us with choices where both versions are equally standard:

She need not do it. / She does not need to do it.
I helped them mend the fence. / I helped them to mend the fence.

Or one version may be standard for some areas and not for others:

a They have just got a new car.
b They have just gotten a new car.
c She now lives outside Scotland.
d She now lives outwith Scotland.

The form of (b) is standard in American English, that of (d) in Scots English.

But as with informal spellings, there are forms in grammar where the assessment of correctness depends on style and personal judgment:

Who did they elect to speak for them?	(Whom . . .)
His sister is younger than him.	(. . . he)
The data is just not available.	(. . . are . . .)
Neither of them were present.	(. . . was . . .)

While the parenthesised alternatives are preferable in certain circumstances (such as formal writing), all of these are used freely by educated people and must be regarded as acceptable within Standard English. But we should be prepared for honest disagreement in such matters, and there are plenty of further choices where the 'popular' version raises far more doubts about its admissibility:

If anyone has lost their ticket, they should apply to the box office.

Between you and I, Fred has refused.

Her results are widely different than yours.

Although choices such as these loom large in discussions of standard and non-standard grammar (and we shall return to them in Chapter Sixteen), they form a tiny minority of grammatical features. For the most part, the line between standard and non-standard is clear, though we depend heavily upon our schooling to learn which is which, and we do not find it as easy as we do with spelling to check in case of doubt. In general, our success at appreciating the difference is shown by our ability to recognise (and enjoy) the occasions when non-standard grammar is deliberately introduced in the context of Standard English discourse: for example, when Mrs Margaret Thatcher accuses some politicians of being 'frit' or when President Reagan proclaims 'You ain't seen nothing yet' (whether or not we recognise the Al Jolson echo). We can even take over into Standard English an expression which embodies both non-standard spelling and non-standard grammar:

He has written another whodunnit.

Standard and slang

With this last example, we pass from grammar to vocabulary and at once confront the phenomenon already noted: the relation of style and tone to our judgment on whether a word is acceptable as Standard English. For most of us, *whodunnit* is decidedly colloquial, to be used without hesitation in familiar talk and writing but scarcely to be introduced in place of 'detective novel' or 'crime story' if we are writing an article on literature or speaking in a court of law. Much closer to the borderline would be an adjective like *doddery:*

He was feeling doddery, so she helped him to a seat.

Most people would regard the word as part of Standard English, though some would feel it too informal to be used in (say) a sermon or a report to a health authority. On the other hand, though the words *posh, yob, phony* are widespread and well known, many people would not regard them as Standard English at all but rather as belonging to an outcast *slang* status, like the italicised words in the following:

They like mixing with *swells* and *nobs.*
She accused him of being a *mingy jerk.*
The two comedians *creased* their audience.
He made a living by *flogging* encyclopaedias.

We are thus making a distinction between colloquial (or informal) usage and slang; but there is of course some overlap, in that it is unusual to find slang words used outside colloquial speech while it is quite usual to pepper one's colloquial speech with slang, and opinions will often sharply differ as to whether a given word is colloquial or slang. But while slang can be regarded on the one hand as being at the extreme end of the colloquial range (so that we may hesitate to introduce slang words into conversation unless we know our addressees very well), slang has its outcast status in part only because it is daring, racy, new, and (at its best) excitingly imaginative. In other words, it is often not standard because it has not yet had sufficient general currency. Slang (again at its best, we must insist) can in fact be regarded as the poetry of ordinary people, pressing language beyond their ordinary experience of it. 'The two comedians *creased* their audience' or 'I was *fingered* by a *grass*' may strike us as slangy rather than poetic, but 'Tonight the wind *gnaws* with teeth of glass' will strike us as poetic rather than slangy (even without our knowing that it was written by Laurie Lee).

Consider the following discussion that takes place in George Eliot's *Middlemarch* (1872):

> 'But' — here Rosamond's face broke into a smile which suddenly revealed two dimples. She herself thought unfavourably of these dimples and smiled little in general society. 'But I shall not marry any Middlemarch young man.'
>
> 'So it seems, my love, for you have as good as refused the pick of them; and if there's better to be had, I'm sure there's no girl better deserves it.'
>
> 'Excuse me, mamma — I wish you would not say, "the pick of them".'
>
> 'Why, what else are they?'
>
> 'I mean, mamma, it is rather a vulgar expression.'
>
> 'Very likely, my dear; I never was a good speaker. What should I say?'
>
> 'The best of them.'
>
> 'Why, that seems just as plain and common. If I had had time to think, I should have said, "the most superior young men". But with your education you must know.'
>
> 'What must Rosy know, mother?' said Mr Fred, who had slid in unobserved through the half-open door while the ladies were bending over their work, and now going up to the fire stood with his back towards it, warming the soles of his slippers.
>
> 'Whether it's right to say "superior young men",' said Mrs Vincy, ringing the bell.
>
> 'Oh, there are so many superior teas and sugars now. Superior is getting to the shopkeepers' slang.'
>
> 'Are you beginning to dislike slang, then?' said Rosamond, with mild gravity.
>
> 'Only the wrong sort. All choice of words is slang. It marks a class.'
>
> 'There is correct English: that is not slang.'
>
> 'I beg your pardon: correct English is the slang of prigs who write history and essays. And the strongest slang of all is the slang of poets.'
>
> 'You will say anything, Fred, to gain your point.'
>
> 'Well, tell me whether it is slang or poetry to call an ox a *leg-plaiter*.'

'Of course you can call it poetry if you like.'
'Aha, Miss Rosy, you don't know Homer from slang. I shall
invent a new game; I shall write bits of slang and poetry on
slips, and give them to you to separate.'

Without being as perverse as Fred Vincy, we might agree with
him to the extent of wondering whether the highly technical,
highly specialised language of experts within their own field
might be regarded as a sort of 'slang'. If we look back at the
samples given in Chapter Four, what status should we assign to
the stock-market term *short-covering* in (2), the golfing verb *eagled*
in (7), *bit image* in (10), *transponder* in (12), not to mention *vidwan*
in (3)? The impression of 'insider talk' is somewhat similar to that
conveyed by slang, and it is this aspect of such words which
makes them unwelcome if they are introduced into non-
specialised contexts. But our reaction to such expressions is more
usually captured by labelling them *jargon* rather than slang. Both
are terms largely of disparagement, but with 'jargon' we designate
the difficult words of the expert, with 'slang' the deliberately ir-
reverent words of the nonchalant.

British and American standards

There are many other words that we might question in these
Chapter Four passages, however, without calling them either
slang or jargon. There are in particular the purely regional words
in the Scots poem (5) and in the Yorkshire dialect passage (14).
Perhaps indeed, we should regard *vidwan* in (3) as less musical
jargon than a regional word familiar in Indian culture. This
reminds us that, as we have seen with spelling and grammar,
Standard English has regional branches, especially the British
branch and the American. Far more than in spelling and grammar, these two have differences in their 'standard' stock of words.
Although these differences are rapidly declining with the increased commonality of culture spread by the media, many stead-
fastly remain, such as *gas(olene)* (American) beside *petrol* (British);
sidewalk (A), *pavement* (B): *candy* (A), *sweets* (B); *comforter* (A), *eider-
down* (B). Neither member of these pairs is to be regarded as 'more
standard' than the other; each is equally standard but within different systems. In any event, the differences are usually not so
polarised as these examples. It is far more common to have

preferences than mutual exclusions. Thus *mail* is commoner in American English, *post* is commoner in British English; but *mail* and *post* are both used in both systems. The word *automobile* is almost exclusively American, but *car* is used equally in American and British English. When we further reflect that, as within Standard British English, there are style constraints in Standard American English too, such as those determined by relative formality, we can see that standards in vocabulary present us with considerable complexity. And if our English is basically British or basically American, we need to be especially wary with the 'marginal' vocabulary in the other system. Americans cannot easily tell when they can safely use *lolly* for 'money', or *grotty* for 'unpleasant', nor can the British easily acquire a feel for *jerk* or even *guy*. Needless to say, as further national standards develop (Australian English is an obvious candidate), the breadth and complexity of Standard English vocabulary must inevitably increase.

At this point, it may be helpful to recapitulate by giving in full the interesting definition of Standard English as it appears in the most recent unabridged Webster dictionary (*Webster's Third*). The definition has four subsections:

 1: the English taught in schools;
 2: English that is current, reputable, and national;
 3: the English that with respect to spelling, grammar, pronunciation, and vocabulary is substantially uniform though not devoid of regional differences, that is well-established by usage in the formal and informal speech and writing of the educated, and that is widely recognised as acceptable wherever English is spoken and understood;
 4: all words entered in a general English language dictionary that are not restricted by a label (as *slang*, *dial*, *obs*, *biol*, *Scot*).

Variation in sound

There is one feature in the Webster definition that we have not yet discussed: to the uniformity of spelling, grammar and vocabulary, Webster adds *pronunciation*. We have left this matter of pronunciation to the end, precisely because it is the aspect of English where (in our view, as opposed to Webster's) the concept of standard is least applicable. That is natural enough when one considers the nature of pronunciation. Distinctions in vocabulary, grammar, and spelling are inclined to be discrete and absolute: 'I said *friend* not *offend*', 'I said *I would know* not *I don't know*', 'The word is spelled *conceive* not *concieve*'. By contrast, pronunciation is protean: differing from person to person, indeed from one person speaking slowly (or emphatically) to the same person speaking fast (or casually); and the gradations of 'difference' can be big and obtrusive or infinitesimally small, observable only to the trained ear of a phonetician. So an *absolute* uniformity in pronunciation would be difficult to achieve and is almost inconceivable.

Moreover, the sounds we give to words, the way we say *mother* or *dad* or *I'd love some of that:* these are so personal as to be inalienable from our sense of identity itself. Pronunciation in fact less resembles spelling than it resembles handwriting: this too, as we saw in Chapter Eight, is highly variably as well as highly personal. As with handwriting, we find it more useful to speak of *care* and *clarity* in pronunciation than to speak of (or seek for) uniformity. In short, the two main systems of 'transmission' that we distinguish in this book — spelling and pronunciation — are on a sharply different footing, and one of the advantages of the rather irregular, arbitrary, and frequently unphonetic spelling of English is that it can be understood throughout the world, irrespective of the actual sounds used by a given reader — in Leeds or Los Angeles, Ottawa or Otago — if he or she were to read it aloud.

We acquire our pronunciation, quite unconsciously, from those around us: our family and our playmates. We do not even know what we sound like, and the first time we hear a recording of a family conversation, we often recognise the voices of everyone in the group — except our own. Moving, perhaps temporarily, outside our normal environment, we may have attention drawn to what strikes our new companions as a strange pronunciation and we may even be teased about it; sometimes we are intimidated into taking on, chameleon-like, the pronunciation used in our new environment. This is doubtless the mechanism by which, in any society, pronunciation achieves whatever 'uniformity' there is. But however much our accent becomes blurred by such imitation, we may continue throughout life to withdraw at will into our original local dialect — as into our own home: when we want to be particularly private and personal, or when we want to declare our basic commitment, identity, and loyalty.

Given his own origin, background, and subsequent envelopment into a national context, it is understable that D H Lawrence was interested in such dual tendencies, and they are explored in *Lady Chatterley's Lover*. For example:

> 'Why do you speak Yorkshire?' she said softly.
> 'That! That's non Yorkshire, that's Derby.'
> He looked back at her with that faint distant grin.
> 'Derby, then! Why do you speak Derby? You spoke natural English at first.'
> 'Did Ah though? An' canna Ah change if Ah'm a mind to 't? Nay, nay, let me talk Derby if it suits me. If yo'n nowt against it.'
> 'It sounds a little affected,' said Hilda.
> 'Ay, 'appen so! An' up i' Tevershall yo'd sound affected.'

We may be tempted to think that by 'natural English' Hilda means nothing more than *her* English, the kind of English that comes naturally to *her*. But there is more to it than that. Although there is nothing like the uniformity of standard pronunciation that we find in grammar, vocabulary, and above all spelling, there is some general consensus about a *range* of pronunciation that is more widely acceptable than other kinds of pronunciation. It is the range that we associate with (and expect from) the educated: whether these be television news readers, political leaders, doctors, lawyers, or schoolteachers.

Since, however, one of the marks of the educated is that their English falls recognisably within this range of pronunciation, we are undoubtedly involved in some circularity. This has long been recognised. As the American scholar, R O Williams, put it in the late nineteenth century: 'If pressed to say definitely what good American English is, I should say, it is the English of those who are believed by the greater number of Americans to know what good English is.' That in fact applies not just to pronunciation but to Standard English as a whole.

We may say, in short, that Standard English is that kind of English which draws least attention to itself over the widest area and through the widest range of usage. It is particularly associated with the English that is *intended* to have the widest reach, and in consequence it is traditionally associated most of all with English in not just a *written* form but a *printed* form. In fact, the standards of Standard English are determined and preserved to a far greater extent than most people realise by the great publishing houses.

This fact should remind us that, invaluable as Standard English is as a communication system, and vital as it is that all of us should acquire it, we make no aesthetic or moral claims for it. Standard English is neutral in these respects. It can be used to stir up hatred and to spread messages of harmony alike. Standard English can be made to sound ugly, boring, or stale; and it can equally sound beautiful, uplifting, exciting. We adopt it for its efficacy as an instrument; the uses we make of the instrument are our own responsibility.

SOME FOLLOW-UP WORK

1 List a dozen vocabulary items and a dozen features of grammar belonging to your own 'repertoire' of English which you would not consider standard. Match them with the standard versions and give examples of occasions when you would consider it more appropriate to use the standard or the non-standard forms.

2 In the light of your own experience, discuss the views on dialect expressed by Lawrence's Hilda and Mellors.

3 Refer back to what was said about phatic communion in Chapter Two. To what extent is the concept of Standard English helpful or otherwise in this respect?

4 At the end of Chapter Four, we considered the various passages quoted there in connection with such matters as style and tone. Rereading them now with Standard English in mind:
a) Write a narrative version of sample (1) in Standard English, beginning: 'Her father asked Kathleen what was the matter with her.'
b) Sample (4) is already in Standard English. Without departing from Standard English, write a version that is more in tune with your own taste.
c) Finally, comment on the changes that you introduced in both (a) and (b).

5 Some examples were given of differences within Standard English as between Britain and the United States. Give some further examples — in vocabulary, grammar, and spelling — from your own experience and reading.

6 If there is a British Standard English and an American Standard English (but with a great deal that is common to both), to what extent do you believe there is a Standard . . . English, filling the blank with *Irish, Australian,* or any other national adjective you please? Give examples, and justify your claim.

7 Pursue the argument advanced by George Eliot's Fred Vincy, giving some examples of what he might consider as 'shopkeepers' slang' today, or the 'slang' of poets. Re-examine the samples given at the beginning of Chapter One, and justify (or refute) his concept of 'the slang of prigs who write history and essays'.

8 Read through an issue or so of a current popular newspaper, noting and attempting to explain the introduction of non-standard language features.

The power and complexity of words

The relations that we bear to the words of our mother tongue and to its grammar are quite different. In our daily face-to-face dealings with colleagues at work, friends, and the family at home, we are never really aware of English grammar. With words this is different: we know that we have to name a thing if we want it; we know that occasionally we do not know the name of a thing and then have to ask for it; we are aware that a word can hurt, excite, decide a case. Words work. Similarly, when we are travelling to another country, it is words we need first to get anything, anywhere. We are conscious of words, conscious of their power, conscious of their need for our survival.

We may not attribute the same degree of mystical significance to the word as we find it expressed in the opening lines of the Gospel according to St John (in the New English Bible version): 'When all things began, the Word already was. The Word dwelt with God, and what God was, the Word was.' But compared to grammar, there is a special relationship between us and the word, founded on the mystery that a name calls up an entity in the world around us, and vice versa. When tiny children have grasped that a particular string of sounds is related to an object around them, and when they utter their first word, we know that with this first step they have acquired the key to the world. Once this intuitive mental operation has been performed, it will be repeated again and again. One word is the key to language and it is therefore not surprising at all that the word *word* itself can mean 'speech' or 'language' in a number of languages. Compare: '*Et maintenant, je donne la parole au metteur en scène.*' — '*Das Wort hat der Abgeordnete Schmidt.*'

Gradually children learn more and more names for things and

build up a world of their own in which every object has a name. The more words they learn, the more their little world will become similar to our own. But we all know that this building-up process is never completed. The stock of words of a language — its *vocabulary* or *lexicon* — is so immense that no individual has a total knowledge of it. We all know only a fraction, the size of this fraction varying from one person to another, though we share a considerable part. We may therefore say that the whole of the English vocabulary exists only within the English speech community taken together.

Name and referent

The experience that a name and a referent (what is named) call up each other is so basic to our existence that it accounts for certain attitudes that we display with respect to words. We tend to regard the link between the name and the referent as natural, as inevitable, it could not be otherwise. Words, as the English philosopher John Locke put it 300 years ago in *An Essay Concerning Human Understanding*, 'come to excite in Men certain *Ideas*, so constantly and readily, that they are apt to suppose a natural connexion between them'. A dog can only be called a dog, and a spade only a spade; nothing else. Occasionally, we may even go so far as to describe what we feel as this natural connection: 'The sea is called the *sea* because the water stretches on and on and on, just like s - e - e - e.' Or 'a pot is called a *pot* because it is open in the middle and has walls on the sides', etc, etc. This feeling that the link between the two is necessary makes us believe that there is a right and correct name for every thing, every quality, every action. Another consequence of this idea is the evocative power that is attributed to words. This can manifest itself in a number of different ways.

Take, for example, incantations and charms. In various countries of Europe there are still areas where special men or women are called upon to cure such ailments as styes, shingles, or warts, by means of verbal incantations. Conjurers often begin their tricks by pronouncing some words that are supposed to work magic. Most of us are familiar with the incantatory *abracadabra* uttered on such occasions. Spells in fairy tales are another case in point. In the famous German folk tale *Rumpelstilzchen*, for instance, the correct guessing of the dwarf's name by the king's bride destroys its bearer. The belief that the mere mention of a name has the magic power to make the referent actually appear on the scene has even become proverbial in some languages. The French say *Quand on parle du loup, on en voit la queue*; the Germans *Wenn man vom Teufel spricht, dann kommt er.* This belief helps us to understand why in some speech communities the mention of a particular name is avoided and circumlocutions are used instead. This is, for instance, common for the names of certain animals that are feared or regarded as foreboding ill luck or disaster. Thus a bear may be referred to as 'the brown one,' and the crew of a ship may fear the sight of 'the little fellows' (*rats*). The development of the names for the weasel in the Romance languages is an interesting case in this respect; for example, the Italian *donnola* literally means 'little woman'. It now also becomes understandable why the name of the devil should not be used, and why the name of God is treated with such respect.

The close natural connection assumed to hold between a name and its referent also makes us confound the two. That is, we transfer the attitude that we have for a particular word to its referent, and equally, when we like or dislike something, or someone, we tend to see the pleasure or discomfort reflected in the name. We may think that we are sophisticated enough to distinguish between the two. But the transfer is so common that it is difficult to avoid. Which of us can say that we have never found a particular name very pleasing or likeable because the person so called was especially dear to us? Who has not had the experience of disliking a particular name because someone with that name was disloyal or dishonest? For most people, the choosing of a name therefore becomes very important. Parents ponder with enormous seriousness before deciding what to call their baby. Actors and actresses think hard to find a stage-name that will in itself be pleasing to the public. Not all people are linguistically as mature as Juliet:

> What's Montague? It is nor hand, nor foot,
> Nor arm, nor face, nor any other part
> Belonging to a man. O, be some other name!
> What's in a name? that which we call a rose

By any other name would smell as sweet;
So Romeo would, were he not Romeo call'd,
Retain that dear perfection which he owes
Without that title: Romeo, doff thy name;
And for that name, *which is no part of thee*,
Take all myself.

Romeo and Juliet, Act II, scene 2

Since attributing features of the referent to its name (and vice versa) is so common, some people may take advantage of it and exploit it for their own purposes. This is why the issue has to be brought to our attention and why we need to be aware of it. Advertising, for instance, thrives on our belief in an affinity between name and referent. When a soap called *Sunlight* came on the market, long before we all had washing-machines, the implication obviously was of laundry hung out, cleaned and dried in open sunlight. And do oranges of the name *Sunkist* not look and taste better because they were kissed by the sun during ripening? Can one not feel the cleaning effect of a *Kleenex*? Advertising is only one relevant field; others are for example politics and religion. Language awareness and awareness of our attitude towards it thus become important.

Reality shaped by words

The nomenclature attitude — the belief that words are simply labels for objects, qualities, and movements — often underlies our first ventures into learning another language. We expect that each word in our mother tongue will be matched by one in French or Russian or whatever the language is that we are learning. And at the beginning stage, our expectation seems to be confirmed: *a car* is *une voiture* in French, *ein Auto* in German; *a door* is *une porte*, *eine Tur* respectively; for *to open* the French say *ouvrir*, the Germans *offnen*; and what we call *fast* is *vite* in French and *schnell* in German. But when we progress further, we find that the French call a flower *une fleur*, and a blossom also *une fleur*. How odd, we think; surely a flower and a blossom are not the same thing; how can the French manage with only one word? We discover that water can be deep in French (*profond*), but there is no word for *shallow*. One has to say *peu profond* ('hardly deep').

The Germans, on the other hand, do not distinguish between jam and marmalade as we do. What they spread on their rolls and slices of bread is *Marmelade*, whatever kind of fruit preserve it is. They can, of course, differentiate between strawberry jam, raspberry jam and marmalade by forming compound words: *Erdbeermarmelade, Himbeermarmelade, Orangenmarmelade*. A German would not see any reason why *Orangenmarmelade* is so special that it deserves a completely different word, one that does not immediately link it to the *Marmelade*-group. In learning German, we also find that the word corresponding to parents is *die Eltern*, but that one cannot say *ein Elter* ('a parent'). A further German example for which we do not have a one-word translation in English is *Geschwister* ('brothers and sisters'). If someone tells you that he or she has *zwei Geschwister*, this means that there are three children in the family and the speaker could have either two brothers, or two sisters, or one brother and one sister. The further we penetrate into another language, the more complicated it becomes, the more we realise that the nomenclature equation does not hold. We discover that things do not always have to be seen in the 'English way'. A language thus is and mediates a particular view of the world.

Let us look at this more closely. We do not know how language began, and scholars can only speculate. There is no evidence. Most of us first encounter language in the form of only one particular language: Chinese or Swedish or Hungarian or English. All human beings are endowed with the faculty of speech. Yet which particular language they will actually acquire depends on the linguistic environment. Every human being is born into a community and first learns the language of that community. As human beings, we perceive in the world around us a myriad of objects, shapes, smells, noises. In order to communicate our perceptions to other human beings, we have to be able to refer to them. But in fact, the phenomena around us are not so much discrete, separable 'things' as a constantly changing flux. In consequence, naming is in part an arbitrary segmentation of continual and ever-changing phenomena. Where does the chin end and the cheek begin? We need not be surprised to find that other people's perceptions differ greatly from our own. In a given speech community, language is the means by which we achieve some kind of agreement as to what is relevant to name in the environment

around us and how to classify our perception and experience of
the world. Let us recall points made in Chapter One.

Lexicalisation

Communities are, for instance, conditioned by the geographical
area where they live, the climate surrounding them, the social and
cultural systems they have inherited. The perceptions of a community are guided by its interests. It may therefore single out perceptions and *lexicalise* them, that is, encapsulate them in the form
of a noun, verb, or other part of speech. This then becomes a *word*
or *lexical item* for something which another community might not
think of lexicalising. The white substance that we call snow, for
instance, has a deeper relevance in the geographical area where
the Eskimos live than in Britain where we may have experience
of it for a few weeks in winter. The conditions of snow are therefore relevant to the Eskimo people, whether it is new, wet, dry,
hard, etc, and each kind may be lexicalised. In English, on the
other hand, glaciers seem not to have struck its speech community members until fairly recently. This is suggested by the fact
that there was no native English word for them: *glacier* and *crevasse*
are both adopted from French. One may therefore reasonably expect that 'interest' or 'relevance' areas of a language community
are relatively densely lexicalised because different aspects of a
phenomenon or an object are focused upon. Just think of the
words for means of transport in our time and those common in
centuries past. We are fascinated by the different names for horses
that Chaucer uses in the Prologue to his *Canterbury Tales*: *amblere,*
hors, mere, palfrey, rouncy, stot. In the nineteenth century there was
a wide range of carriages, and people differentiated between a
barouche, a *brougham,* a *calash,* a *carriole,* a *coupé,* a *diligence,* a *gig,*
a *landau,* a *phaeton,* a *victoria.* Compare with this the names for
types of car that we are familiar with nowadays.

Societies differ in their beliefs and in their rules of propriety and
decency. There are therefore certain things that one should not
talk about. Yet this does not make the referent and the need to
name it disappear. Speakers tend to observe the societal decency
code, and when the need arises to talk about the tabooed referent,
they create new lexical items. Some may be jocular at first, but

often they become generally accepted and thus conventionalised. Foreigners who come to England, for instance, are always amazed at what they regard as 'fanciful' names for *toilet*. What they are looking for in public buildings, theatres, restaurants or pubs may be called *cloakroom*, *Gents*, *Ladies*, *lavatory*, *powder room*, *public convenience*, *rest room*, *WC*, or of course *toilet*.

Death is something that few of us like to talk about. No wonder therefore that we have lexicalised the passage from life to non-life in so many different ways. Some expressions for *die* are for instance: *decease*, *expire*, *succumb*, *pass away*, *be gone*, *be no more*, *close one's eyes*, *depart this life*, *give up the ghost*, *go the way of all flesh*, *join the majority*, *meet one's Maker*, *kick the bucket*, *bite the dust*, *push up the daisies*. In the case of *toilet* and *die*, we have two perceptual situations lexicalised as one word each. As we see from the above examples, however, lexicalisation is not restricted to single words. It can also avail itself of two or more words which are then knitted or moulded together to form one lexical unit, as in *cloakroom*, *rest room*, *be no more*, *close one's eyes*.

Relevant areas such as taboo attract the speakers' imagination and lead to a constant supply of new lexicalisations in which different facets of the same phenomenon, event, or object are presented. One might compare this linguistic situation to a state of siege: the act of dying is assailed by language, and each new lexicalisation is an attempt to capture it. The battle area becomes a *lexical field* where one perceptual unit is expressed by different lexical items that are all very close in meaning. By an assault of synonyms, the speakers of a language try to tackle a specific perceptual bastion.

In the cases of the Eskimo words for snow, the wealth of English expressions for *toilet* and *to die*, we have tried to account for the fact that some areas of our perception are more richly lexicalised in one language than in another. But this cannot be the whole story. Our mother tongue is handed down to us as something that generations of speakers before us have used and into which they have integrated their lexicalised views of the world (consider *sunrise*) and into which we will incorporate ours (consider *orbit* or *program*). Why does English have a number of different words for the colour *red*? What is so special about the perception of this colour that there are such lexical items as *crimson*, *purple*, *ruddy*, *sanguine*, and *scarlet*, whereas there is virtually only *green* for the colour green? We do not know, just as there is no explanation of why, with specific reference to human hair, English speakers have lexicalised only *auburn*, *blond*, and *brunette*. For the other colours, compounds like *dark-haired*, *grey-haired*, *red-haired*, *white-haired* are used. We thus find in a language *primary lexicalisations* (e.g. the simple words *auburn*, *blond*, *brunette*) and *secondary lexicalisations*, or word-formation: that is, lexical items coined out of primary lexicalisations (e.g. the compound words *dark-haired*, *grey-haired*, *red-haired*, *white-haired*).

Human perception is obviously determined by biological factors, by the ways in which our mind and senses work. It is directed towards the world around us where some objects are clearly delimited, above all those that can be moved without being destroyed, and others merge with each other. And it is guided by our interests. All this is reflected in language, in the way we single out aspects of our perception and experience of reality and encapsulate them in lexical units. A chair and a table can easily be recognised as different objects and are given different names, *chair* and *table*. There are of course many actual chairs and tables in this world; they come in different sizes, colours, materials. We abstract from the varying physical features of these objects, retain what is permanent and essential as a mental image (for instance, that a table is a man-made object with a flat top and one or more legs), and encapsulate all this in the word *table*. In the case of such words as *cheek*, *nape*, *forehead*, on the other hand, we cannot really say where the part of reality that has been lexically singled out begins and ends. In such cases, the concrete area referred to by the word may even gradually change, above all when the word is not often used for reasons of societal decency. Such a referential shift can be illustrated with the French word *la cuisse*. Where does a thigh end or start? At the hip? The Latin word *coxa* meant 'hip', and the French word *cuisse* which goes back to Latin *coxa* means 'thigh'.

When we make the world our own by classifying it through language, human perception functions as a yardstick. We perceive, for instance, differences in size, colour, shape. So we have lexical items where these aspects predominate. Size is criterial in *big*, *small*, *tall*, *tiny*, *dwarf*, and *giant*; colour in *auburn*, *blond*, *albino* and *blush*; shape in *straight*, *oval*, *round*, *circle*, *triangle*, *to roll*, and *zig-zag*. We capture lines of human descent in the terms of parental relations: *father, mother, son, daughter,* etc. We are aware that things are a functioning assembly of parts, and we give names to the different parts: a tree has a *trunk,* a *branch,* a *twig,* a *leaf;* a knife has a *blade,* an *edge,* a *handle.*

What all this is demonstrating is that there is some order and coherence in lexicalisation. There is great complexity, and coherence may therefore be difficult to detect, but it is there. And it must be there. Without the control of parameters, we would have chaos, and nothing that could be remembered and passed on to fellow human beings. What we have is very different. However amorphous it may seem to ordinary speakers, the lexicon of every language is highly structured, and structured in complex ways.

The dynamic nature of meaning

In the illustrative examples given above, we had nouns, adjectives, and verbs; that is, certain classificatory parameters cut across word classes. So far, we have mostly dealt with nouns referring to concrete objects in reality. Let us now look at more complex examples to bring out some other features that characterise the lexicon of a language.

When we lexicalise a perception or experience, what we are doing is to impose an artificial impression of neatness and unity rather arbitrarily on a whole general and complex moving scene, with setting and participants. Take the noun *family.* Here we capture the fact that it concerns human beings (factor 1), that there is a common source (factor 2), from which by blood relation (factor 3) descendants are issued (factor 4). We might say that these are four essential factors for the noun *family.* What is left unspecified is, for instance, the number of descendants. This leaves room for applications to different situations: in the sentence, *Almost every family in this street owns two cars,* the interpretation of *family* would be 'a group of people consisting of the parents and children'; in *She comes from a family that has farmed this area of the country for 300 years,* the interpretation of *family* would be something like 'all the descendants over 300 years from one pair of ancestors'. Perceptions progress by detecting similarities and differences. So we find, for instance, that there are other phenomena which seem to have some similarity to a family as described above, e.g. animals and plants. In a sentence like *The lion belongs to the cat family*, we have applied the word to a case where factors 2, 3, and 4 hold, but where factor 1 would either be ignored or reinterpreted as 'animals'. When we speak of the Indo-European language 'family' to which English belongs, our basis for applying the word *family* to a group of related languages must be the factors 2 and 4, ignoring factors 1 and 3.

Or let us look at the word *bunch*, as in *a bunch of flowers, a bunch of grapes, a bunch of keys*. What has been lexicalised here seems to be an unspecified number (factor 1), of things (factor 2), of the same kind (factor 3), occurring (growing, fastened, grouped) together (factor 4). In expressions like *a bunch of girls, a bunch of students*, we show that we perceive some similarity between the group of girls or students and the *bunch* of flowers, grapes and keys. In applying *bunch* to people, we have extended its meaning. Yet it is not quite clear how far we have expanded it. *A bunch of girls, a bunch of students* sounds all right. But could we apply the word to all possible groups of people? Imagine a social occasion attended by members of the royal family or important statesmen. A commentator might say: *The royal party* (*The group of visiting statesmen*) *is moving to take their seats.* Could a reporter or journalist use *bunch* instead of *party* or *group*? It would sound highly improper and undignified. Perhaps it is that the things referred to by *bunch* (flowers, grapes, keys) are usually relatively small and therefore there would be a clash if we applied it to people of importance.

Let us illustrate some further characteristics of the lexicon with the verb *to drink* and the adjective *clever*. In a sentence like *Drink your coffee before it gets cold, drink* is used to encapsulate the perception of 'taking a liquid into one's mouth and swallowing it'. But in a sentence like *He doesn't drink*, where the verb has no object, the normal interpretation is 'to take an *alcoholic* liquid into one's mouth and swallow it': that is, what was generic in our first example (a liquid) has become specific. As a further development, in a sentence like *He drinks*, again a use of the verb without an object, the meaning has become pejorative: not only does he drink alcohol but he does so habitually and possibly too much.

A pejorative extension has occurred also with *clever*. In a sentence like *She was a clever girl and went to university*, it is quickness of understanding and learning in a human being that are the essential factors in the meaning of *clever*. These qualities can be transferred from the human being to the action which displays them. Therefore we can also speak of *a clever answer, a clever solution,* etc. People are always very sensitive to each other's mental capabilities. Quickness of mind may therefore also be regarded as *too* quick, as being not thorough enough, not entirely sincere, as merely intended to impress someone else. This accounts for such uses as in *Are you trying to be clever? Too clever by half,* and I *don't like his clever tricks,* where the choice of the adjective *clever* expresses criticism and disapproval.

What emerges from our discussion of *family, bunch, to drink* and *clever*? The major part of the vocabulary of our mother tongue that we gradually acquire is always already created; that is, we learn how to use words that already exist in the speech community. In a sense, we are presented with the lexicalised perceptions and experiences of the generations of speakers that preceded us. This means that in the majority of cases, we are not performing the lexicalisation process; we are presented with the results. We have to explore, puzzle out what has been encapsulated in them. This can only be done by watching very carefully how our mother tongue is used. Thus we may, for instance, first hear and understand *bunch* in the phrase *a bunch of flowers* and derive from this use that the meaning of *bunch* is something like 'a number of, several' applied to flowers. We may later come across the expression *a bunch of keys.* We store this use of the word but at the same time our mind starts working on what the similarities are between flowers and keys that they could both be used in combination with *bunch*. We may come up with a hypothesis that is something like 'collected, or fastened together'. When we then hear someone talk about *a bunch of grapes,* we may at first be puzzled but then quietly adjust the factor 'collected or fastened together' so as to cover also 'clustered, grown together'. Thus bit by bit the different possibilities of use are built up in us. The ways a word is used constitute its meaning. In *bunch,* as in *family, to drink,* and *clever,* and as in fact in most vocabulary items, the meaning is multi-faceted, not single but radiating out, with different faces shining in different lights: in other words, with different meanings on different occasions.

On the way to building up the different senses of a word, we may of course also go astray. When we have heard *a bunch of flowers* and *a bunch of keys*, we may abstract from these uses the idea that *bunch* is used for a number of objects that can be held in the hand. This could then lead us to talk about *a bunch of marbles* or *a bunch of pills* or *a bunch of coins*. Other speakers would look puzzled and they might say something like 'Ah, you mean . . .', and this would signal to us that our hypothesis on the use of *bunch* was not quite correct, and did not conform to other speakers' use, and that we needed to make a slight shift towards something like 'collected, fastened, or grown together' but not necessarily held in the hand.

Let us assume that we had also incorporated into our stored knowledge about the use of *bunch* that it can be used for a group of people as in *a bunch of girls, a bunch of students*, where there is no question of 'fastened' or 'grown together', but where the idea of being assembled or clustered applies. Let us then assume that we come across a phrase like *a bunch of thugs, a bunch of muggers*. As with *girls* and *students*, *bunch* is here applied to a group of people. Yet the mental image called up by the use of *bunch* and a group of *thugs* or *muggers* may also call up our experience that *thugs* and *muggers*, when they are met with in small groups, are usually up to something nasty. Therefore our understanding of *a bunch of thugs* or *muggers* could be simply a group of them, but an understanding co-present could be 'a group of thugs (or muggers) putting their heads together and planning their next attack'. We would thus have co-present a potential shift from a mere clustering to a clustering for a specific purpose, a mischievous one. The possibility of this shift is there, latent, waiting to be picked up by the speakers of the language. If it is, a slight change towards a pejorative sense of *bunch* would have taken place, as we noted it earlier for *to drink* and *clever* in such instances as *He drinks* and *Are you trying to be clever*?

This demonstrates that the meanings of words are never fixed; they are in a dynamic state of existence in the minds of the speakers of a language. We have the impression that some factors are rather fixed and permanent, while others seem to be of a tentative nature, ready in the wings, so to speak, to come on stage. The very way in which they have this potential precludes them from ever becoming permanently fixed. As we said earlier, words are perceptions, experiences of our world, cast into one unit through the process of lexicalisation. What is encapsulated in a lexical item is an abstraction from a complex experience. The abstraction enables us to apply the lexical item to other similar experiences. How many and which factors of a concrete situation survive in the abstraction process we do not know. Nor do we know whether they have all the same status or whether some have more importance and centrality than others. The only thing that seems to be clear is that the relation between them is dynamic, not fixed, so that what we regarded as a factor in *a bunch of flowers, a bunch of keys,* the fact that these are things, for instance, can be changed to cover human beings as in *a bunch of girls.* This does not prevent us, however, from imagining that there are some fixed and permanent meaning factors.

This seems to be confirmed in some uses of a word, where we believe we detect the same conglomerate of meaning factors. In the same way, we imagine the permanence of our identity, although this is also constantly changing. Human beings cannot live without the illusion of the permanence of things. When the use of a word is extended or cannot be extended in a specific way, we discover additional meaning factors that we had previously overlooked. It is through the use and the possibilities of use of a word, and through the contrast with other words, that in hindsight we discover what might be meaning factors. Take for example the contrast between *bunch* and such words as *bundle, pile, heap.*

Vocabulary expansion

We conclude, then, that a language is permanently in flux. It has to have this flexibility so that the speakers can adapt it to the changing world around them, refer to the changes in their society, and express the attitudes they feel towards fellow speakers, their beliefs, behaviour, etc. Words may therefore fall out of use and others may come in; new uses of words emerge. Our reaction to such changes varies according to whether we are young, middle-aged, or elderly. On the whole, we all seem to be quite forbearing with respect to old words, as when grandfather is reminiscing about broadcasts of the 1936 Olympics: 'We couldn't get close enough to the wireless, we were just about glued to it.' And fussy old aunt Lucy may remember dressing up for her first social party: 'There I was, primping and preening in front of mother's bedroom mirror.' The greater leniency displayed towards dated or old language may be linked to our social behaviour of showing the elderly respectful tolerance. But while there may be such forbearance, we may also encounter a quite different attitude, being more interested in, and stirred by, what is up and coming than by what is on the way out. New uses of words are usually accepted and absorbed readily by the younger generation who are indeed very often the source of them. Neologisms tend to be welcomed less enthusiastically by the older generation whose instinct may be to oppose them as improper language use.

Let us turn, then, to the question of how the lexicon of a language is expanded. This question has already been answered in part, but we shall now look at it more systematically. All languages basically use the same linguistic devices (borrowing, meaning extension, word-formation, and word-invention), but they use them to varying degrees. Which process of enrichment is used also depends on the state of development of the language concerned. Thus, in the Middle Ages and during the Renaissance period, when the English vocabulary was not yet developed enough to absorb the immense changes in society and the vast progress in human knowledge and learning, one of the major ways in which the vocabulary was enriched was by borrowing words from other languages, above all from French, Latin, and Greek. The borrowings were so substantial that scholars often talk about the resultant mixed character of the English vocabulary, with its three different vocabulary layers. The oldest and most basic is the native, Anglo-Saxon layer, which is characterised by simple words of one or two syllables like *bread, butter, clean, do, go, help, open*. The second consists of early borrowings from French and Latin that became fully integrated into English; these are not nowadays recognisable as borrowings (except by experts) because they resemble the words of the first layer in again being short; for example, *act, aim, beef, clear, polish, punish, sudden, veal, very*. In both these layers, where words have more than one syllable, the stress is usually on the first. The third and more recent layer comprises later borrowings from French, Latin, and Greek which most of us could somehow recognise because they are usually longer and the position of the stress is more variable; compare *agenda, diploma, envelope, examine, hesitate, incumbent, surreptitious*. The English of our own time is a fully developed cultural language and borrowings no longer play the key role they had in earlier stages of the language.

Among the other ways of expanding the vocabulary, we may first mention word invention; that is, new primary lexicalisation. It is rather rare, and this may be because, in a fully developed language, we usually respond to the need for newly lexicalised perceptions or experiences by extending meanings within the existing word stock, or by forming new words from existing ones. But new primary lexicalisations can occur in specialised vocabulary areas. A case in point is the new item *googol*, invented about 1940 by the American mathematician Edward Kasner to refer to the number 10 raised to the power of 100 (10^{100}).

Turning to meaning extension, we commonly find words being transferred from concrete reference to an abstract one. A recent example is the figurative or metaphorical use of the word *umbrella*. We all know the concrete object that we open to protect ourselves against rain. From this comes the transferred sense of the word as we find it in a sentence like *The drug squad was operating under the umbrella* ('protecting power or influence') *of the United Nations*.

Recent examples to illustrate secondary lexicalisation, that is, the processes of word-formation, are: *arrestee, baby boomer, baby break, chatline, to chainchew, geep* (a cross between a goat and a sheep), *gloomster*.

Although we cannot predict how the meaning of some words may be stretched at a certain period of time, which meaning may be transferred, and which new words may be coined by word-formation processes, there is something that we can predict for all these processes of vocabulary expansion. Whatever becomes lexicalised bears a relation to the existing vocabulary in the sense that the perception or experience to be lexicalised is singled out as something relevantly similar or dissimilar enough to something else already lexicalised to deserve a special name in that speech community.

Mastering the vocabulary

Let us then summarise. The lexicon of a language encapsulates the perceptions and experiences of a whole language community and thus its culture. It is structured in very complex ways. For its speakers, it is always something already made and in existence; and at the same time, it is always in the making, in a state of being created, because it is never static. Where does this leave us, the speakers of the language, in trying to master it?

We are all aware that the total vocabulary of our mother tongue is vast and that we have internalised only part of it. This does not worry us, because we know that no single individual can master the total lexicon of a language, just as no human being can be in possession of all the knowledge in the world. The extent and depth of command of the particular words that we have at our disposal vary enormously according to our age and social surroundings. There is also a difference between the words a person understands, the *passive* vocabulary, and the words a person actually uses, the *active* vocabulary. In general, the passive vocabulary must be much bigger than the active vocabulary, and it is very doubtful if the vocabulary command of a native speaker can ever be measured. One of the difficulties would be to decide on the basis unit of measurement. Do we know a word when we know just one sense of it? What does knowledge of different senses in fact mean? Unknown words or senses may immediately be guessed when they are presented in an appropriate context, but remain impenetrable in isolation.

At all stages of our life the command of words which we think we actually have, either passively or actively, will be very mixed. There will be words or even whole sectors of the lexicon which we know well and in every detail; there will be others where we will just have a vague idea of what the word is about; and there will be many stages in between. The process of learning new words and new senses of words is never complete. We might distinguish three types of vocabulary in which we all operate as we interact with different social groups:

1 A sector of vocabulary will be shared with the whole speech community. It covers all the necessities of everyday life such as eating, shopping, travelling, chatting to one's neighbour over the garden fence, etc. We might call this the **core vocabulary**. In size, it is likely to be much bigger than the other two types of vocabulary.

2 Then, there is something that we might call the **private vocabulary**. This is an 'insider' vocabulary which is shared only with family and close friends. The items of this type are not un-

derstood by outsiders, because they came into being through a personal experience shared by the members of the group. One family we know, for instance, uses the word *peedee* whenever something should not be discussed in the presence of strangers. It was picked up during a visit to France: the phrase *pas devant* (*les enfants*) was used by a French couple whenever they talked money. The phrase appealed to the English family; it became abbreviated to *p.d.* and then used as a family word. Another instance is the use of the word *beatitude* within one particular group. It is uttered whenever there is a mishearing, and it goes back to an occasion when *He'll catch you* was misheard and the nonunderstanding hearer asked 'Did you say *beatitude*?'

3 The third type of vocabulary is the one that is shared with groups that pursue special interests, e.g. mountain climbing, tennis, physics, gardening, etc. We may call this the **specialised vocabulary**, and any individual may have several specialised vocabularies, because we have different hobbies, jobs, and fields of interest.

In view of the fact that we will inevitably master only parts of the lexicon of our mother tongue, do we feel let down by not having a full command? In general, there is no such feeling; we are not particularly concerned. Yet there are situations in which the limitations of our vocabulary knowledge are brought home to us. For instance, when we receive a form or a letter from the tax office, the electricity board, the bank manager. We may have to ask somebody or consult a dictionary in order to understand some of the words used, because they do not belong to any of our vocabularies but obviously have a place within a specialised vocabulary area mastered by the writer. Again, in extreme emotional situations, we may literally become 'speechless' and anxiously struggle to find the right word to say. There are other occasions when we experience the opposite: a poem, a speech, a verbal settling of a dispute, by the very choice of words, may all of a sudden give us insight into perceptual and factual differences that we had not noticed before. They were produced by people who know that, in order to succeed, they have to give to their use of words the same care and attention they give to dress, manners, and other forms of social behaviour. They know that it is *range* that matters. Range means having a choice of words to select from on a given occasion, and choice also implies knowing dif-

ferences. None of us is satisfied with having only one or two out-
fits to cover our body so as to observe rules of decency and give
us warmth. We like to have a range of different clothes, carefully
chosen for size, cut, and colour, to put on to suit the weather or
social occasion. So too, we need to have choice in our vocabulary
if we are to be ready for different social or business occasions.

Language comes as naturally to us as the movements of our
body, and so we tend to forget how very special language is.
Language is the key to knowledge and the knowledge of words
provides its own incentive, just as knowledge itself does. When
we are shown a friend's garden and admire the roses, sweet peas,
the dahlias and the larkspurs, we are likely to pause over the one
flower whose name we do not know. And just because we know
all the others, we will ask for the name of this one. 'Ah, so that's
a columbine!' If we are told by our doctor the name of our ail-
ment, however odd the long Greek word may be, we tend to feel
that we have some control over it, just by knowing the name. But
language is at the same time the key to interpersonal relations and
the driving force in them. Here the knowledge of differences between words is as vital as in all other fields. We have to know
the difference between *a quarrel* and *an argument*, between *to nag*
and *to criticise*, in order not to hurt people by saying that they
were having *a quarrel* when they would have said they were just
having *an argument*; by accusing someone of *nagging* when *criticising* would be more appropriate. So we have to know the range of
words that English has for such situations in order to pick the
most appropriate one. Often our vocabulary command is such
that we have no choice of words, or only a very limited choice;
and we may not adequately understand the subtle differences between the words we 'know'. But our addressee may have a much
fuller range and take offence by our choice of word, not knowing
how limited our lexicon is and that we did not mean to hurt. We
had no choice. Many of our interpersonal difficulties are language-
based and it is our misfortune that we are usually not aware of
it.

It is in the common core vocabulary that the command of range
is especially vital. This is the sector of vocabulary where many of
the verbs, adjectives, and abstract nouns are so flickering and
evasive in their meaning. None of us knows exactly how much
and how deeply we have mastered this area. We do not know

whether, after the language-acquisition stages in our youth, we later make any substantial progress in building up this area further. In our adult life we are generally too busy to give much thought to our command of this core vocabulary; we are more preoccupied with the specialised vocabularies that we need for our profession and recreation. This is why the study of the lexicon has such a crucial role in the teaching and learning of the mother tongue at school: to widen, differentiate, and build up the range of that part of the vocabulary which we should all share and which so critically determines the quality of our interpersonal relations.

SOME FOLLOW-UP WORK

1 Study the language of advertising on posters, in public transport, and in magazines, and collect product names that suggest what the product is supposed to achieve.

2 You have started to learn another language. Give examples of words where you can show that your mother tongue and the foreign language classify reality differently.

3 Give a list of words that you regard as taboo, and try to group them so as to show which topics are avoided in your society. Think of the words or phrases you use instead and match them with the corresponding taboo word.

4 Explain the differences in shade expressed by the adjectives *crimson, purple, ruddy, sanguine, scarlet,* illustrating their use in each case. You may use a desk dictionary to help you.

5 Name all the parts of a book; a flower; a chair; a bicycle.

6 *Bunch* is a word to refer to a number of things just as *family* refers to a number of people seen as a unit. Make a list of other words used for a group of things and a group of people. Work out what each of them means, paying special attention to the differences between them.

7 We have seen that *drink* and *clever* can have a slightly derogatory meaning. Think of three other verbs and three other adjectives that express a somewhat negative attitude.

8 List some words that your grandparents used and that you yourself would no longer use. Try to account for the changes.

9 The major word-formation processes in English are compounding (as in *arm-chair*), prefixation (as in *undo*), suffixation (as in *helpless*), clipping (as in *phone*) and blending (as in *motel*). Provide three further examples for each process.

10 Give examples of a private vocabulary that you share with your family or your friends, discussing their use and possible origin.

11 *To quarrel, to dispute, to argue, to disagree*: differentiate these words and make one sentence with each, so as to bring out the difference.

12 You want to stop someone from nagging, but you want to be polite about it. Think of alternative ways of expressing *nag* and in consequence set out what you understand to be the meaning of this verb.

Words and dictionaries

*I*n the previous chapter, we stressed that none of us as individuals can know the total vocabulary of our language: it is too vast. Moreover, during the whole of our lifetime we go on acquiring new words and learning new uses and senses of words. We do this basically in three ways. The situational or linguistic context may give us an immediate insight into the meaning of a word we do not know. Thus, a tool may actually be in front of us, and we hear it being referred to. Or a passage in a novel that depicts a far-away countryside may contain a word we have never encountered before, but from the other words used within the text, we guess that the unknown word must be the name of a flower. We may leave it at that, and later encounters with the word will complete our picture: what kind of flower it is, what its colours may be, etc. Another possibility is that we ask a friend. If someone talks about the *'pristine* condition of a book' and the context does not give us any clue as to the meaning of the adjective *pristine*, we can ask and be given an explanation of the meaning. This may either be a kind of paraphrase like 'something that has not been used', or simply another adjective regarded as synonymous in the particular context, e.g. 'new' or 'undamaged'. And finally we may consult a dictionary. Thus, if we are puzzled by the use of the verb *to boot* in the context of computers, we could look up the item — and thus find that it means 'to load into a computer's memory'.

For most people a dictionary is *the* arbiter of the language: they think that it contains all the words of the language, specifies all and the correct meanings of words, and gives the correct spelling and pronunciation for each lexical item. This widespread belief in an almost biblical authority of the dictionary is reflected in the way we use the word: e.g. 'I looked it up in *the* dictionary', 'There's no such word: it isn't in *the* dictionary', '*The* dictionary spells it . . .'. We refer to it as if there was only one unique book. Such unique reference (*the* dictionary, as we also speak of *the* Bible, *the* sun, *the* moon, *the* earth) may have made sense when the first English dictionary appeared, but in our day there are scores and scores of dictionaries. The fact that many of us still speak of '*the* dictionary' may reveal that we feel a need for some guidance in language matters and appeal to the dictionary as *the* linguistic institution of authority.

But the belief that a dictionary lists all the words of a language with their meanings is a pipe-dream.

In Chapter Ten, we have seen that a language is always in the making and yet at the same time also something already made, created. We have shown what this intrinsic characteristic of language means for the vocabulary of a language, and in particular for the meaning of words. Let us now briefly consider how far the very nature of language predetermines what is feasible in dictionary-making and what the basic problems are that all lexicographers have to face. For the better our understanding is of dictionaries, of their extreme usefulness, and of their inherent limitations, the more profitable will be the use that we can make of them.

Data, selection, meanings

The nub of any description of the vocabulary of a language is an interdependent triad: the database, the word-selection, and the description of meanings.

The word stock of a language is vast; it varies regionally and socially; many words are in common use, others are quite rare. A substantial part belongs to special fields of knowledge; some words are old or obsolescent, others are neologisms. Where do we start if we want to record the lexicon of a language?

As we said earlier, the lexicon of a language exists only within the minds of all its speakers taken together. All individual utterances, whether spoken or written, are concrete manifestations of this lexicon. However many such utterances we collect, they will never make up the total potential lexicon. It is thus in principle not possible to get at the whole of the vocabulary, to encompass all its units and senses.

The most easily accessible sources are written texts and they have therefore been used as the bases for dictionaries. The choice of texts then, for instance literary ones, scientific ones, etc, becomes important, for it influences the sample of words that will be included in the dictionary. The trouble is that it is hard to know what choice of texts will yield a relatively trustworthy and representative picture of the vocabulary of a language.

Modern technology has made it possible to record language and we may therefore also use spoken texts as databases. Since some colloquialisms and slang expressions may not appear in print, and since neologisms are usually first heard in speech, spoken databases could well supplement written ones. But using recorded oral evidence is expensive in time and money, and spoken language has in consequence been little used in the making of modern English dictionaries.

In any case, whatever our database and however big it may be, there is no guarantee that all the senses of a particular lexical item will have been recorded. Lexicographers therefore must complement their textual evidence with their own knowledge of the language.

The next step in the preparation of a dictionary is the *word-selection*. That is, the lexicographical team will look at all the words found in their database, study their uses and meanings, and decide in each case whether to list the item or to exclude it. If one ignored the meanings of words, the selection could be based on the frequency of occurrence of word forms. Yet for general dictionaries that describe the meanings of words — and these are our concern here — this is unacceptable.

For practical purposes, dictionaries are limited in size. The selection of the word list for a dictionary is a very complex process and a certain degree of arbitrariness can never be avoided. Factors which tend to influence the choice, and which account for the fact that general-purpose dictionaries still vary considerably in their word lists, are:

1 the planned size of the dictionary;
2 the envisaged users, their age, their educational background, their specific fields of interest which will determine which

specialised vocabulary areas will be covered, e.g. photography, numismatics, etc;

3 the publisher's data bank or citation files. Publishers with a long tradition in dictionary-making usually have good files for neologisms, etc;

4 the words included in those dictionaries that are regarded as competitors;

5 internal consistency. As we have seen in Chapter Ten, words bear a relationship to other words. The exclusion or inclusion of a particular item will therefore affect related items: if it has been decided, for instance, that Mr should be included, then the other titles (*Mrs*, *Miss*, *Ms*) will also have to be included in a good and consistent dictionary.

All this makes it imperative that we study the introduction to a dictionary very carefully to see what the actual coverage of vocabulary is, and whether it is what we are looking for, e.g. the common core of both British and American English; or this common core as well as the special terminology of the natural sciences, etc.

The last member of the triad is the description of *meaning*. As we have seen in Chapter Ten, the meaning factors that allow us to use a particular lexical item in a specific situation are not a predetermined fixed set. On the contrary, these factors become revealed and salient in relation to other words. Thus, by contrasting *bunch* with *bundle*, *cluster*, *group*, etc, we are able to establish some of the necessary factors in the meaning of the noun *bunch* that are sufficient to use it. But there are always other potential contrasts that may bring out another factor. We cannot anticipate, capture, and describe a contrast that is only there as a potential. The discussion of the noun *bunch* has also revealed that the interrelation of the meaning factors that we established for this word are so complexly shifting that it is difficult to say where one configuration ends and another begins. A singling out of one meaning or several may thus be perceived as an arbitrary separation. Yet this is exactly what is done when the meaning of a word is described in sense 1, sense 2, etc in a dictionary.

Descriptions of the meaning of words in a dictionary, or definitions, could therefore be regarded as a lexicographical device to decompose something that is not really decomposable. The device as such does not correspond to language reality as we experience it. It is artificial and the decomposition cannot be done without a certain amount of arbitrariness. This also explains why there cannot be a 'correct' way of describing the meaning of a word or of establishing the 'correct' meanings of a word. All definitions are attempts at capturing something that in its very nature is evasive. Looked at from this angle, the senses in a dictionary definition are marks of orientation for the use of a word. Some such marks or sequences of marks may be more appropriate and hence better than others.

Let us now, after this general outline of the intricate problems that any team of lexicographers is faced with, look at some English dictionaries in more detail. Dictionaries vary with respect to the number of words they include and the amount of information they provide for each lexical item. It is evident that the shorter the dictionary entry for a word is, the less trustworthy it will be: the lexicographer will have had to make too many oversimplifications and therefore easily misleading statements about the meaning of words. By contrast, the longer the entry, the more the lexicographer is able to outline the different shades of meaning and their stylistic value. And finally, the bigger the number of specialised vocabulary areas included and the greater the detail of their coverage, the more the lexicographical team will need consultant specialists for various fields of knowledge.

The OED (2nd edition, 1989)

The most comprehensive dictionary of the English language is *The Oxford English Dictionary* (originally called *The New English Dictionary*). The work for it was begun in 1857 and the first of its great volumes appeared in 1888, the last in 1928, with a Supplement in 1933. The planning for a new supplement to record the language of the twentieth century started in 1957, and the four new supplement volumes appeared between 1972 and 1986. When the last supplement volume had gone to press, work began to computerise the original dictionary and its supplements. 1989 saw the publication of the second edition of the *OED*. It consists of twenty volumes; the original dictionary and its five supplement volumes have been integrated; some 5,000 new items have been added, and the earlier awkward transcription system to indicate pronunciation has been replaced by the symbols of the International Phonetic Association. The total number of entries of the *OED* now amounts to more than 325,000.

The *OED* is the most 'authoritative' dictionary of the English language, and indeed constitutes one of the greatest lexicographical achievements of all time, coming to serve as a model for other major dictionaries. But it must be carefully understood on what basis its authority rests. The purpose of the dictionary was to record the history of all the English words that have been in the language from about 1150. The ambitious undertaking endeavoured:

1 to show for each individual word in what forms and with what meanings it occurs as an item of the English vocabulary;
2 the trace the development in form and in meanings up to the present time;
3 to provide textual evidence for these facts and to illustrate them by a selection of quotations ranging from the first observed occurrence of the word to the latest;
4 to provide an etymology for each word that was strictly based on historical fact.

In order to achieve this goal, thousands of books were read by devoted volunteer helpers on both sides of the Atlantic; millions of words were scrupulously copied with their contexts onto standardised citation slips and the latter sent to Oxford. Sir James Murray and his colleagues then examined these millions of quotations illustrating the *use* of the words to be defined, and abstracted from the way a word was used a statement of how it was used — that is, its meaning in each particular context. The process adopted was exactly the one that we should use if we encountered in our reading a word that we had never met before. Let us assume that we find the word *clop* in the following contexts while we are reading:

1 'Do get me a *clop*,' she said, smacking her lips, but her brother, with a scornful glance up at the branches, said that there were none ripe yet.
2 The fashionable colour this spring is green in all shades: *lime, clop, moss, olive* . . .

3 People seeking refreshment on hot days have discovered a new passion: clop-juice.

4 This year's Indonesian clop yield has been the best since 1980.

What we can conclude from these text examples is that a *clop* is a noun and the name of an edible green(ish) juicy tropical fruit grown (for example) in Indonesia. And if there were no further evidence in the shape of textual references, this would be as much as we could say. We would have done our best to give a full description of the meaning of the word from the evidence that was available to us. Yet if we have been slipshod and have not noticed other references to *clop* which might have helped to define *clop* more closely, or if we have been too lazy or too shortsighted and have not had many other books searched for references to the word, then the 'authority' of our dictionary is small.

Let us now see how a dictionary entry in the *OED* is structured. The noun *character* gets practically the whole of a large three-column page to itself (the verb occupies a further half-column, and other related or derived words like *characteristic*, *characterize*, etc take up more than three columns in addition). The entry for the noun begins with the word *character* itself (technically called the *headword* or *lemma*) printed in bold black letters to set it off from the rest of the entry. It is followed by an indication of its modern pronunciation, given within brackets and in the symbols of the International Phonetic Association. The next piece of information is *sb.*, indicating that it is a noun (substantive). Now that the lemma *character* has been identified grammatically, the description of the word's history can begin. We first have an account of the different spellings of the word: in the fourteenth and fifteenth centuries the spelling was *caracter*, in the sixteenth century there were a number of different spellings, *caracter*, *caractere*, *carracter*, *carractre*, *charecter*, *character*, and in the seventeenth century four different spellings occurred, *caracter*, *carecter*, *charracter*, *characture*. The modern form, *character*, thus goes back to the sixteenth century. Not even spelling, we note, is a matter of dogma: 'right' or 'wrong' must be judged on the recorded evidence. We are then given an etymological note, telling us that the noun was adopted during the Middle English period from French *caractere*, itself an adaptation from Latin *character*, which in turn goes back to Greek. We are even given the meanings of the original Greek word: 'instrument for marking or graving, impress, stamp, distinctive mark, distinctive nature'.

After this introductory section, the entry proceeds to deal with the ways the noun *character* has been used since the Middle Ages. This account of usage is in two main sections (always denoted in this dictionary with roman numerals) and nineteen subsidiary sections (in arabic numerals), several of which are subdivided (a, b, c . . .). An obelisk (†) at the head of any subsection indicates that the usage to be described has become obsolete, and so it is easy to run through any entry to take note only of current uses. In the present case, the two main sections are described as literal senses (I) and figurative senses (II). The subsections of the literal senses that are not marked as obsolete are:

> **1.a.** A distinctive mark impressed, engraved or otherwise formed; a brand, stamp.

As though to emphasise that the lexicographer does not speak with the voice of oracular infallibility, there follows a selection of the quotations from which the definition has been abstracted, beginning with one dated about 1315 and ending with one from 1875. These quotations (too lengthy, of course, for us to reprint here) are not mere illustrations; they provide the raw material of the evidence and we can thereby evaluate the definition given. Sense **1.b.** amply supports what we said earlier about the difficulties of separating off senses of words because they often shade into each other. Although figurative senses of the word are dealt with in section II, we are given a figurative sense under **1.b.** because it is felt to be close to **1.a**:

> **b.** *fig* with distinct reference to the literal sense.

The earliest quotation dates from 1586 and is from Marlowe's *Tamburlaine*:

> Thou . . . by characters graven on thy brows
> . . . Deserv'st to have the leading of an host.

The other uses in the first section are:

> **2.** A distinctive significant mark of any kind; a graphic design or symbol.
> **3.a.** *esp* A graphic symbol standing for a sound, syllable, or

notion, used in writing or in printing; one of the simple
elements of a written language; e.g. a letter of the alphabet.

Sense **3.c.** shows the integration of the new supplements, providing a use in the field of computers, for which the quotations begin
from the middle of the twentieth century:

> **c.** *Computers.* One of a set of letters, digits, or other symbols
> which can be read, stored, or written by a computer and used to
> denote data; also, a representation of such a symbol by means
> of a small number of bits, holes on punched tape, etc., arranged
> according to a specified code and taken as a unit of storage.
> **4.** *collect.* **a.** *gen.* writing, printing.
> **b.** The series of alphabetic signs, or elementary symbols,
> peculiar to any language; a set of letters.
> **c.** The style of writing peculiar to any individual; handwriting.
> **d.** Kind or style of type or printed letter.
> **5.** A cabbalistic or magical sign or emblem; the astrological
> symbol of a planet . . .
> **7.** A cipher for secret correspondence.

The progression of senses from **1** to **7** shows greater and greater
specialisation. The general 'distinctive mark' of **1** has become a
secret sign in **7**.
   Section II describes the uses **8** to **18** of which some are already
obsolete, and again the sequence of meanings progresses from
the more general to the more specific. The very first sense in this
figurative section is not quite obsolete, but regarded as *archaic* in
general use:

> **8.a.** A distinctive mark, evidence, or token; a feature, trait,
> characteristic.

In the case of the **b** sense, we note that the subject field for which
this use is characteristic is explicitly mentioned at the beginning,
as in the case of **3.c.** *Computers*; in this case, Natural History:

> **b.** now *esp* in *Natural History*. One of the distinguishing features
> of a species or genus . . .
> **9.** The aggregate of the distinctive features of anything; essential
> peculiarity; nature, style; sort, kind, description.
> **11.** The sum of the moral and mental qualities which distinguish
> an individual or a race, viewed as a homogeneous whole; the
> individuality impressed by nature and habit on man or nation;
> mental or moral constitution.

12. . . . Moral qualities strongly developed or strikingly displayed; distinct or distinguished character; character worth speaking of.

In **12**, we note a peculiarity: the word to be defined, *character*, is used within the definition. This practice is generally avoided in definitions because of its obvious circularity, as though one were to say 'a dog is a dog'. When such cases occur in a dictionary, they are never the first sense in a definition, but, as is our example, in a later one. The lexicographer assumes that the dictionary entry is read as a text sequence, so that the users when they reach sense **12** have incorporated the specific meaning of the item. In addition, the item in question is not used on its own, as in a definition, but is always specified further. In the instance above, these specifications are the premodification 'distinct or distinguished' and the postmodification 'worth speaking of'. The next current sense is **13**:

13.a. The estimate formed of a person's qualities, reputation: when used without qualifying epithet implying 'favourable estimate, good repute'.
b. is a *transferred* sense of things.
14.a. A description, delineation, or detailed report of a person's qualities.
c. *esp* A formal testimony given by an employer as to the qualities and habits of one that has been in his employ.
15. Recognized official rank; status, position assumed or occupied. Now influenced by sense 17.

The addition at the end 'Now influenced by sense 17' is a further indication that it is extremely difficult to isolate one sense without covering another. A further instance is **16.b.** below:

16.a. A person regarded in the abstract as the possessor of specified qualities; a personage, a personality.
b. *colloq.* A person, man, fellow (freq. slightly derogatory: cf. sense 18).

The earliest quotation for this sense dates from 1931 and is taken from Damon Runyon's *Guys & Dolls*:

Marvin Clay is a most obnoxious character. . . . The paymaster must be a very dishonest character.

To continue:

> **17.a.** A personality invested with distinctive attributes and
> qualities, by a novelist or dramatist; also, the personality or
> 'part' assumed by an actor on the stage.
> **18.** *colloq.* An odd, extraordinary, or eccentric person.

The earliest quotation dates from 1773 and is taken from Oliver
Goldsmith's comedy *She Stoops to Conquer*:

> A very impudent fellow this! but he's a
> character, and I'll humour him.

Again, senses **16.b.** and **18.** are very close and one may wonder
why they are distinguished. In both cases, the definition is
preceded by the label *colloq.* The claim that *character* in these senses is colloquial may sound like a personal opinion (which would
have no place in a modern dictionary); but in fact, the lexicographical team have based the claim on a careful weighing of
the textual evidence, not merely to gauge the meaning but also
to decide whether it occurs chiefly in colloquial or formal or legal
or dialectal usage.

Webster's Third

The other major dictionary of the English language was published
in the United States. It is *Webster's Third New International Dictionary*. It has about 2,700 pages and 460,000 entries. This figure is
much higher than that given for the second edition of the *OED*.
But comparing the number of words in different dictionaries is
not easy. Are we counting 'entries' or 'headwords', for example?
This takes us right back to the basic issues in lexicology and lexicography. What is a word? We would say that it is a linguistic
unit that has a form (the sound sequence or the written sequence
of letters) and a meaning. It resists any insertions between its constituents: a *'useful* knife' cannot be made into *usesful*, however
many uses the knife may have. It is the smallest element in a
sentence that has positional mobility, e.g. *Father loves mother;
Mother loves father; Father, mother loves.* But things are not as easy
as that. Take the word *blackbird.* We recognise the parts *black* and

bird in it, but a *blackbird* is different from a *black bird*. What has happened is that a particular species of black bird has been lexicalised in the compound *blackbird* and it does not include *crow* which is also a black bird. Therefore the noun *blackbird* refers to a specific bird, and not, like *black bird*, to any bird that is black in colour. How about *red wine*? Is it just any wine that looks red or does it refer to a specific type of wine?

There are many such cases in a language where it is very difficult to decide whether we have to do with one word (a secondary lexicalisation) or two that have been juxtaposed according to the syntactic rules of that language. In the case of *blackbird* the syntactic combination *black bird* has become lexicalised to *blackbird*. Since any language is always in the making, there are many intermediate stages in such lexicalisation processes. When lexicographers scan texts to extract from them the lexical items that they will list in their dictionary, their interpretation as to whether something is already lexicalised or not yet will obviously vary. Yet this is not the only source of variation. If two lexicographers were to read the same new book and compile a list of words to be added to the next edition of their dictionary, the two lists would show considerable differences. No lexicographer who has been assigned a reading programme will have present in his or her mind the words or senses of words already listed in the dictionary while scanning texts for new words and senses. Therefore the word collections will vary. The contrast of catchment between the *OED* and *Webster's Third New International Dictionary* amply illustrates the imponderabilities of word selection in lexicography mentioned earlier. *Webster's Third*, as it is commonly referred to, was published in 1961 and has had three supplements: *6,000 Words, 9,000 Words* and *12,000 Words*. The entry for *character* in *Webster's Third* is as follows:

¹**char·ac·ter** \'karȧktə(r), -rēk- *also* 'ker-\ *n* -s [alter. (influenced by L *character*) of earlier *caracter*, fr. ME, fr. MF *caractère*, fr. L *character* mark, sign, distinctive quality, fr. Gk *charaktēr*, fr. *charassein* to sharpen, cut into furrows, engrave; akin to Lith *žerti* to scratch, scrape] **1 :** a distinctive differentiating mark: **a :** a conventionalized graphic device, token, or symbol typically single or simple in form esp. impressed or engraved as an indication of ownership or origin or capable of being impressed or engraved **b :** a device indicating a special characteristic or relationship ⟨the ∼ of the fish is often used to indicate early Christians⟩ **c :** a graphic symbol (as a hieroglyph, ideograph, alphabet letter, punctuation mark, or shorthand mark) used as a unit in writing or printing ⟨a typewriter keyboard with special ∼s⟩ ⟨mathematical ∼s⟩ **d :** a conventionalized figure, representation, or expression ⟨a medieval ∼ of

Christ⟩ **e characters** *pl, obs* **:** SHORTHAND **1** *Roman Catholi-
cism* **:** an indelible mark impressed on the soul by the sacra-
ments of baptism, confirmation, and holy orders by which the
recipient is empowered to produce or receive something sacred
g : a cabalistic, magical, or astrological emblem ⟨charms, images, ~*s* stamped of sundry metals —Robert Burton⟩ **h :** a
particular set of letters or other symbols used in writing **:** AL-
PHABET **2 :** CHARACTERISTIC: as **a** (1) **:** one of the essentials of
structure, form, materials, or function that together make up
and usu. distinguish the individual **:** any feature used to separate distinguishable things (as organisms) into categories (2)
: the detectable expression of the action of a gene or group of
genes — see UNIT CHARACTER (3) **:** the aggregate of distinctive
qualities characteristic of a breed, strain, or type **b :** the complex of accustomed mental and moral characteristics and habitual ethical traits marking a person, group, or nation or serving to individualize it ⟨it depended wholly on the governors' individual ~*s* whether their terms of office were equitable or
oppressive —John Buchan⟩ ⟨to comprehend the full ~ of these
United States —Ruth Suckow⟩ **c :** main or essential nature
esp. as strongly marked and serving to distinguish **:** individual
composite of salient traits, consequential characteristics, features giving distinctive tone ⟨each town came to have a ~ of
its own —Sherwood Anderson⟩ ⟨the president had taken those
measures which gave to Union war policy its controlling ~
—*Dict. of Amer. History*⟩ **3 a :** WRITING, INSCRIPTION,
PRINTING; *also* **:** what is represented in such writing, inscription, or printing **b :** style of writing or printing esp. in
physical qualities ⟨you know the ~ to be your brother's
—Shak.⟩ **c :** a private mode of communication in writing **:** CI-
PHER **4** *obs* **:** APPEARANCE **:** outward and visible quality or trait
5 : a piece of printer's type that produces a character **6 :** POSI-
TION, RANK, CAPACITY, STATUS ⟨in the ~ of a slave⟩ ⟨his ~ as a
town official⟩ **7 a** *archaic* **:** a description, delineation, or
detailed account of the qualities or peculiarities — now used of
a person, but formerly of a thing ⟨give the police a ~ of the
thief⟩ **b** [trans. of Gk *charaktēr*] **:** a descriptive often satiric
analysis usu. in the form of a short literary sketch of a human
virtue or vice as embodied in a representative human being, of
a general type of human character (as a busybody, an old
man, a country bumpkin), or of a quality of a particular place
or thing — most frequently applied to the form as it developed
in 17th century English and French literature **c :** a written
statement as to the behavior, habits, and competence of an
employee given by an employer **8 a :** a person regarded as
characterized by or exemplifying distinctive or notable traits
: PERSONAGE, PERSONALITY ⟨Caesar is a great historical ~⟩
⟨the Toronto financier . . . an almost fabulous ~ in Canadian
mining circles —J.D.Hillaby⟩ **b :** personality as represented
or realized in fiction or drama ⟨a play weak in ~ but strong in
plot⟩; *also* **:** a given representation or realization of this kind
⟨the main ~ in the novel⟩ **c :** the personality or part which an
actor recreates **d :** characterization esp. in fiction or drama
⟨a novelist good in both ~ and setting⟩ **e :** a unique, extraordinary, or eccentric person ⟨the cheery, cheeky, undefeata-
ble ~ — the cockney —*London Calling*⟩; *esp* **:** a dramatic role
calling for the representation of such a person **f** *slang* **:** PER-
SON, INDIVIDUAL, MAN ⟨an underworld ~⟩ ⟨romantic ~*s* will
often camp out on the site —Jacquetta & Christopher Hawkes⟩
9 : reputation esp. when good ⟨his association with evil
companions detracted from his ~⟩ **10 :** a composite of good
moral qualities typically of moral excellence and firmness
blended with resolution, self-discipline, high ethics, force, and
judgment ⟨that stiffening of the moral fiber which we call ~
—F.A.Swinnerton⟩ ⟨his eldest brother . . . had not ~
enough to reproach me —John Galsworthy⟩ **11 :** the crimp
of wool fiber esp. with respect to its evenness **12** *of a dog*
: style of action or deportment in field trial

syn SYMBOL, SIGN, MARK, NOTE: CHARACTER is likely to suggest a simple form or shape, sometimes the individual forms or
devices that constitute signs or symbols. CHARACTER is likely
to be used in reference to familiar conventionalized patterns.
⟨*characters* include letters of the alphabet, digits, simple
musical notes, and so on⟩ SYMBOL, sometimes interchangeable
with CHARACTER, is likely to stress the fact that the device in

question means or stands for something ⟨a *symbol* is a sign, figure, or physical object the meaning of which is established by convention —Kurt Seligmann⟩ ⟨in the expression *Cu,* the *C* and the *u* are *characters; Cu* is the *symbol* for copper⟩ SIGN may be used to designate something less arbitrary and conventional than CHARACTER, something that hints by its form at what is meant, as arrows as direction markers ⟨*symbols* and *signs,* then, may be seen to differ in this wise: signs are proxy for the objects they represent; symbols are "vehicles for the conception of objects" —W.V.O'Connor⟩ MARK may be close to CHARACTER in suggesting simplicity; it usu. indicates something that is arbitrarily and conventionally adopted ⟨consignee *mark* — a symbol placed on packages for export, generally consisting of a square, triangle, diamond, circle, cross, etc., with designated letters ... for the purpose of identification —*Marine Corps Manual*⟩ NOTE, except in reference to musical notation or perhaps to punctuation marks, is now uncommon as a synonym for CHARACTER. In various subjects use of these words is determined more by convention than by consideration of exact meanings and shades of connotation.
    syn see in addition DISPOSITION, QUALITY, TYPE
— **in character 1 :** in accord with a person's normal or usual qualities or traits **2 :** befitting a role or character type
— **out of character 1 :** not in accord with a person's normal or usual qualities or traits ⟨his rude behavior was quite *out of character;* he was generally meticulously well-bred⟩ **2 :** unbefitting a role or character type ⟨the protagonist's curtain speech in act II was so *out of character* it was omitted after the first performance⟩

By permission. From Webster's Third New International Dictionary © 1986 by Merriam-Webster Inc., publisher of the Merriam-Webster ® dictionaries.

General-purpose dictionaries

For ordinary use and ordinary everyday needs, the *OED* and *Webster's Third* are too comprehensive; we need a shorter, more compact dictionary. There are many such dictionaries and here are samples of the entry for *character* from some of the best:

Oxford Concise Dictionary of Current English (7th edition, 1982)

chǎ'racter (kǎ'rǐk-) *n.,* & *v.t.* **1.** *n.* distinctive mark; (in *pl.*) inscribed letters or figures; graphic symbol, esp. denoting sound or idea; (arch.) style of such symbols used in a language; (Computers) group of symbols representing letter etc. **2.** characteristic (esp. Biol., of species etc.); collective peculiarities, sort, style; person's or race's idiosyncrasy, mental or moral qualities; distinction, individuality. **3.** moral strength, esp. if highly developed or evident; reputation, good reputation (∿ **reference, witness,** (attesting to this); ∿ **assassination,** malicious destruction of person's reputation); ∿ (**sketch,** brief) written description of person's qualities; testimonial. **4.** personage, personality; person portrayed in novel, drama, etc.; part played by actor or (arch.) hypocrite; **in, out of,** ∿, appropriate to these or not, (of action etc.) in accord or not with person's character. **5.** eccentric or noticeable person (*quite a character*); ∿ **actor** (who impersonates eccentric or unusual persons). **6.** Hence ∿LESS *a.* **7.** *v.t.* (arch.) inscribe; describe. [ME, f. OF *caractere* f. L f. Gk *kharaktēr* stamp, impress]

Longman Dictionary of the English Language (1984)

character /ˈkarəktə *n* **1a** a distinctive mark, usu in the form
of a stylized graphic device **b** a graphic symbol (eg a hieroglyph, punctuation mark, or alphabet letter) used in writing or
printing **c** a symbol (eg a letter or number) that represents
information; *esp* a representation of such a symbol in a code
that can be understood by a computer **2a** (any of) the mental
or moral qualities that make up and distinguish the individual
b(1) a feature used to separate distinguishable things into categories; *also* a group or kind so separated ⟨*people of this* ~⟩
⟨*advertising of a very primitive* ~⟩ **b(2)** an inherited characteristic determined by a gene or group of genes **b(3)** the sum of
all the distinctive qualities characteristic of a breed, strain, or
type ⟨*a wine of great* ~⟩ **c** the distinctive or essential nature
of something ⟨*the building of new estates gradually changed the
whole* ~ *of the town*⟩ **3a** a person marked by notable or conspicuous traits ⟨*one of the real* ~s *in Westminster today*⟩ **b**
any of the people portrayed in a novel, play, film, etc **4** (good)
reputation ⟨~ *assassination*⟩ **5** moral strength; integrity ⟨*a
man of* ~⟩ **6** *archaic* REFERENCE **4b** (statement about a person's
qualifications) **7** *informal* a person ⟨*some* ~ *has just stolen her
purse*⟩ **synonyms** see ¹TYPE [ME *caracter*, fr MF *caractère*, fr
L *character* mark, distinctive quality, fr Gk *charaktēr*, fr
charassein to scratch, engrave; akin to Lith *žerti* to scratch] –
characterful *adj.* **characterless** *adj* – **in/out of character**
in/not in accord with a person's usual qualities, traits, or behaviour

Chambers English Dictionary (new edition, 1988)

character *kar'ək-tər* (*Spens., Shak.*, etc. *-ak'*), *n.* a letter,
sign, figure, stamp, or distinctive mark: a mark of any
kind, a symbol in writing, etc.: writing generally,
handwriting: a secret cipher: one of a set of symbols,
e.g. letters of the alphabet, numbers, punctuation
marks, that can be arranged in groups to represent
data for processing (*comput.*): any essential feature or
peculiarity: a quality: nature: personal appearance
(*obs.*): the aggregate of peculiar qualities which constitutes personal or national individuality: esp. moral
qualities: the reputation of possessing these: a formal
statement of the qualities of a person who has been in
one's service or employment: official position, rank,
or status, or a person who has filled it: a person noted
for eccentricity or well-marked personality: a personality as created in a play or novel (*Shak.* **char'act**) or
appearing in history: a literary genre, consisting in a
description in prose or verse of a human type, or of a
place or object on that model, a dominant form of
literature in the 17th century under the influence of
Theophrastus and the theory of humours: a person
(*slang*). — *v.t.* (*arch.*) to engrave, imprint, write: to
represent, delineate, or describe. — *n.* **characterīsā'-
tion, -z-.** — *v.t.* **char'acterise, -ize** to describe by
peculiar qualities: to be a distinguishing mark or

quality of. — *ns.* **char′acterism** a characteristic: a characterisation; **characteris′tic** that which marks or constitutes the character: the integral part of a logarithm. — *adjs.* **characteris′tic, -al.** — *adv.* **characteris′tically.** — *adj.* **char′acterless** without character or distinctive qualities. — *ns.* **char′acterlessness; characterol′ogy** the science or study of the variety and development of character: **characterol′ogist; char′actery** (in *Shak. -ak′*) (*arch.*) writing: impression: that which is charactered. — **character actor** one who plays character parts; **character assassination** the destruction of a person's reputation by slander, rumour, etc.; **character essay; characteristic radiation** the wavelength of radiation that characterises a particular substance; **characteristic X-rays** see under X; **character literature; character part** a stage or film role portraying an unusual or eccentric personality type; **character sketch** a short description of the main traits in a person's character. — **in character** in harmony with the part assumed, appropriate: in keeping with the person's usual conduct or attitudes: dressed for the part; **out of character** not in character, unlike what one would expect from the person concerned.   [Fr. *caractere* — L. *character* — Gr. *charakter*, from *charassein*, to cut, engrave.]

Collins Concise Dictionary (2nd edition, 1988)

character (′kærɪktə) *n.* **1.** the combination of traits and qualities distinguishing the individual nature of a person or thing. **2.** one such distinguishing quality; characteristic. **3.** moral force: *a man of character.* **4. a.** reputation, esp. a good reputation. **b.** (*as modifier*): *character assassination.* **5.** a person represented in a play, film, story, etc.; role. **6.** an outstanding person: *one of the great characters of the century.* **7.** *Inf.* an odd, eccentric, or unusual person: *he's quite a character.* **8.** an informal word for **person:** *a shady character.* **9.** a symbol used in a writing system, such as a letter of the alphabet. **10.** Also called: **sort.** *Printing.* any single letter, numeral, etc., cast as a type. **11.** *Computers.* any such letter, numeral, etc., each of which can be represented uniquely by binary code. **12.** a style of writing or printing. **13.** *Genetics.* any structure, function, attribute, etc., in an organism that is determined by a gene or group of genes. **14.** a short prose sketch of a distinctive type of person. **15. in** (*or* **out of**) **character.** typical (or not typical) of the apparent character of a person. [C14: < L: distinguishing mark, < Gk *kharakter* engraver's tool]   —′**characterful** *adj.*   —′**characterless** *adj.*

Reader's Digest Great Illustrated Dictionary (1984)

char·ac·ter (kárriktər || kə-ráktər) *n.* **1**: The combination of quali-
ties or features that distinguishes one person, group, or thing from
another. **2**. One such distinguishing feature or attribute; a characteristic. **3**. The moral or ethical nature of a person or group.
4. Moral or ethical strength; integrity; fortitude. **5**. The quality of
being distinctive or outstanding: *an old house of great character.*
6. Status; capacity; role: *in his character as a father.* **7**. *Informal.*
a. A person: *There's some character at the door asking to see you.*
b. A person who is amusing or eccentric. **8**. A person portrayed in
a drama, novel, or other artistic piece. **9**. *Archaic.* A reference; a
testimonial. **10**. A symbol or mark used in a writing system, such as
a letter of the alphabet. **11**. *Printing.* A letter, punctuation mark,
numeral, or the like, cast in type and usually occupying a fixed
amount of space. **12**. A style of printing or writing. **13**. *Genetics.*
Any structure, function, or attribute determined by a gene or group
of genes. —See Synonyms at **disposition, quality, type**. —**in** (or
out of) character. Consistent (or inconsistent) with the usual nature of a person.
~*adj.* **1**. Specialising in roles portraying odd, eccentric, or unusual
personality types: *a character actor.* **2**. Calling for the abilities of
such an actor: *a character part.*
~*tr.v.* **charactered, -tering, -ters**. **1**. To portray, describe, or represent. **2**. *Archaic.* To write, print, engrave, or inscribe. [Learned re-
spelling of Middle English *caracter,* from Old French *caractere,*
from Latin *character,* character, mark, instrument for branding,
from Greek *kharaktēr,* engraved mark, brand, from *kharassein,* to
brand, sharpen, from *kharax* (stem *kharak-*), pointed stake.]

Webster's Ninth New Collegiate Dictionary (1989)

¹char·ac·ter \'kar-ik-tər\ *n* [ME *caracter,* fr. MF *caractère,* fr. L *character* mark, distinctive quality, fr. Gk *charaktēr,* fr. *charassein* to scratch,
engrave] (14c) **1 a** : a conventionalized graphic device placed on an
object as an indication of ownership, origin, or relationship **b** : a
graphic symbol (as a hieroglyph or alphabet letter) used in writing or
printing **c** : a magical or astrological emblem **d** : ALPHABET **e** (1)
: WRITING, PRINTING (2) : style of writing or printing (3) : CIPHER **f**
: a symbol (as a letter or number) that represents information; *also* : a
representation of such a character that may be accepted by a computer
2 a : one of the attributes or features that make up and distinguish
the individual **b** (1) : a feature used to separate distinguishable
things into categories; *also* : a group or kind so separated ⟨people of
this ~⟩ ⟨advertising of a very primitive ~⟩ (2) : the detectable expression of the action of a gene or group of genes (3) : the aggregate of
distinctive qualities characteristic of a breed, strain, or type ⟨a wine of
great ~⟩ **c** : the complex of mental and ethical traits marking and
often individualizing a person, group, or nation ⟨assess a person's ~ by
studying his handwriting⟩ **d** : main or essential nature esp. as
strongly marked and serving to distinguish ⟨excess sewage gradually
changed the ~ of the lake⟩ **3** : POSITION, CAPACITY ⟨his ~ as a town
official⟩ **4** : a short literary sketch of the qualities of a social type **5**
: REFERENCE 4b **6 a** : a person marked by notable or conspicuous
traits : PERSONAGE ⟨a notorious campus ~⟩ **b** : one of the persons of a
drama or novel **c** : the personality or part which an actor recreates **d**
: characterization esp. in drama or fiction **e** : PERSON, INDIVIDUAL
⟨some ~ just stole her purse⟩ **7** : REPUTATION **8** : moral excellence
and firmness ⟨a man of sound ~⟩ **syn** see DISPOSITION, QUALITY, TYPE
— **char·ac·ter·less** \-ləs\ *adj* — **in character** : in accord with a person's
usual qualities or traits — **out of character** : not in accord with a person's usual qualities or traits

Webster's New World Dictionary (2nd College Edition, 1970)

char·ac·ter (kar′ik tər) *n.* [ME. *carecter* < OFr. *caractere* < L. *character*, an engraving instrument < Gr. *charaktēr* < *charattein*, to engrave] **1.** a distinctive mark **2.** *a)* any letter, figure, or symbol used in writing and printing *b)* the letters of an alphabet, collectively **3.** *a)* writing or printing *b)* style of printing or handwriting **4.** *a)* a mystic symbol or magical emblem *b)* a code or cipher **5.** a distinctive trait, quality, or attribute; characteristic **6.** essential quality; nature; kind or sort **7.** the pattern of behavior or personality found in an individual or group; moral constitution **8.** moral strength; self-discipline, fortitude, etc. **9.** *a)* reputation *b)* good reputation [left without a shred of *character*] **10.** *same as* CHARACTER SKETCH (sense 1) **11.** a statement about the behavior, qualities, etc. of a person, esp. as given by a former employer; reference **12.** status; position **13.** a personage [great *characters* in history] **14.** *a)* a person in a play, story, novel, etc. *b)* a role as portrayed by an actor or actress **15.** [Colloq.] an odd, eccentric, or noteworthy person **16.** *Genetics* any attribute, as color, shape, etc., caused in an individual by the action of one or more genes —*vt.* **1.** to write, print, or inscribe **2.** to characterize **3.** [Archaic] to represent; portray —*SYN.* see DISPOSITION, QUALITY —**in** (or **out of**) **character** consistent with (or inconsistent with) the role or general character

American Heritage Dictionary (2nd College Edition, 1985)

char·ac·ter (kăr′ək-tər) *n.* **1.** The combination of qualities or features that distinguishes one person, group, or thing from another. **2.** A distinguishing feature or attribute; characteristic. **3.** The combined moral or ethical structure of a person or group. **4.** Moral or ethical strength; integrity; fortitude. **5.** Public estimation of someone; reputation. **6.** Status, capacity, or role: *in his character as a father.* **7.** *Informal.* A person who is peculiar or eccentric. **8.** An important, influential person; personage. **9.** A person portrayed in a drama, novel, or other artistic piece. **10.** A description of a person's attributes, traits, or abilities. **11.** A formal written statement as to competency and dependability, given by an employer to a former employee; recommendation. **12.** A symbol or mark used in a writing system. **13.** *Computer Sci.* **a.** One of a set of symbols, as letters or numbers, arranged to express information. **b.** The multi-bit code representing such a character. **14.** A style of printing or writing. **15.** A symbol used in secret writing; a cipher or code. **16.** *Genetics.* A structure, function, or attribute determined by a gene or group of genes. —*adj.* **1.** Capable of acting in roles that emphasize traits markedly different from those of the performer himself: *a character actor.* **2.** Of or calling for the abilities of a character actor: *a character part.* —*tr.v.* **-tered, -ter·ing, -ters. 1.** To write, print, engrave, or inscribe. **2.** *Archaic.* To portray, describe, or represent. —*idiom.* **in** (or **out of**) **character.** Consistent (or not consistent) with someone's general character or behavior. [ME *carecter* < Lat. *character* < Gk. *kharaktēr* < *kharassein*, to inscribe.]

Random House College Dictionary (revised edition, 1988)

char·ac·ter (kar′ik tər), *n.* **1.** the aggregate of features and traits that form the individual nature of some person or thing. **2.** one such feature or trait; characteristic. **3.** moral or ethical quality. **4.** qualities of honesty, courage, or the like: integrity: *It takes character to talk up to a bully like that.* **5.** reputation. **6.** good repute. **7.** an account of the qualities or peculiarities of a person or thing. **8.** a formal statement from an employer concerning the qualities and habits of a former servant or employee; reference. **9.** status or capacity. **10.** a person, esp. with reference to behavior or personality: *a suspicious character; a weak character.* **11.** *Informal.* an odd or eccentric person. **12.** a person represented in a drama, story, etc. **13.** *Literature.* (esp. in 17th- and 18th-century England) a formal character sketch or descriptive analysis of a particular human virtue or vice as represented in a person or type. **14.** a part or role, as in a play, motion picture, or the like. **15.** *Genetics.* any trait, function, structure, or substance of an organism resulting from the effect of one or more genes as modified by the environment. **16.** a significant visual mark or symbol. **17.** a symbol as used in a writing system, as a letter of the alphabet. **18.** the symbols of a writing system collectively. **19.** *Computer Technol.* **a.** any symbol, as a number or letter that represents information and, when encoded, is usable by a machine. **b.** a pattern of ones and zeros representing the relationship of positive and negative pulses in a computer. **20.** a style of writing or printing. **21.** **in or out of character,** in or out of harmony with one's nature or disposition. —*adj.* **22.** *Theat.* representing or portraying a marked or distinctive personality type: *character actor.* —*v.t.* *Archaic.* **23.** to portray; describe. **24.** to engrave; inscribe. [< L < Gk *charaktēr* graving tool, its mark = *charak-* (var. s. of *charáttein* to engrave) + *-tēr* instrumental suffix; r. ME *caractere* < MF < L, as above] —**char′ac·ter·ful,** *adj.* —**char′ac·ter·less,** *adj.*
—**Syn. 1.** CHARACTER, INDIVIDUALITY, PERSONALITY refer to the sum of the characteristics possessed by a person. CHARACTER refers esp. to moral qualities, ethical standards, principles, and the like: *a man of sterling character.* INDIVIDUALITY refers to the distinctive qualities that make one recognizable as a person differentiated from others: *a man of strong individuality.* PERSONALITY refers particularly to the combination of outer and inner characteristics that determine the impression that a person makes upon others: *a man of pleasing personality.* **5.** name, repute. See **reputation.** **16.** sign, figure, emblem.

Funk & Wagnalls Standard College Dictionary (1977)

char·ac·ter (kar′ik·tər) *n.* **1.** The combination of qualities or traits that distinguishes an individual or group; personality. **2.** Any distinguishing attribute; characteristic; property. **3.** Moral force; integrity: He has no *character.* **4.** Reputation; also, good reputation. **5.** Status; capacity: in his *character* as president. **6.** A personage. **7.** A person in a play, novel, etc. **8.** *Informal* An eccentric or humorous person. **9.** A detailed description of a person's qualities or abilities. **10.** A written recommendation given by an employer to a former employee. **11.** A figure engraved, written, or printed; mark; sign; letter. **12.** Style of handwriting or printing. **13.** A form of secret writing; a cipher. **14.** *Genetics* Any structural or functional trait in a plant or animal resulting from the interaction of genes and regarded as hereditary in origin. — **in** (or **out of**) **character** In keeping (or not in keeping) with the general character or role. — *v.t.* **1.** To write, print, or engrave. **2.** *Archaic* To represent; portray. [< MF *caractere* < L *character* < Gk. *charaktēr* stamp, mark < *charassein* to sharpen, engrave, carve] — **char′ac·ter·less** *adj.*

The dictionaries from which these samples have been taken are all general-purpose dictionaries that record the Standard English of our time. A close comparison of all the samples will reveal many interesting similarities and differences. Let us draw attention to some of them in order to gain more insight into the complex and condensed linguistic information that is packed into every dictionary entry. In all the samples, different printing types as well as upper-case and lower-case letters have been used to differentiate the different types of information given and to make them perceivable for the dictionary user. The headword (like related items at the end of the entry) is printed in bold type; grammatical information (in this case, that the word is a noun) is always in italics, and the definitions always in normal type. Another common feature is that all the dictionaries have grouped the first three pieces of information in the same order: headword, pronunciation, word class. They constitute the 'address' of the lexical item; with these three pieces of information, it has been identified and can then be described further. All dictionaries similarly indicate the origin of the word, some near the beginning, others at the end (*tennis*, for instance, probably goes back to the imperative of the French *tenir* 'to hold'). When a sense of a word is restricted to a specialised vocabulary area, this is explicitly stated before the actual definition, e.g. *Printing, Computers, Genetics, Literature*. Stylistic indications, e.g. *informal, colloquial, slang*, are also given, either before or after the sense in question.

What are major differences? The way the pronunciation is given differs: *Collins Concise Dictionary* uses the IPA symbols, the other dictionaries have a transcription system that tries to respell the word on the basis of the most common correspondences between sound and spelling in English. *Chambers English Dictionary* is the only one in which the different senses of the word are not numbered, but only separated by punctuation. It is also the only one that mentions Spenser's and Shakespeare's use of language. This is a well-known characteristic of this dictionary and illustrates our earlier point: every good dictionary tries to cater for specific user groups and emphasises certain vocabulary areas. In addition, some of the dictionaries, e.g. the *Longman Dictionary of the English Language*, occasionally illustrate a sense of a word by an example. Again, such examples of usage are signalled by a different fount (*italics*) and/or specific brackets.

The *OED* entry retraced the history of the noun *character*. Since all ten of our dictionaries were published long after the *OED*, does this mean that they follow the order in which the *OED* lists the senses of the word, simply omitting the obsolete ones? By no means. Some of the dictionaries start with the concrete and older sense of the word, others list the abstract one first. We have seen earlier that distinguishing different senses of a word at a particular period is a very difficult and somewhat arbitrary and artificial process, because they fade into each other and are thus often co-present. We cannot reproduce this co-presence in a dictionary but have to give the senses in a linear order. There are, in fact, various ordering principles in lexicography: long established senses before more recent ones; literal before figurative ones; common before rare ones. A further alternative is the 'logical' principle of ordering the meanings so as to explain the development from one sense to another. In the *OED* entry for the noun *character* we can see the interaction of some of these principles.

Another difference is in the treatment of derived words. There is a verb of the same form derived from the noun *character*. Some dictionaries treat both within the same entry, others give them an entry each and then differentiate the headword by a raised figure, e.g. [1]**character**.

And finally, we have to mention a feature that is more common in American general-purpose dictionaries than in British ones: a synonym section at the end of an entry. We have such sections in the *Reader's Digest* dictionary, in *Webster's Ninth New Collegiate Dictionary*, and in the *Random House College Dictionary*.

Learner's dictionaries

General-purpose dictionaries like the ones we have illustrated are obviously much too difficult for foreign learners of English. The language used in the definitions presupposes a command of the vocabulary (words like *aggregate, ethical, trait*) that learners do not yet have. There are numerous dictionaries for all types of learners, but three of them (with their smaller derivatives) are outstanding. They are: the *Longman Dictionary of Contemporary English, Collins Cobuild English Language Dictionary* and the *Oxford Advanced Learner's Dictionary of Current English*. The special features that characterise this type of dictionary are:

1 They concentrate on the common core standard vocabulary of English.

2 The definitions are written in simple English suited to the student's command of the language. For the *Longman Dictionary of Contemporary English* there was even developed a special defining vocabulary. This consists of about 2,000 words (printed at the end of the dictionary) by means of which the 55,000 words and phrases of the dictionary are explained. A learner who has mastered the defining vocabulary can therefore be expected to understand all the definitions in the dictionary.

3 The three learner's dictionaries pay special attention to the ways the words are used grammatically. Traditional dictionaries tell the user the word-class membership of an item ('sb'), and in the case of verbs, whether they are transitive or intransitive. Our three learner's dictionaries give much more grammatical information: they tell the user whether a noun is countable or not, which prepositions it takes with complements, whether a verb can be used in the progressive form, whether an adjective can be predicative, etc.

4 Again, these dictionaries give guidance on the appropriate use of words stylistically. Style labels, explicit usage, and language notes provide this guidance.

5 In order to help the learner understand all this information, these dictionaries provide many example sentences that illustrate the uses of a word.

Here are the entries for the noun *character* from these three dictionaries so that they can be compared with those from the general-purpose dictionaries:

Longman Dictionary of Contemporary English (new edition, 1987)

char·ac·ter /'kærɪktə'/ *n* 1 [C;U] the combination of qualities which make a particular person, thing, place, etc., different from others; nature: *The twins look alike but have very different characters.* | *A tendency not to show emotions is supposed to be part of the British national character.* | *a man of good character* | *When they pulled down the old houses in the centre of the town, the whole character of the place was changed.* | *I can't understand why she did that — it's quite* out of character.

(=not at all typical of her behaviour) —compare CHAR-
ACTERISTIC², PERSONALITY (1)   **2** [U] a combination of
qualities that are regarded as valuable or admirable,
such as high principles, honesty, etc.: *a woman of great
character | a nice old house with a lot of character*   **3** [C]
a person in a book, play, etc.: *It's a good story, but I find
some of the characters rather unconvincing.*   **4** [C] the
opinion that other people have about a person; REPUTA-
TION: *a newspaper story that blackened* (=damaged) *his
character | character assassination* (=cruel and usu. un-
just destroying of someone's character) | *The defendant
is a man of previous good character.* (=does not have a
criminal record)   **5** [C] *infml* **a** a person: *She's a
strange character.* | *(derog) Some character just walked
up and stole my bag.* **b** an odd or humorous person:
*She's a real character | quite a character — she has us in
fits of laughter.* | *a well-known* **character actor** (=one
who often plays odd or humorous people)   **6** [C] a letter, mark, or sign used in writing or printing: *a notice
printed in Chinese characters | The characters on my type-
writer are too small. | Our new printer operates at 60
characters per second.*   **7** [C *usu. sing.*] *fml* official position; CAPACITY: *He was there in his character as a town
official.*   **8** [C] *old-fash, esp. BrE* a usu. written statement of a person's abilities; REFERENCE: *My employer
gave me a good character.*

Collins Cobuild English Language Dictionary (1987)

character /ˈkærəˌktə/, **characters**. 1 The charac-   N COUNT : USU
ter of a person, group of people, place, etc consists of   WITH POSS
all the qualities they have that combine to form their   = nature
personality or atmosphere. EG *There was another
side to his character... People were affected by the
character of New York.*

2 If you say that someone is behaving **in character**,   PHR : USED AS AN
you mean they are behaving in the way you would   A
expect them to behave, knowing how they usually   = in keeping
react to things. EG *Such a gesture would be in
character with Smithy's behaviour.* ● If you say that   ● PHR : USED AS
someone is behaving **out of character**, you mean   AN A
that they are behaving in a way which you would not
expect, knowing how they usually behave or react to
things. EG *Her reading glasses had bright green
frames, which seemed out of character.*

3 If something has a particular **character**, it has that   N UNCOUNT : USU
particular quality. EG *We need to emphasize the*   + SUPP
radical character of our demands... Concessions are   1 identity
not always purely negative in character... He lit   = nature
*several candles, giving the meeting a clandestine
character.*

4 When you talk about **the English character**, the   PHR
Irish character, etc, you are thinking of the qualities   = make up,
that people from a particular country or race are   psyche
believed to have. EG *...the independence of the Spanish character... Acting is not in the English character.*

5 If you describe someone as being of **high charac-**   N UNCOUNT : ADJ
ter, **good character**, etc, you are emphasizing how   + N
much they are respected by other people. EG *All*   1 reputation
complaints were withdrawn, acknowledging   = good name
*McKinley's irreproachable character... ...beautiful
women of high character.*

6 Your **character** is your personality, considered especially in relation to how honest and reliable you are. ᴇɢ ...*a confidential assessment of Mr Charles Boon's character... He was asked to write a character reference for Mr Stevens.*

N COUNT : USU
POSS + N

7 If someone has **character**, they have the ability to deal effectively with difficult, unpleasant, or dangerous situations; used showing approval. ᴇɢ *It takes considerable character not to just give up and go home... I think Jenny has great strength of character.*

N UNCOUNT
† strength

8 If you say that a place has **character**, you mean that it has a special, interesting, and unusual quality that makes you notice or like it; used showing approval. ᴇɢ *'I like this place,' she declared. 'It's got character.'... ...an old house of great character.*

N UNCOUNT
= atmosphere

9 The **characters** in a film, book, or play are the people that the film, book, or play is about. ᴇɢ *...the tensions that develop between the two main characters.*

N COUNT : USU PL
† person

10 A **character** is 10.1 a person, especially when you are mentioning a particular quality that he or she has. ᴇɢ *He's a strange character, my friend Evans... ...a seedy character with a cigarette butt jammed behind his ear.* **10.2** a very interesting, unusual, or amusing person. ᴇɢ *Dooley was a local character... She was a real character.*

N COUNT : USU
ADJ + N
† person

N COUNT : USU
ADJ + N
† personality
= eccentric

11 A **character** is also a letter, number, or other symbol that you write or print. ᴇɢ *...the twenty-six characters of the English alphabet.*

N COUNT

Oxford Advanced Learner's Dictionary of Current English (4th edition, 1989)

char·ac·ter /ˈkærəktə(r)/ *n* **1** [C] **(a)** mental or moral qualities that make a person, group, nation, etc, different from others: *What does her handwriting tell you about her character?* ○ *His character is very different from his wife's.* ○ *The British character is often said to be phlegmatic.* **(b)** all those features that make a thing, a place, an event, etc, what it is and different from others: *the character of the desert landscape* ○ *The whole character of the village has changed since I was last here.* ○ *The wedding took on the character of* (ie became like) *a farce when the vicar fell flat on his face.* **2** [U] **(a)** striking individuality: *drab houses with no character.* **(b)** moral strength: *a woman of character* ○ *It takes character to say a thing like that.* ○ *Some people think military service is character-building.* **3** [C] **(a)** (*infml*) person, esp an odd or unpleasant one: *He looks a suspicious character.* **(b)** (*approv*) person who is not ordinary or typical; person with individuality: *She's a real/ quite a character!* **4** [C] person in a novel, play, etc: *the characters in the novels of Charles Dickens.* **5** [C] reputation, esp a good one: *damage sb's character.* **6** [C] letter, sign or mark used in a system of writing or printing: *Chinese, Greek, Russian, etc characters.* **7** (idm) **in/out** of **character** typical/not typical of a person's character(1a): *Her behaviour last night was quite out of character.*

Special dictionaries

We have concentrated in this chapter on dictionaries which seek
to describe the general use of the English vocabulary, but of
course there are many dictionaries as well that provide special information of various kinds. For expert guidance on pronunciation,
there is the world-famous *English Pronouncing Dictionary* (originally
by Daniel Jones, and now in a revised edition by Susan Ramsaran,
1988). If one's interest is in the history of a word's form and
meaning, one goes to an *etymological* dictionary, such as the *Oxford
Dictionary of English Etymology*, edited by C T Onions (1966), or the
Concise Oxford Dictionary of English Etymology, edited by T F Hoad
(1986). Or if one is interested in slang, one would consult Eric
Partridge's *Dictionary of Slang and Unconventional English* (now in
its eighth edition, prepared by Paul Beale, 1984), and the *Dictionary
of American Slang* by H Wentworth and S B Flexner (1975).

All these books about words have one thing in common: the
entries are arranged alphabetically, that is, according to the spelling. From one point of view, this is very convenient: we know
exactly where to find all about a word, provided only that we
know the word to begin with, and have a reasonably good idea
how to spell it. Yet occasionally, our principal problem is not to
find the exact meaning of a word but to find the exact word for
a meaning which is floating, so to speak, in our heads. What we
want then is not an alphabetically arranged dictionary but something more like a *classified* telephone directory in which all house-
painters (for example) are brought together, whether they are
called Abbot or Young. Word-books of precisely this kind exist,
the best known being *Roget's Thesaurus*, originally compiled by
Peter Mark Roget and first published in 1852. It is still the most
widely used thesaurus of the English language. Suppose, for instance, in the middle of writing we are suddenly stuck for the
'right' word: we know it has to do with *growing smaller*, but this
is as far as we can get, though we have the irritating feeling that
the word is on 'the tip of the tongue'. With the *Thesaurus* to hand,
we can easily settle our problem. It will present us with the lexical
fields for the notion of 'growing smaller'. We can either turn
directly to the sections dealing with relative size or be guided to
them by looking up any common associated word in the index.
We find a whole set of words in the required field of meaning:
lessen, reduce, condense, contract, attenuate, dwarf, wane, diminish,

decrease, shrink, dwindle, and several others. These are items from this lexical field relating to verbs alone. Should we need a noun or an adjective instead, we would also find the respective lexical fields for these word classes.

A thesaurus does not usually give definitions of the individual words, and if we come upon one in the list that is unfamiliar, we must turn to a good dictionary to find exactly what it means. But since our 'passive' knowledge of words is always much greater than our 'active' use of words, it is often enough merely to see a word in a list to know that it is just right for our needs.

It is clear, then, that there are many books which we *ought* to consult about words, books which can enlarge our experience by making us see our world in greater detail and which can help us to communicate our experience of it to others with greater precision.

SOME FOLLOW-UP WORK

1 Here are some everyday expressions using the adjective *mean:*

Uncle Tom has always been very mean with money.
It was mean of you to switch off the television set and
send the children to bed.
I feel rather mean for not having helped more.
She makes a mean beef curry.
He's no mean administrator.

Try to abstract from these examples the meanings of the
word and write a dictionary definition. Before you compare
your definition with one in a dictionary, think whether there
are other meanings of the word in addition to those
illustrated. If you find some, add them to your dictionary
definition.

2 Look up the adjective *mean* in *Roget's Thesaurus* and note all
the expressions that you are given for the sense 'miserly'.
Try to differentiate the meanings of the words given. Then
compare your explanations with the definitions provided in
your dictionary.

3 Study several dictionaries in your library to see how up to date they are. When were they last revised? Which areas of the English vocabulary do they claim to cover?

4 The dust jackets and the introductions of dictionaries often highlight the number of entries they have, in order to outdo each other. Argue that it is not the number of entries of a dictionary that is its most important characteristic.

5 On p. 106, we distinguished between 'grammatical words' and 'lexical words'. Use a general-purpose dictionary and compare the definitions given for a lexical word like *thin*, *house*, etc and a grammatical word like *the*, *and*, etc. Is the lexicographical method of description equally effective for both types? In what ways does the presentation of 'definition' differ between them?

6 Compare the definitions for *character* in the three learner's dictionaries quoted in this chapter and state similarities and differences.

7 Which treatment of *character* do you prefer, taking account of all the dictionaries quoted in this chapter. Explain the reasons for your preference.

8 In trying to keep up to date by including new words, dictionaries at each revision have to be relieved of some meanings of words (and some words themselves) because they have become rare or obsolete. Take any four consecutive pages of a one-volume dictionary and consider carefully how much material you might recommend to be discarded for this reason.

How do we learn grammar?

In Oliver Goldsmith's play, *She Stoops to Conquer* (1773), Tony Lumpkin sings a song which begins:

> Let school-masters puzzle their brain
> With grammar, and nonsense, and learning.

Why should anyone be so contemptuous about learning grammar as to connect it in the same breath with nonsense? One reason may be that the grammar traditionally taught was actually the grammar of Latin (and this did not end with Goldsmith's time), so naturally it could seem to have little relevance to English. A second reason follows from this. If English does not make a good many of the distinctions found in Latin grammar (we may recall the discussion of *Vir dixit puellas advenisse* in Chapter Eight), the impression is quickly formed that English presents us with very little grammar to be learned. Furthermore, since we already speak our mother tongue before ever we go to school, we have apparently already learned what grammar there is to learn anyway!

Well, oddly enough, one of the comments on Tony Lumpkin's song is: 'I loves to hear him sing, because he never gives us nothing that's low.' This reminds us that, as we saw in Chapters Eight and Nine, there is in fact plenty for us to learn about the grammar of *Standard English* when we get to school. Not only that: but in the learning of *English* grammar (as opposed to Latin grammar partially applied to English), we find that English has a very great deal of grammar, much of it extremely interesting and subtle.

All the same, it is still true that we have acquired an impressive knowledge of grammar before our schooling begins. Let us take as an example the following authentic remark of a five-year-old boy:

Eric and me's just buyed lots of fings.

This is the sort of thing that tickles an adult (and also warms the heart — of a parent at any rate) precisely because of the 'quaint' way in which the child makes *mistakes* in the allegedly non-existent grammar of English. In fact, the proud parent ought to feel pride in the quite remarkable amount of grammar the little boy has *correctly* mastered. He has mastered the ordering of sentence elements perfectly, having placed the subject *Eric and me* in front of the verb *[ha]s buyed* with the object *lots of fings* in its correct place after the verb. A different arrangement would indeed have made 'nonsense', and we can ignore the fact that he has probably never heard the terms 'sentence elements', 'subject', 'verb', or 'object' — and would certainly not know what these grammatical labels mean.

Even the components of the phrases which operate as the sentence elements have been put in correct grammatical sequence. The child's verb expression is *[ha]s just buyed* not *just has buyed* or *buyed just has*; his object is *lots of fings* not *of lots fings* or *fings of lots*. His subject shows an even subtler grasp of ordering: the polite relegation of the speaker reference to the end — *Eric and me* rather than *me and Eric*.

He seems also to have acquired a sense of English *aspectual* expression, correctly selecting the *perfect* '[ha]s buyed' with the item *just*, where if the adverbial had been *last week* he would doubtless have selected the simple past:

Last week Eric and me buyed lots of fings.

Equally, if the adverbial had been *always*, he would probably have used the simple present to indicate that the action is habitual:

Eric and me always buy lots of fings.

We are guessing at the child's competence here, of course, but the guess is made plausible by the fact that the attested sentence shows the correct use of what many people would regard as the more difficult verb form, the perfect *has buyed*.

We are not overlooking the *errors* of grammar that the little boy makes. He seems to have little idea of *concord*: the fact that some verb forms (*is, has, plays*) can be correctly used only with a singular subject and that otherwise a plural form must be substituted:

One kitten is / has / plays . . .
Two kittens are / have / play . . .

Nor does he seem to realise that personal pronouns have a subject form and an object form; he uses *me* (in 'Eric and me') instead of the correct *I*, though the form of his subject would have been all right in an object phrase ('Mum helped Eric and me'). But since in both respects his grammatical deviance is shared by thousands of adults who have not learned (or who carelessly ignore) standard grammar, we should not be too hard on the five-year-old. And in one respect what he has got wrong tells us how much he has in fact correctly learned: *[ha]s buyed* is wrong, but it shows that he has mastered the inflexion of regular verbs: *love/loved, play/played, warm/warmed*.

The power of analogy

We can in fact make a significant generalisation from the evidence of the child's sentence 'Eric and me's just buyed lots of fings'. This is that he has achieved the remarkable insight of *analogy*. We have no reason to believe that he had heard this particular sentence before in its entirety and was merely repeating it as a parrot might. Rather, he seems to be able to take other people's sentences apart, identify the functions and forms of the various parts, and then make up new sentences of his own, putting pieces that he needs for his immediate communicative purpose into particular places in what we can imagine as a quite abstract *pattern*. He does not know the term 'subject', but he knows that a sentence needs one, and he knows what its relation is to the rest of the sentence. He *generalises* by *analogy* to a highly impressive extent, and it is not surprising that he still has to learn that *buy* is not merely irregular but unparalleled among our verbs in having *bought* correspond to the *(e)d* forms he has identified as normal.

We shall return presently to look more closely at these concepts of analogy, generalisation, and pattern, but first let us pause to note the hint of uncertainty introduced into the last paragraph. 'We have no reason to believe', we said; the child 'seems to be able . . .'. The uncertainty is very well justified, because the question posed in the title of the present chapter is, we fear, largely unanswerable: at any rate, on present knowledge. There are many *theories* as to how a child acquires the grammar (and other features) of the native language, but no one actually knows. It is fairly obvious that parrot-like imitation plays a part; but it is equally obvious that it is a relatively small part. It is obvious that analogy plays a part and that this is a rather important part; but analogy cannot plausibly account for everything. Explicit teaching by parents and peers must surely play an important role ('Not *fings*, darling: *things*; can you say *things*?' 'Not *buyed*, darling: it's *bought*'); but just as surely, we must learn a vast amount that we were never taught.

Take, for instance, the subject phrase *Eric and me* in the child's sentence. Never mind that it should have been *Eric and I*: how does anyone learn that self-reference is done with a special set of words *I, me, my*? A child seems to begin self-reference with his or her own name ('Robbie want dat', 'Dat's Robbie's'), and adults seem to appreciate the child's problem in this respect by using the name instead of a pronoun too: 'Molly have another drink?' rather than 'Will *you* have another drink?' But at some stage, the child makes the linguistic leap from something like 'Eric and *Robbie's* just buyed lots of fings' to 'Eric and *me's* just buyed lots of fings'. This leap is all the more remarkable in that, although we must have been addressed scores of time as *you*, we do not seem to make the mistake of saying things like 'Eric and *you*' when we mean 'Eric and *me*'.

The discussion of the child's sentence has by no means exhausted the evidence of sophisticated learning that it presents. There is the grasp of *number* (that is, singular and plural), such that since we have *lots of fings*, we can reasonably presume that the child would have been able to speak equally of a singular *fing*, and even that he would not have used the quantifier *lots of* if his brother and he had bought only *two or three* 'fings'.

But in some respects the evidence is inadequate. He has used the active voice *[ha]s buyed* (as distinct from the passive 'Lots of fings has been buyed'), but we cannot assume that he might equally have been able to use the passive, though he doubtless understands its meaning when someone else uses it. In other words, just as we noted the distinction between a very large *recognition* knowledge in vocabulary and a more modest *productive* or *active* knowledge, so it must be in acquiring grammar that we recognise structures, patterns, and forms long before we start actually using them ourselves.

There is a further difficulty in hypothesising how a child learns the mother tongue. The evidence strongly suggests, as we have said, the early ability to analyse stretches of language into component parts. But we have very little idea of how the child conceptualises either the stretches themselves or the resultant components. In attempting here to see grammar learning from the child's point of view, it is obviously better to speak of the little boy's learning that '*has* can be appropriately accompanied by a word ending in *d*', than of his learning that 'the past participles of verbs end in *d*'.

The latter is an alternative way of stating the fact, but it is essentially not just an *adult's* but a *grammarian's* way: an attempt to find some abstraction to which a great many disparate facts of language can be referred. The facts themselves may be, from one point of view, 'loved, swallowed, played, eaten, bought, put, found, had,' etc; from another point of view, 'the form of the verb that enters into construction with a part of the verb *to have* in forming the perfect' (and it will be realised that 'a part of the verb *to have*' is itself an abstraction from *have, has, had*). For these and other statements, 'past participle' is a convenient shorthand expression, and because most of us have to make abstractions of this kind from time to time, we find it useful to have at our fingertips a grasp of simple and widely understood grammatical terminology. It is not just grammarians who need to be able to use such terms, any more than it is just engineers who need to be able to use such a word as 'thread', instead of attempting a vague (and inaccurate) description of 'little grooves running parallel to each other at a slight angle from the diameter of a bar in such a way that one piece of metal can encircle the bar and move across it'. But 'thread' is an abstraction that we learn to make, of course, long after we have been screwing parts of toys together as we made models. In the same way, we learn to fit *has* and *played* together long before we have heard of a 'past participle'.

What the child seems to learn is that utterances constitute patterns, and to learn also that disregard of these patterns produces utterances that listeners do not understand: it is just babble, nonsense.

The use of nonsense

We can however make use of what is literally nonsense to set up a hypothesis as to how we learn the role of what we may later learn to call parts of speech like *adjective* or parts of sentences like *subject* or *adverbial*. Take the following string of items:

1 croatation ungleshably polanians pleakful ruggling plome rit will the in be the

Although we recognise individual grammatical words as 'English' here, and some individual lexical words which *might* be English (*pleakful*, for example, is in various ways more English than, say *lufkaelp* would be), there is no recognisable relationship between the 'words'. They seem to form only a random, shapeless list. Now, consider them rearranged as follows:

2 Plome the pleakful croatation will be ruggling polanians ungleshably in the rit.

It is at once obvious that the second arrangement is less nonsensical than the first, and this is because every 'word' now falls into some sort of *pattern* that is recognisably English. We do not know what *rit* means, yet if we were to replace it by a word that we do know, we would choose one like *nest* or *bag* or *office* or *terror*: we would not be satisfied with 'in the politely' or 'in the of' or 'in the beautify' or 'in the then'. So what is it that *rit* has in common with *nest* and *office* that it does not have in common with *beautify* or *then*? Clearly, one answer is that *rit* is a noun, and we must now see that we have recognised *rit* as a noun not because we knew about a noun being 'the name of a person, place or thing', but because *rit* is used in (2) in the framework where words like *office* but not *then* frequently appear and 'make sense'. We cannot know that *rit* is the name of a person, place or thing in (1), and even in (2) we do not know what exactly *rit* is the name of.

According to their state of language development, a group of students will be able to replicate the items in (2), replacing those they do not (and cannot!) know, not merely by items that they know, but by items which 'make sense' in the sequence as a whole:

	a	b	c	d
2	Plome	the pleakful	croatation	will be ruggling
3	Then	the artful	delegation	will be muddling
4	Suddenly	the fine	horse	will be facing
5	Probably	the young	publisher	will be reading

	e	f	g
2	polanians	ungleshably	in the rit.
3	politicians	unpardonably	in the street.
4	picnickers	shyly	in the field.
5	manuscripts	through	in the evening.

There are two quite different kinds of grammatical identity here. The vertical sets *a* to *g* each comprise items grammatically identical (*a* and *f* adverbs; *b* adjectives; *c*, *e*, and *g* nouns; and *d* present participles of verbs), and the horizontal structures are grammatically identical too. But there is a vital connection between the two kinds of identity: *fine*, for example, is grammatically the same as *artful* only because both appear in the same 'horizontal' structure ('the *b c*') in the same position, *b*. If on the other hand we replaced *pleakful* by *fine* in the arrangement (1), we could not assign it to a vertical set at all, since arrangement (1) does not display any horizontal structures: it might be a verb ('the croatation will *fine* polanians' — when they offend) or equally a noun ('the pleakful *fine* will plome the polanians ungleshably'). There are three other points that we should not miss here. First, the horizontal arrangements (2) to (5) are structural, but it must be noted that they display not just *a* structure but *structures*. That is to say, we do not — as we have seen — need to consider the whole of (2) to decide that *rit* is a noun: the little sub-structure '(in) the rit' is enough for that. Similarly, if we rearranged the ending of (1) to read 'will the in be the rit', we should have enough structural guidance to conclude that *in* is a noun too. The all-important notion that English has structures within structures is one that we shall develop further presently.

The second point is this. Arrangement (3) is closer in form to (2) than is (4) or (5), and this draws attention to the fact that there is a 'grammar' within the word as well as between words. Such words as *croatation* and *delegation* have their noun character suggested by their form alone, even before we see them identified as nouns by their use in a structure. Moreover, the correspondence between the noun *delegation* and a related verb *delegate* would lead us to postulate a verb *croatate*, just as the relationship of *unpardonably* to *pardon* would lead us to interpret the 'internal grammar' of *ungleshably* as concerning something which cannot be *gleshed*.

Making sense

The third point is more obvious than the other two but ironically far harder to explain. The words students will enter in the vertical columns will not only be grammatically appropriate as we have seen (an adjective in place of another adjective, a verb in place of another verb), they will be entered with an eye on whether they 'make sense' in the horizontal arrangement. Thus (4) above makes 'horizontal' sense in that we know what a *fine horse* might look like, can imagine it in a *field*, *facing picnickers*, and seeming to do so rather *shyly*. Contrast an alternative:

4a   Recently, the square horse will be reading buses darkly in the sea.

Such a version, in our game of extending the pattern of (2), is highly unlikely, not because we (children and adults alike) do not enjoy playing with nonsense linguistically, but rather because it is actually a great deal more difficult to invent the studiously impossible (4a) than it is to invent (4). This seems to suggest that 'making sense' comes first in our linguistic priorities, and we are prepared to accept all kinds of grammatical or lexical deviance provided we can guess the intended meaning. If, however, we are confronted with nonsense such that we cannot even imagine a possible world in which the sentence would make sense ('recently *will be* reading'? a *square* horse'? 'reading *buses*'?), then in spite of the fact that we understand the individual words and we recognise the grammar as correct (in 4a both these conditions are met), we reject the sentence as gibberish. As a further example, compare the following pair:

Colourful crimson poppies grow abundantly.
Colourless green ideas sleep furiously.

The grammar is identical in the two sentences, the words are familiar in both; but only in the former do the meanings of the words fit together to make a meaningful whole.

Let us look at a deeper irony in the same connection. Imagine being told:

My daughter's two flointles have disappeared.

This seems perfectly straightforward — except that we do not know what a flointle is; a pet or a toy, perhaps. So we ask, only to be told that *flointles* is the girl's word for *parents*. Now, though we know all the words in the sentence, it is no longer straightforward:

My daughter's two *parents* have disappeared.

The sentence entails that the speaker must be one of the girl's parents, so how could he or she be uttering a statement that makes sense? In other words, however it is that we learn grammar, it must be accompanied simultaneously with learning the meanings of words and with having the ability to make sense with both.

But while grammar and vocabulary are thus interdependent, we have good reason to regard grammar as being a more important prerequisite. The same words with the same meanings add up to very different sentences if the grammar is changed. Consider the effect of switching subject and object in:

The farmer killed the wolf.
The wolf killed the farmer.

Again, if a sentence has comprehensible grammar but one incomprehensible vocabulary item, we know how to ask the question that should make the sentence as a whole comprehensible. For example:

The car was gackulented by snow.

This has a clear grammar and will have a clear meaning once we are told what *gackulented* means. But even without knowing this word, we know from the grammar alone that the following sentence has the same meaning as the first:

Snow gackulented the car.

Equally, we know from the grammar alone that the following sentence is a denial of the first:

It wasn't snow that gackulented the car.

Again, we can ask well-formed and intelligent questions from our knowledge of the grammar alone:

Did snow gackulent the car?
Was anything else gackulented by snow besides the car?
Did the snow do anything except gackulent the car?

On the other hand, if instead of the clearly grammatical sentence ('The car was gackulented by snow'), we had the same words arranged with no recognisable grammar, none of these consequences could follow:

By gackulented the was car snow.

It would not now occur to us to ask what *gackulented* means, since it would not help us to make sense of the 'sentence'.

In contrast to this last *gackulented* example, which has no recognisable grammar, let us return to the comment on Tony Lumpkin in *She Stoops to Conquer*:

I loves to hear him sing, because he never gives us nothing that's low.

This is fully comprehensible and has a recognisable grammar, though it is not the grammar of Standard English, which would require correction of the concord between *I* and *loves*, and correction too of the double negative (from 'he *never* gives us *nothing*' to 'he *never* gives us *anything*'). But we are correcting from one grammatical system, which accepts *I loves* and double negatives, to another grammatical system, that of Standard English, which does not. The sentence becomes more widely acceptable in the process but it does not become more comprehensible.

Grammar and standard grammar

If on the other hand we correct the double negative and say it is wrong because 'two negatives make a positive', we are guilty of a mis-statement because we allege that the grammar offends in the matter of comprehensibility. And this, as we have just seen, is patent nonsense — one of the instances of nonsense that Tony perhaps had in mind when he associated grammar-teaching with nonsense. If a child says 'I haven't done no homework,' the teacher has yet to be born who will reply (without sarcasm), 'Oh good, I'm glad you've done it.' The two negatives here do not make a positive: they make a quite emphatic negative, but they make an unsatisfactory English utterance because the usage does not conform with educated conventions.

So learning the grammar of our native language is even more complicated than we have allowed, since it involves learning several systems of grammar — at least to a level of *recognition* knowledge — and also learning that one of these systems, that of the standard language, must have pride of place for a number of important functions. It is not that uneducated or non-standard expressions like 'he never gives us nothing' has *no* grammar. A man who goes to be interviewed for a job as a clerk wearing an open-neck shirt is wrongly dressed for the occasion, but no one would say that he is not wearing clothes. Most of us are fairly easily convinced that, although none of our close friends thinks we are objectionable when we are wearing a T-shirt at a party, a potential employer almost certainly would, if we were thus dressed at an interview. In just the same way, we come to be aware of which grammatical conventions pass muster among our friends and which need adjustment when we are in touch with a wider circle.

An appeal to our sense of conformity, convention, and fashion will often make sense to us where talk of 'This is meaningless' or 'Don't you know that two negatives make a positive?' would not. There is more convention than logic in matters of dress, and the same applies to language. And the conventions of language are nearly as changeable as those of dress. In Charles Dickens's time, it was correct for the young clerk to say, 'He don't look well,' just as it was correct for him to wear a frock coat and top hat. It is convention that makes 'They have forgotten it' acceptable where 'They have forgot it' is not acceptable. It is not that one form is more 'logical' or even more 'grammatical' than the other: the two differ simply in following different conventions, as we can see if we compare our usage in 'They have got it' which has the very participial form of which we disapprove in 'They have forgot it'. Logic might insist that we fall in with the Americans in saying both *forgotten* and *gotten* or that we fall in with some British dialects in saying both *they have forgot* and *they have got* (which might arguably entail our saying also *they have spoke* and *they have wrote*). Pure reason might equally suggest that, if it is a cold day,

I may go for an interview in a roll-neck sweater; whereas if it is hot, I may go in a T-shirt. But the conventions of human behaviour are not all determined by logic and reason, and language is part of human behaviour.

Tony Lumpkin's song in *She Stoops to Conquer* went on to say that the school-masters' brains were puzzling over. 'Their *Qui's* and their *Quae's* and their *Quod's'*. Much of our feeling that English grammar is somehow unreal results from the way in which grammarians have traditionally looked at English through the lattice of categories set up in Latin grammar. The extent to which we have remained unconvinced that English has a grammar like Latin is probably the basis of the popular fallacy that English has very little grammar at all.

Different language, different grammar

English, as we have seen, is certainly not without grammar, but this does not mean that it has the same grammar as Latin — or any other language for that matter. Just as the vocabulary of every language is distinct and peculiar, so is the grammar of a language. There is so common a failure to grasp this point, that it is worth pausing for some elementary discussion of it.

In English, we have three verb expressions which we can distinguish as 'simple present', 'progressive present', and 'emphatic present'. Compare 'I play — I am playing — I *do* play ', 'I work — I am working — I *do* work'. In some languages there is only one single verb-form corresponding to these sets of three: for example, in French, we have *je joue* and *je travaille*; in Russian, *ya igráyu* and *ya rabótayu*. The first thing that we should note is this: the fact that the French and Russians do not possess three separate verb-forms does not mean that they cannot express these distinctions. They most certainly can, but it is not done, as in English, by a change in the verb-form. Americans, after all, do not normally use special fish knives and forks as people do in Great Britain, but this does not mean that Americans cannot eat fish.

The second thing to note is that, in making these distinctions by other means than a change in the verb, the French feel no obligation to give three different names to the verb they use when they make them. 'Je travaille chaque jour,' someone may say where we might use the simple present, 'I work each day.' 'Je travaille en ce moment,' someone might say on the other hand, where in English we should be more likely to use the progressive form, 'I'm working at present.' Thirdly, we might hear a French person say, 'Je travaille — je vous l'assure,' where we could use our emphatic present, 'I *do* work.' In English, the three verb-forms need three labels, but naturally the French do not call *je travaille* 'simple present' in the first case, 'progressive present' in the second, and 'emphatic present' in the third; they do not need three labels for a single verb-form, merely because English has to use three different verb-forms.

This sounds obvious, yet until very recently it has been common to talk about English as though it made its distinctions in precisely the same way as Latin does. There are grammars still in print today which give one label to *came* in 'I came yesterday' ('indicative') and another label to the same form in 'If I came tomorrow, would you see me?' ('subjunctive'). Similarly, we find a sentence such as 'I gave the dog a bone' described as containing one noun in the 'accusative' (*bone*) and the other in the 'dative' (*dog*). On the other hand, in 'I gave the dog away', *dog* would be called 'accusative' — the same form having two labels — while in the sentence 'I gave a bone to the dog', *to the dog* would be called 'dative' — two different expressions (*the dog* and *to the dog*) thus having the same label.

If you know Latin, you can see some sort of justification for this terminological distinction. In translating 'I gave *the dog* away' into Latin, one would require the accusative form *canem*, but in translating 'I gave *the dog* a bone', one would require the dative form *cani*. Analogously in German, the definite article would be different in the two sentences, thus justifying two labels, accusative and dative:

Ich habe *den* Hund weggegeben.
Ich habe *dem* Hund einen Knochen gegeben.

But since in English we have *the bone* in both sentences, there is no point in having labels like accusative and dative. In the same way, the French would regard it as nonsense to call *je travaille* 'simple present' in one sentence and 'progressive present' in another (and very difficult to remember, if they did not mentally translate into English to test out which was which). Nor even for Germans and Russians (whose languages have accusative and dative distinctions) is it helpful when they are learning English to be told that our language distinguishes accusative from dative also: they would expect a 'dog-em', 'dog-i' contrast which does not exist. Worse, it could be positively misleading. If French children were in fact taught to call *je travaille* 'simple' in one sentence and 'progressive' in another, merely on account of the general context, they would naturally be predisposed to think that the 'simple progressive' distinction in English is to be achieved similarly, and they would say things like, 'Do not disturb me: I work.' An English-speaking child who learns to call *dog* 'accusative' or 'dative' according to the general context is hindered from understanding that in German (or Russian) the accusatives and datives that are supposed to correspond are quite differently distinguished, with formal inflexional endings.

We may go further and claim that, even where English has inflexional differences (*I — me, she — her*, and so on), these should not be referred to as 'nominative' and 'accusative'. True, in these instances, we certainly can talk of *cases*, and we need two labels for the two forms. But to call them 'nominative' and 'accusative' would be to suggest that these labels would have the same application as they have in Latin or German or Russian grammar, where there are not two but four or five case forms to distinguish and where 'nominative' and 'accusative' form a set along with additional labels such as 'dative', 'ablative', 'prepositional', and the like. The meaning of 'accusative' in a two-term system, nominative/accusative, is bound to be different from the meaning of 'accusative' in a four- or five-term system. For English, therefore, it is better to speak of a *subject* case and an *object* case.

Let us consider an analogy. Two friends travel by train from Münster to Frankfurt; they must be in one of two classes of compartment — first or second. When they are 'translated' to a transatlantic flight at Frankfurt, they must be assigned to one of *three* seat-classes: 'first', 'club' (or 'business'), and 'economy'. The two sets of categories have one label in common, 'first class', but this does not mean that if they travelled *first* on the train, the two friends will travel *first* on the plane. They may feel that for their taste or income, the appropriate equivalent to *first* on the train is *club* by air. The identity of the label 'first' is not much help: in the one case it operates in a two-term system, in the other in a three-term system.

So too, if we call *her* an 'accusative' in expressions like 'I obey *her*', 'I am like *her*', 'I sat with *her*', the term 'accusative' may actually hinder us when we translate into another language which has an accusative along with several other cases and in which the word for *obey* takes the dative, the word for *like* the genitive, and the word for *with* the ablative — as they do in Latin.

SOME FOLLOW-UP WORK

1 Collect some examples of young children's speech and analyse them carefully so as to assess how much grammar has been learned and how much remains to be learned.

2 Explain and illustrate the process of *analogy*, not restricting yourself to matters of language.

3 We can say 'a round table' and 'he rounded the bend', but *pleakful* is likely to have only one grammatical function by reason of the affix *-ful*. What other affixes are there which seem to restrict words to particular grammatical functions?

4 'It is the pleakful croatation that will plome be ruggling polanians.' Attempt other variations upon arrangement (2), checking their acceptability in the corresponding lines (3) to (5) on p. 179.

5 In arrangements (2)–(5), it will be seen that while columns *b* and *c* are fixed in relation to each other, as *c* is in relation to *d*, the columns *a*, *f*, and *g* permit some mobility. How much and with what effect?

6 Try to write definitions of noun, adjective, and adverb, with reference only to the positions that each of these can take up in relation to other words. (If your definition leaves you equating *railway* and *new* because both can occur between *the* and *station*, you have not gone far enough!)

7 A good many grammatical words like *through* and *in* can be either adverbs or prepositions. How can one tell? How many

utterances can you think of in which there is a similarity of position as in 'We ran up a hill' and 'We ran up a bill'?

8 Which categories in French grammar have no relevance for English, and which categories are equally necessary in describing both English and French? (You may substitute for French any language you prefer to compare, such as German, Russian, Japanese.)

CHAPTER 13

Patterns and constructions

*I*f we could give only a partial and hesitant answer to the question 'How do we learn grammar?' we must be similarly modest in turning to the question 'What is the grammar we learn?' Quite apart from the fact that it would require several hundred pages to give anything like an adequate description of English grammar, it is no part of our purpose in this book to tackle such a task: any more than it is to offer a description of the English vocabulary (i.e. to present the reader with a dictionary). Rather, as with the vocabulary, so with the grammar, our aim is to set down and discuss some basic principles, so that the reader is in a better position to use a dictionary effectively and rewardingly — and to consult a grammar likewise.

This chapter is not the first in which we have introduced grammatical concepts, relying on the reader's knowledge of such things as *noun* and *verb*, *subject* and *object*, *tense* and *aspect*. But now we shall look at such abstractions a little more systematically, formally establishing acquaintance with the widely familiar terms for the parts of a sentence. Let us consider the following example:

> The new tenant has painted the smallest bedroom during the past week.

Obviously, from one point of view the 'parts' of the sentence are *words*; and there are twelve such parts in this sentence. Just as obviously, however, this is not a very relevant fact (unless we are constrained to a word-count in sending an international telex): some words belong together in contrast with other words. One such clustering is to divide the *subject* ('The new tenant') off from the *predicate* (the rest of the sentence). Another is to see the whole sentence as comprising grammatical *elements* — in this example a *subject*, a *verb*, an *object*, and an *adverbial:*

> The new tenant [S]
>   has painted [V]
>   the smallest bedroom [O]
>   during the past week [A].

Even without knowing such terms as *object* and *verb*, we feel that this set of word clusters makes grammatical sense where considering the sentence as comprising twelve separate words did not. This intuition is derived from our awareness, as competent speakers of the language, that we treat the clusters as *meaningful* wholes in that they *refer* as wholes to recognisable entities or actions. Moreover, it is easy to see that they are separable as *grammatical* wholes:

> *Who*   (has painted the smallest bedroom)?
>   *The new tenant.*
> *What*   (has the new tenant painted)?
>   *The smallest bedroom.*
> *When* (has the new tenant painted the smallest bedroom)?
>   *During the past week.*

Note also our ability to focus upon the *who/what/when* units with the *cleft-sentence* construction:

> It is *the new tenant* that has painted . . .
> It is *the smallest bedroom* that the new tenant . . .
> It is *during the past week* that the new tenant . . .

We cannot comparably demonstrate that the V element, *has painted*, constitutes a cluster, though of course we have the negative evidence in the two words concerned being the sole residue after we have shown that the other words operate as clusters.

The groups of words functioning in this example as the elements S(ubject), V(erb), O(bject), and A(dverbial) are called *phrases*; we have *noun phrases* as S and O, a *verb phrase* as V, and a *prepositional phrase* as A. Noun phrases are so called because they have a noun as their main constituent, preceded by a *determiner*, plus optional *premodification* (typically an adjective) and followed by optional *postmodification* (for example a relative clause or prepositional phrase). Noun phrases may thus be very short or indefinitely long:

> *The tenant* has painted the smallest bedroom.
> *The new tenant* has . . .
> *The new tenant from Japan* has . . .
> *The new unmarried tenant from Japan who moved in recently* has . . .

The constituent of the noun phrase that we call the *determiner* may be one of the articles or demonstratives or possessives:

> *A* new tenant . . .
> *That* new tenant . . .
> *Our* new tenant . . .
> *Mary's* new tenant . . .

With plural nouns and uncountable nouns, the determiner may be 'zero'; contrast:

> *New tenants* have rented the rooms upstairs.
> *Butter* is becoming very expensive.

It may seem as though this last subject is not a noun phrase at all but simply the noun *butter*, but we must insist that it is not mere pedantry to insist that even this subject is indeed a noun phrase. The very real meaning of the silent 'zero' determiner can be seen by extending the example:

> A: *'Butter* is becoming very expensive.'
> B: 'Well, certainly *this saltless butter* seems expensive.'

B's response makes it clear that the subject of A's sentence was rightly understood to mean *all* butter, butter in general; B agrees only to the extent of a subset of all butter, '*this saltless* butter'.

Prepositional phrases have a structure that requires little explication: they consist of a *preposition* (such as *in, from, for, at, with*) and a noun phrase, this latter having the same structure and potentiality for expansion as any other noun phrase.

Meanings and the verb phrase

The verb phrase is concerned to express various things about a verb — things such as *tense* and *modality* and *voice*. In our example about the new tenant, the verb phrase concerns the verb *paint;* but before a verb can function in a verb phrase, it has to express more than just its lexical meaning, and *tense* is the minimum:

The tenant *painted* the bedroom.

As with *butter* as a subject, we must see this not as just the one word *painted* but as *paint* + 'past'; so too with:

Tenants always *paint* rooms before they settle in.

This is *paint* + 'present', since the V element here just as clearly distinguishes present from past as *painted* distinguishes past from present. But of course the verb phrase is often an actual string of words:

The tenant *has painted* the bedroom.
    . . . *has been painting* . . .
    . . . *had painted* . . .
    . . . *is painting* . . .
    . . . *will paint* . . .
    . . . *may have painted* . . .
    . . . *must have been painting* . . .

These examples illustrate differences of tense, aspect, and modality, but all of them in the *active* voice. Because our model sentence has an object, the *transitive* verb phrase could be made *passive* with the object turned into the subject:

The bedroom *has been painted* by the new tenant.
    . . . *is being painted* . . .
    . . . *will be painted* . . .
    . . . *must have been painted* . . .

As these illustrate, the passive voice can show the same range of tense, aspect, and modal distinctions as the active. These differences are complex and subtle, but if we extend the model sentence with a range of different adverbials, we can help to pinpoint the shifts of meaning that can be expressed:

Tense   Future: She tells me that she *will paint* the room *tomorrow.*
            Present: She *is painting* the room *at this moment.*
            Past: She *painted* the room *last week.*

Pluperfect: She *had painted* the room *before her husband arrived.*

Aspect   Habitual: She *always paints* with a special kind of brush.

Progressive: She *is painting* the room *at this moment.*

Perfect: She *has painted* the room *very recently.*

Modality   Possibility: She *may paint* the room *perhaps.*

Permission: I told her that *she may paint* the room *if she wishes.*

Obligation: She *should paint* the room *because it looks so gloomy.*

Necessity: I told her that *she must paint* the room *because she had promised.*

There are several other modal verbs (*could, would, might,* for example) and other modal meanings (volition and ability, for example). We notice that the future is often tinged with modal meaning such as intention or volition, as in:

He says *he will pay* promptly.

A purer expression of future can be achieved by using *be going to* or by combining *will* with the progressive:

She *is going to paint* the room tomorrow.
She *will be painting* the room tomorrow.

Modal meanings often depend on context (such as the presence of a particular adverbial) and sometimes vary according to the *person* of the subject. Thus with the first person, *may* usually connotes possibility, but with the second person it more usually connotes permission:

I *may see* the director after the meeting.
You *may see* the director after the meeting.

Meanings and the noun phrase

Turning to meaning distinctions carried by the noun phrase, we should mention that between *specific* and *generic* meaning. Consider the following sentences:

He's chasing *pigeons* from his fruit trees.
Penguins live in the Antarctic.

In the former, reference is made to some specific pigeons that are, on a specific occasion, gobbling the subject's fruit. In the latter, reference is made to the habitual whereabouts of the genus of birds called penguins. The zero determiner (together with the tense form of *live*) steers us away from thinking that the speaker has some particular penguins in mind. Contrast:

Some penguins were being fed when we visited the zoo.

Generic meaning is often accompanied by the definite article, so that the following is superficially ambiguous:

My sister is studying *the elephant*.

Either she is writing a book about elephants (generic), or she is looking intently at a particular elephant (specific), perhaps one performing in a circus.

Another important distinction in the noun phrase is that between *restrictive* and *non-restrictive* modification:

He was wearing *a red tie*.
He was wearing *the tie that his daughter had given him*.
Mary is visiting *her elderly parents*.
Mary is visiting *her parents who live in Wales*.

In the first two sentences, the modification is restrictive: a red tie (not a brown or blue one), the particular tie which he had received as a present from his daughter. In the second pair of sentences, the modification is non-restrictive; Mary has only one set of parents, so neither 'elderly' nor 'who live in Wales' serves to distinguish them.

The roles of sentence elements

Such meaning distinctions in the noun phrase must in turn be distinguished from the meanings carried by noun phrases in respect of their roles as sentence elements such as subject and object. But before we look at the meanings of such roles, there are more sentence elements that should be mentioned and illustrated. One is the *complement*, which, as the term suggests, fills out our knowledge of some other element. For example:

My sister is *a student.*
My sister is *highly intelligent.*

Here the complement (C) tells us more about the subject (S), and as we note from these examples, a C may be realised by a noun phrase or by an adjective phrase. A complement may also fill out our knowledge of an object (O):

They made James (O) *their new president* (C).
The acid turned the paper (O) *quite red* (C).

There are very few verbs like *make* and *turn* which enable us to express an object complement, but there are several which admit two objects. Where there is only one object, it is almost always the *direct object*; but where there are two, the other is the *indirect object*. Compare:

She bought *a beautiful scarf.*
She bought *her brother* a beautiful scarf.

Where a sentence has an object, the *role* of subject is usually *agentive*, in other words, the subject 'does something' — for example, buys a scarf. The direct object by contrast has the role of merely being *affected*, while the indirect object can be called the *recipient* or *beneficiary*, naturally enough when one considers paraphrases:

She bought *her brother* a beautiful scarf.
~ She bought a beautiful scarf *for* her brother.
Miss Yamamoto was teaching *the children* English.
~ The children were learning English *from* Miss Yamamoto.
They sent *the neighbours* an invitation.
~ They sent an invitation *to* the neighbours.

The subject can also have an agentive role where the verb is *intransitive* (i.e. does not take any object):

Steffi trained vigorously for months.

But subjects may also be *affected* or *recipient*; for example, when they are functioning with passive verb phrases:

The room was painted by the new tenant. (affected)
The neighbours were sent an invitation. (recipient)

And there are many other sentences in which the subject is equally in no way agentive:

I had a cold.
Their daughter owned a large car.
The monument stands in the market square.
That jar contains coffee.
It's awfully cold in here.

Nor are direct objects always affected; contrast:

I destroyed *the letter*.
I typed *the letter*.

In the latter case, it is more reasonable to regard the object as *resultant* than affected.

Finally in the matter of roles, we should consider the adverbial (A) element. This is used to express a wide range of meanings within a sentence. For example, it can say *where* something happened, *when* it happened, *how* it happened, *why* it happened, and even assess the *truth* of whether it happened or not. To illustrate each of these in turn:

He parked his car *near the corner*.
        . . . *in the early evening*.
        . . . *carefully*.
        . . . *to do some shopping*.
        . . . *no doubt*.

Since none of these added meanings excludes in principle any of the others, the adverbial is unique among sentence elements in being permitted multiple inclusion. There can be as many A elements as the sentence requires and as our sense of style allows. For example, we could combine all of the above in one sentence:

No doubt (A1), he *carefully* (A2) parked his car   *near the corner* (A3) *in the early evening* (A4) *to do some shopping* (A5).

Grammatical economy

We shall return presently to such issues of sentence expansion, but first let us look at the converse, sentence compression. Once we have established that we are talking about *the new tenant*, we do not need to repeat this noun phrase in the next sentence; we can replace it by the relevant *personal pronoun*, 'he' or 'she':

> *The new tenant* has painted the smallest bedroom during the past week. Next *she* will be painting the bathroom.

Similarly we can replace *the smallest bedroom* by *it*:

> The new tenant has painted *the smallest bedroom* during the past week; *it* hadn't been painted for years.

There are *proforms* also for expressions of place, time, and other adverbials:

> *That* is *why* he parked *there then*.

There is one whole section of a sentence that can also be replaced by a proform; this section is called the *predication* (to be carefully distinguished from the predicate), comprising the main verb of the verb phrase plus the rest of the sentence:

> They should *release the hostages unconditionally*, but they won't *do so*.

The words *do so* here correspond to the predication *release the hostages unconditionally* (and not of course to the predicate 'should release the hostages unconditionally'). This type of compression can often be expressed by *ellipsis*, without any proform:

> She said she was *visiting her elderly parents in Wales*, and I think she is.

Here we understand after *is* the italicised portion that follows *was*.

But as well as providing an economic way of referring to what is *known*, proforms are a convenient device for referring to the unknown:

> *Who* painted the bedroom?
> *What* has the new tenant painted?
> *When/where/why* did he park his car?

The 'unknown' does not of course arise only when we are asking questions; we often need to refer to people or things we do not know or do not care to identify, and for this we have a range of *indefinite* pronouns. For example:

There is *someone* at the door.
If *anyone* calls, say I'll be back soon.
They lost *everything* in a fire.

Grammatical complexity

We have seen that a sentence comprises a Subject, a Verb, and then (according to the nature of the V element) such possible additional elements as Object, Complement, and Adverbial. In most of our illustrative sentences, the S, O, and A elements have taken the form of phrases, but in some they have had the form of units which themselves have elements such as S, V, etc. For example, the A element in:

She should paint the room *because it looks so gloomy.*

Here, in addition to the conjunction *because*, the A consists of the S *it*, the V *looks*, and the C *so gloomy*. Such sentence-like units within sentences are called *clauses,* and we now illustrate the way in which clauses can operate instead of phrases as sentence elements:

Subject: *That Mary* (S) *won* (V) *the first prize* (O) totally astonished even her greatest admirers.

Object: He discovered *that he* (S) *had left* (V) *his keys* (O) *at home* (A).

Complement: The result will be *that inflation* (S) *will rise* (V) *further* (A).

Adverbial: *If she* (S) *had taken* (V) *her car* (O), she would have been home by now.

Clauses can also function within phrases; thus in the following sentence, the object is a noun phrase, part of which (the postmodification) is a relative clause:

We are now selling *the little house which* (O) *we* (S) *bought* (V) *last year* (A).

Clauses thus operating in a *subordinate* capacity within a sentence are often abbreviated, appearing without a subject and with the verb either non-finite (that is, lacking a part showing tense contrast as in *has* or *sat*) or completely absent. For example:

Subject: *Driving* (V) *the car* (O) always relaxed him.
Object: She wants to *visit* (V) *the Far East* (O) *next year* (A).
Adverbial: He is a bright child, *though sometimes* (A) *rather lazy* (C).

But full clauses need not always be subordinate within a sentence. Discourse often involves *compound sentences* in which clauses are *coordinate:*

> Jacqueline has accepted a post in Germany *and* her present job is being advertised.
> The university term began a few days ago *but* lectures won't start till next week.

Coordination can link smaller units than clauses. We can have: coordinated subjects, as in:

> *Two cars* and *a bus* were involved in the accident.

Coordinated verbs, as in:

> The ship *pitched* and *rolled* in the heavy sea.

Coordinated objects, as in:

> The burglar stole *a camera, a clock,* and *some jewelry.*

We can also coordinate adverbials and complements, as well as parts of elements: 'a *young* and *vigorous* child', '(she) *can* and *must* finish (the poem)'. Predications may also be coordinated, as in:

> I shall either *wash the car* or *do some gardening.*

Another way of treating two or more units as on an equal grammatical footing is by *apposition,* but whereas coordination is for units with different reference, apposition is a way of expressing the same reference in different terms. The terms may be merely juxtaposed as in:

> Let me introduce *Martia, my sister-in-law.*

Or the alternative formulation may be indicated by such devices as *or (rather), that is, better,* and *namely:*

> He *muttered* or (rather) *mumbled* something about it.
> They were *disrupting the meeting* — *heckling the speaker,* that is.

Items in apposition may be in immediate sequence or be separated by whole clause elements as in:

The idea struck him as totally absurd *that she should abandon her career so suddenly.*

In place of a clause as subject, we may similarly evoke apposition, using a 'dummy subject', *it*, with the clause it stands for postponed to the end of the sentence:

That he was wrong became obvious.
~ *It* became obvious *that he was wrong.*
To read in such poor light would damage your eyes.
~ *It* would damage your eyes *to read in such poor light.*

In casual spoken English, other pronouns than *it* enable us similarly to postpone the full subject:

She's doing well, *that new sales director.*

Focusing information

All these examples involving separation show apposition being used to displace part of a sentence, or better, to place part of a sentence where it can have greatest communicative impact. This is at the *end* of a clause or sentence, and apposition is by no means the only way we have of achieving it. If we are talking about the sale of a car, there are several potential points on which we might wish to focus: what was sold, who sold it, who bought it, what the price was, when the sale took place, and so on. For example (where *Oi* = 'indirect object' and *Od* = 'direct object'):

A French doctor (S) sold (V) my brother (Oi) an excellent little car (Od) at a bargain price (A1) only a few weeks ago (A2).

Thus arranged, the sentence reaches its climax with A2: when the sale took place. If we wished to focus instead on the bargain price, we could move A2 to initial position, thus ending the sentence with A1:

Only a few weeks ago, a French doctor sold my brother an excellent little car at a bargain price.

Alternatively, we could achieve the same climax by a rewording which ignored some of the original constituents:

My brother bought an excellent little car at a bargain price.

If we wished to highlight the seller, we could move this constituent to final position by using the passive or again by rewording:

My brother bought an excellent little car from a French doctor.
My brother was sold an excellent little car by a French doctor.

Yet a further device for focusing upon a particular constituent is the '*wh*-cleft' construction, where an interrogative word at the beginning acts as a dummy element which alerts the listener or reader to await the answer to whatever the question-word is asking:

What my brother bought from a French doctor was *an excellent little car*.

We cannot use *who* in *wh*-clefts, but where the constituent concerned has human reference, we can analogously anticipate it with a rather 'empty' noun phrase:

The person that sold my brother an excellent little car was *a French doctor*.
The person that bought a car from a French doctor was *my brother*.

The item on which we want to focus in a sentence (and which we thus wish to place at a final climactic point) is obviously the one we regard as most important in the communication, and — just as obviously — this will usually be the one that we expect to be 'news' for our hearer or reader. We therefore tend to construct our sentences so as to move in linear order from the most known to the most unknown, from the 'given' to the 'new':

I've just been talking to *a French doctor*. He tried to sell me *an excellent little car*, and he's willing to sell it *at a bargain price*. A person who may be interested is *my brother*.

One way of introducing news is the *existential sentence* which uses a dummy subject, *there*, followed usually by a form of the verb *be*, and with the substantial item thus in final position:

There's been *a terrible accident*.

This item can then become the 'given', expressed by a pronoun, in a subsequent sentence. For example (continuing to italicise the most salient items):

It happened *near Watford,* when a fuel tanker struck *a coachload of school children.*

Contrast what most would agree is a less effective order:

. . . when a coachload of school children was struck by *a fuel tanker.*

Existential sentences usually involve the verb *be,* as in 'There are two goldfish in that little pool', but certain other verbs of generally 'presentative' meaning are also used:

There came into the room *a strikingly handsome officer.*
There stands near here *a monument to Franklin Roosevelt.*

These have a rather stiff and formal tone, however; and where we want to have these italicised items in final position, it would actually be somewhat more usual to depart from the normal SVA sentence order of English and invert it as AVS:

Into the room (A) came (V) *a strikingly handsome officer* (S).
Near here (A) stands (V) *a monument to Franklin Roosevelt* (S).

Focusing by suppression

Ellipsis and other means of compression also help us to direct attention to the most salient points of discourse, by suppressing items that the context or the conventions of grammar will make reasonably obvious:

Although very frightened, Gloria alone helped the children to safety.
If possible, read this by tomorrow.

In the former, we understand 'Although *she was* very frightened', inferring the subject and tense from the following clause, and inferring the verb *be* from the structure of the *although* clause itself. In the latter sentence however, we understand 'If *it is* possible', inferring with equal confidence the same verb but a different subject and tense.

Informal speech and writing are full of similar short cuts to the main point. 'Another tough day', we note in a diary or groan to a colleague as we leave work ('*It has been* . . .'); 'Another tough day', we warn a colleague in the morning as we arrive ('*This will be* . . .'). 'Feeling better?', we ask a friend who has been off ill. 'How about Garry's?', we may respond on being asked 'Where shall we have lunch today?', meaning something like 'I suggest Garry's Restaurant, if that would suit you', but where the highly compressed formula 'How about Garry's?' reminds us of the extent to which we are able to take linguistic liberties when we are confident that our hearer will understand — and is ready to cooperate in working out our meaning.

Even so brief a synopsis of English grammar as we have presented in this chapter is enough to show the complexity and flexibility of the grammatical devices at our command. Most of this 'command' seems to be acquired naturally, without much effort, if we are native speakers of English. But exploiting the language's grammatical resources to the full requires constant conscious effort if we are to say (or write) all that we want to express in the clearest and most pleasing manner.

SOME FOLLOW-UP WORK

1 A noun phrase may express the same meaning with postmodification or premodification, thus 'an essay to be written during the vacation' may be expressed as 'a vacation essay'. Attempt to rewrite the following noun phrases, replacing the premodification by postmodification, and in each case comment on the advantages or disadvantages in the two versions:
   a) the dark, slimly built, squash-playing chemistry student
   b) a robotic manufacturing system replacement programme
   c) some five per cent redeemable debenture stock
   d) two very seriously cerebral palsied children

2 The meaning of 'You may go' can be expressed in the rough paraphrase 'You are permitted to go'. Explain by similar means what is conveyed by the verb phrases in the following:
   a) I *must tell* you about it.
   b) She *must be* the new sales manager.

c) I *may have caught* a cold.
d) I asked but he *wouldn't tell* me.
e) They *couldn't have fixed* the car without his help.
f) You *ought to read* her latest book.
g) He *wouldn't have got beaten* if he had trained properly.

3 Explain the difference in grammar between the following pairs:
 a) What did you bring the parcel in?
    Why did you bring the parcel in?
 b) He is going to America.
    He is going to visit America.
 c) Are you going to be using the word-processor?
    Are you going to be long using the word-processor?

4 The following was spoken in a broadcast so as to leave two possible interpretations:

   Australians say Fosters are connoisseurs of beer.

 Give the two grammatical analyses and attempt to explain how the broadcaster might have delivered the sentence so as to convey either meaning unambiguously.

5 'The students assembled in the lecture room.' Make a list of other verbs which require a plural subject. Are there verbs whose subject must be singular?

6 a) She made the young man some fresh coffee.
 b) She made the young man a better writer.
 c) She made the young man an excellent wife.
 Show the grammatical difference between (a), (b), and (c) by labelling the elements that follow *made* in each case; then list some further verbs that can take similar constituents to those in (a) and (b).

7 a) In 'To err is human', we understand a general subject for the infinitive clause that would correspond to a full clause like 'That *people* should err (is human)'. Explain the missing elements in the following so as to show their differing grammatical structure:

   Veronica is easy to please.
   Veronica is eager to please.

b) The following sentence has three possible interpretations (each matching a different grammatical structure); provide a plausible context for each interpretation together with a description of the grammar:
   It is too hot to eat.

8 We noted that several A (adverbial) elements could co-occur in a sentence; we also have considerable freedom in positioning them. Write some sentences, in each using more than one of the following, experimenting with alternative positions, and commenting on the resulting differences:

   carefully, that afternoon, naturally, to London, finally, in great indignation, during the evening, if necessary, whenever you wish, utterly, through the woods, then.

9 a) He refused to say how much, when, or even whether the staff would receive.
   b) She has produced a book which has not and could not achieve the distinction of her earlier work.
   c) The young woman departed in anger and a beautiful fur coat.
   Noting that there is something wrong in each of (a), (b), and (c), write on *coordination*, attempting to specify the necessary conditions.

C H A P T E R   1 4

Style and purpose

When we consider some of the purposes of communication, and some of the styles used to achieve those purposes, we may be tempted to doubt what was said at the end of the last chapter: that our grammatical resources enable us to express ourselves 'in the clearest and most pleasing manner'. Let us consider the following, all recent and all written by highly educated people:

a) Within the Litopterna, the affinities of the Colombian species clearly lie within the Proterotheriidae. Macrauchenioid (Macraucheniidae and Adianthidae) specializations of the dentition (including a strongly-developed M^3 hypocone; columnar metaconid and entoconid on the lower molars) are lacking. Conversely, numerous proterothere synapomorphies are present: P^3 molarized, with subequal and widely spaced paracone and metacone; P_3 molarized, with crescentic talonid loph; protocone and hypocone of upper molars strongly joined by lingual crest (Cifelli, 1983a), and upper molar metaconule detached from adjacent cusps. Further evidence for proterothere affinities lies in the skeleton. The astragalus is distinctly specialized over the protolipternid condition, with complete reduction of the fibular shelf, hyperdevelopment of the inferior face of the tibial trochlea, deepening and reorienting of the ectal facet, and modification of the head into a more cylindrical shape.

b) The dianion derived from the keto ester (3) was alkylated in tetrahydrofuran (THF) at −60°C by the slow addition of the t-butyldimethyisilyl ether of 3-iodopropanol (1 equiv.). The esters (4) were isolated as a mixture of diastereoisomers in 75% yield: these isomers and subsequent isomers were not separated since they were eventually converted into one racemate in the radical cyclisation step. Treatment of the esters (4) with sodium hydride in toluene followed by the dropwise addition of 1.3-dibromo-2-methylprop-2-ene gave an alkylated product which was converted into the ketones (5) by treatment with lithium iodide in lutidine [88% from (3)]. Protodesilylation of (5) with aqueous HF in acetonitrile followed by pyridinium chlorochromate (PCC) oxidation in dichloromethane gave the aldehyde (6) in 64% yield for the two steps.

c) While both types of charge can be attacked as fraudulent preferences under section 239 of the Insolvency Act 1986 (if liquidation occurs within six months of creation of the charge), floating charges can also be attacked under section 245 of the Insolvency Act 1986 if liquidation occurs within 12 months of the creation of the charge, unless it is proved that the company immediately after the creation of the charge was solvent, and except as regards any cash paid or goods or services supplied to the company at the time of or subsequent to the creation of and in consideration of the charge.

Clear? Pleasing? Well, unless we are highly expert in the niceties of biology (a), or advanced chemistry (b), or jurisprudence (c), we are in no position to give a *just* answer. If we are not expert in these fields and dismiss the passages as *unclear, unpleasing*, riddled with impenetrable *jargon*, we are giving an *unjust* answer. As we saw in Chapter Four, use-related varieties of language (and use-related these passages certainly are), may be marked both for *content* and for *tone*. In (a), (b), and (c) the content is so specialised that an ordinary reader cannot understand it sufficiently to assess the tone. Moreover, our inability to understand them does not depend on obscure *grammar* so much as on obscure *vocabulary*. This is less noticeable in (c), perhaps, but an alternative legal passage might have contained such law-specific words as *estoffel* and *tort;* and indeed, even in (c), we have words like (*floating*) *charge, preference,* and *creation* used with particular technical senses, for all their apparent familiarity to us.

In any case, these passages are particularly extreme in their degree of specialised language — and they are presented here precisely for that reason. Whether clear to us or not, they clearly have a *purpose:* all are from learned journals, reporting research at the frontiers of their respective disciplines. They are not addressing the general reader; rather, biologist is looking to biologist, chemist to chemist, lawyer to lawyer, in each case assuming in the reader a background of advanced knowledge equal to that of the expert authors themselves. Even so, we the non-experts understand enough to detect a specific and different purpose in each of these passages: and this purpose is even revealed by the grammar.

In (a), the frequent uses of the definite article, along with the present tense of such verbs as *be* and *lie*, persuade us that the purpose of the passage is *generic description:* and this is confirmed by the use of the familiar word *species.* Such other words as we understand, like *the (lower) molars, the (inferior) face,* and *the head,* do not seem to be referring to particular molars, a particular face, or some specific head. And whatever an astragalus is, *the astragalus* is unlikely to be an individual one having its idiosyncrasies pointed out.

In (b), by contrast, the verbs are not merely in the past tense, they are verbs denoting actions (*isolate, separate, convert,* for example), though the actions are reported in the passive voice with the human agent unmentioned — a stylistic feature characteristic of scholarly writing, especially in the sciences. The grammar is thus consistent with the passage being a report of a particular datable experiment, and the occurrences of the definite article are to be interpreted as specific and not, as in (a), generic.

Passage (c) is different again. As in (b), the verbs denote action (*attack, prove, supply*) and are again in the passive. But they do not refer to past actions: rather to possible (*'can . . .'*) present and future actions that may be fulfilled under certain conditions. These features are consistent with the purpose of the passage being *reasoned argument.* In consequence, we should not be surprised to find the grammar of this passage considerably more complex than in (a) or (b) where despite the lengthy noun phrases, densely packed with highly technical vocabulary items, the grammar itself is very simple. Here in (c), every statement is carefully qualified by conditional clauses, and the need to specify conditions for the truth value of what is claimed is even carried into the noun-phrase structure of the concluding line or so — a structure which itself exploits the grammatical possibilities of ellipsis. Note the triple coordination within it (*'at the time of or subsequent to the creation of and in consideration of the charge'*) where we need to anticipate and understand *the charge* after the first two occurrences of the preposition *of.*

Specialised language

Biologists, chemists, and lawyers are not alone in using language that is opaque to the rest of us when they are addressing fellow experts. There are content-marked varieties of English used by nurses addressing nurses, by professional footballers addressing other professional footballers; and it is similar with varieties used among pathologists, plasterers, accountants, sculptors, brewers, and electricians. Even linguists, though engaged with a universal human faculty, can seem rather remote from ordinary language when they are addressing fellow linguists:

> d) If we grant that natural-language sentences systematically under-determine their truth-theoretic content, this being partly fixed by contextual parameters, but if further we require that some account be given of how the output strings of a grammar contribute to determining their truth-theoretic content, then we have to specify the input that they provide to this process. And this in itself is an individuation of intrinsic linguistic content for an expression which is not its reference, nor its existence, nor a truth-value. From this it follows that an articulation of truth-theoretic content for sentences modulo the contribution of contextual parameters has to assume a concept of linguistic meaning — it is that which contributes to reference and extension assignment, disambiguation, etc.

Not least noteworthy here is a preposition — a class of words both small in number and generally speaking shared by the entire speech community — that will be strange to readers inexpert in mathematics, philosophy, or linguistic theory. It is *modulo,* in the last sentence of the passage, and meaning approximately 'with respect to a particular constant'.

But biologists and lawyers, nurses and linguists are frequently obliged to discourse on their specialities to total non-specialists. They are then confronted with the problem of estimating how much simplification and explanation (by means of running definition) may be necessary in order to bridge the gap of knowledge and background between the expert and his or her addressee. A problem aggravated by the need to avoid insult through *excessive* simplification. At the beginning of Chapter One, the first example given showed a scientist in just this position explaining the work of Max Planck to non-specialists. We notice the quiet use of explanatory apposition in the sequence 'definite fixed amounts or quanta'. Compare the impression that would have been given of talking down to the reader if the apposition had been reversed, introducing the term 'quanta' *before* explaining it: 'quanta, that is, definite fixed amounts'. So too, the lawyer in Chapter Four, passage (4), is undoubtedly engaged in the precise formulation of an expert opinion, but just as undoubtedly he or she is aware of a courtroom which includes people who are not expert in law. Legal technicalities are therefore not expressed in legal language but in the ordinary language of forceful argument. Note for example the use of the '*wh*-cleft' construction, together with the *do* auxiliary, to emphasise a point:

> . . . the inspector did not . . . need to say that he was discharging . . . that duty. *What matters* is that he *does* discharge that duty . . .

We see therefore that even where the *content* remains constant (a particular specialist field), a shift in the *purpose* (from addressing fellow specialists to addressing non-specialists) triggers a shift in *style* and *tone*.

And of course it does not stop there. Even the most work-bound lawyers and nurses spend only a part (probably a small minority) of their time discoursing on specialist concerns. They have friends outside their professions, they have hobbies, and they have families. Their reading and their writing, above all their *talk*, are directed to other purposes than their work, and they master a wide range of styles to match.

General language

To some extent, an evening's television represents a microcosm of linguistic purposes and styles with which any normal adult is thoroughly familiar. As does our daily newspaper. Lawyer or nurse, plasterer or biologist, we read news items in one style where the purpose is to inform; a leading article in another, where the purpose may be to persuade; we read articles on health advice, on vacation resorts, on movements in the stock exchange; book reviews, sports reports. We take in our stride the varying styles which accompany the varying purposes of what we read from the front page to the back.

Recalling that sample (7) in Chapter Four was from a report on *golf*, let us compare some further news items on sport from the same paper over the same period of two or three weeks:

e) Ikem Billy tied up in the home straight, and the Liverpool
    student finished second to Ari Suhonen, the Finnish
    record-holder, who clocked '26 seconds I think' over the last
    200 metres to come from fifth position to overtake Billy two
    metres from the line . . . A twisted ankle in a warm-up fall
    forced Billy to miss out on his pre-race preparation. There
    were no signs of problems, however, as he led from the
    break. He took the bell at 53.97 sec and held off Doyle down
    the back straight. A sprint at 200 metres gave him what
    should have been a comfortable two-metre cushion, but 50
    metres from home his head began to roll.

Let us begin by noting the use of apposition here. Just as in the passage about Max Planck the writer quietly equates 'definite fixed amounts' with 'quanta', so here we are quietly reminded (or a reader unfamiliar with athletics is quietly told) that Ari Suhonen is the Finnish record-holder. Rather more indirectly, though plainly enough for anyone familiar with this type of reporting, we are 'reminded' that Ikem Billy is a student from Liverpool — though strictly from a grammatical point of view the subjects of the two coordinate clauses in the first sentence could refer to different persons. We shall come back to other features of style in (e), but for the present let us just note the *resultative* infinitive clauses 'to come from fifth position to overtake Billy two metres from the line'. It is of course possible (again from a strictly grammatical viewpoint) to read these as *purpose* clauses: Suhonen 'clocked' a fast speed *in order to* come from fifth position, and did so *in order to* overtake Billy two metres from the finishing line. But our familiarity with such *to*-clauses in journalism prompts us to read them here as 'and *as a result* came from fifth position and *as a result* overtook Billy'. This is not a grammatical formula found only in sports reporting; in a stock-market report we might read that 'the Dow Jones index fell by 17 points to close at 2735', where it would be absurd to think that the index fell *in order to* close at this figure.

Now let us look at some reporting of cricket:

f) Stewart's innings, full of maturity and fine judgement,
    guided the visitors to the respectable total of 225 for 8 before

bad light ended play 28 overs early. His class shone through the gloom after Darren Bicknell and Grahame Clinton had both fallen leg before while seeking to get off the mark, the latter succumbing to John Lever without offering a stroke.

Stewart bided his time and waited for the bad ball before dispatching it to the boundary. His first 50, off 94 deliveries, contained 11 fours and his 19th, a pull off the front foot off Don Topley, took him into three figures 97 balls later.

Not everything found the middle of Stewart's bat, however, especially early on when both Neil Foster and Lever found enough movement in overcast conditions to keep the predatory cordon of slips on their toes.

Stewart eventually perished when he was caught behind attempting to square-cut the medium-paced Mark Waugh, but not before he had gathered two more boundaries.

Only Monte Lynch batted with an assurance remotely approaching Stewart's. He scored an elegant 40, half of them in boundaries, before he was caught sweeping at John Childs after sharing in a stand of 93 in 29 overs. That was just reward for the left-arm spinner whose admirable line and length had even kept Stewart in check.

Apposition again, we note. The player called 'the left-arm spinner' in the final sentence has already been named (John Childs) in the preceding one. And a similar effect to apposition is created by what we called in Chapter Thirteen non-restrictive modification. 'The medium-paced Mark Waugh' is not being distinguished from another Mark Waugh: rather, the writer is merely noting that Waugh is a medium-paced bowler — without insulting the cricket-fan reader who knows this already. 'The visitors' is also appositive, referring to the Surrey team, named earlier in the report, but here reminding readers that the Essex team were playing on their home ground. Another reason for such apposition is of course what is often called 'elegant variation' — a feature of all styles, not just of sports news — which avoids repetition of the same name for the same referent. Note again the mention of John Childs in one sentence as 'the left-arm spinner' in the next.

We turn now to a third sport, soccer, with a report on a game between Millwall and Wimbledon played on the Wimbledon ground (note 'The visitors' in the second paragraph):

g) The Lions of Millwall clawed their way to the top of the League last night with an 85th-minute equaliser from Tony

Cascarino after Wimbledon had recovered from Eric Young's sending-off to lead through a second-half strike from Alan Cork.

The visitors were subjected to a withering opening bombardment, after eight minutes of which Wimbledon took the lead with a typical mortar bomb of a goal.

Young and Cascarino, jostling for position in the penalty area, were both cautioned before Dennis Wise was able to take a free-kick from which Carlton Fairweather opened the scoring. Brian Horne was clearly at fault, failing to prevent Wise's cross from reaching Fairweather at the far post, but then made partial amends with two impressive saves.

Wimbledon found themselves at a numerical disadvantage after 26 minutes when Young was dismissed for pulling back Teddy Sheringham as the striker accelerated past him.

It took Millwall just 15 minutes to exploit their opponents' disarray and Wimbledon were powerless to prevent David Thompson's long throw from reaching Steve Anthrobus, who scored his first League goal from close range.

The Lions went for the jugular but lack of intestinal fortitude is not among Wimbledon's shortcomings, and the Dons' response was to step heavily on the gas. They were rewarded 10 minutes into the second half when Cork fastened on to a pass from Wise and drew Horne before lifting his shot over the advancing keeper.

Informal tropes

We see more apposition, of course, both in its role of tactfully and unobtrusively supplying information and in its role too of 'elegant variation'. There is a striking example of a different type of elegant variation in the phrase *intestinal fortitude* in the last paragraph: at first sight a strange expression to find in a popular sports report. But the reader, in being forced to 'translate', quickly realises that the writer means *guts*, but has paraphrased this expression (regarded by many as coarse and slangy) and in consequence given the reader some mild amusement.

This point should cause us to reflect on the greater complexity of *purpose* in a sports report (and in most other general use of language) than in the highly specialised texts with which this chapter began — passages (a), (b), and (c). The purpose of (e), (f), and (g) is not only to report events but to entertain and please. Figures of speech more usually thought of as characterising poetry play a prominent part in these reports: particularly *metaphor* and *metonymy*. The latter 'changing the name' device we have already seen with reference to apposition, but there are more studied examples, where a characteristic *sign* of the whole is mentioned instead of directly referring to the whole as such. Thus in (e), the runner 'took the bell' means that he *began the last lap*, with a reference to the conventional bell signal in a multi-lap race. In (f), we are told that 'Not everything found the middle of Stewart's bat', a reference to the match of ball and bat in an ideal stroke and a convoluted way of saying that 'Stewart's batting was not always excellent'.

As to metaphor, this veritably permeates (e), (f), and (g). A lead of two metres is called 'a comfortable . . . cushion' in (e). In (f), the high quality of one player 'shone through the gloom'; the writer speaks of a batsman *dispatching* a ball to the boundary, a metaphor of commerce that seems to be sustained in the use of *deliveries* in the next sentence. The metaphors frequently involve *hyperbole*, such exaggeration seeming to help induce an atmosphere of excitement; in (g), 'the *Lions* . . . *clawed* their way to the top'. Metaphors relating to war and military manoeuvres keep recurring: in (f), players in the slips form a 'predatory cordon', and in (g), there is 'a withering . . . bombardment' including a 'mortar bomb of a goal'. Expressions literal in one sport are introduced metaphorically in discussing another. Thus in (f), 'off the mark' from athletics racing is applied to beginning to win runs in cricket, and in (g), stepping 'on the gas' is from car-racing, going 'for the jugular' is from bloodsports that reach back to the gladiators. There is a further striking example on the same page as that on which (g) appeared:

> Bristol City, who gave the holders Nottingham Forest *a fight* in the semi-finals last year, were *knocked out in the first round* after losing a 2–0 lead at Reading.

The parts we have italicised might puzzle a stranger into thinking that the subject was boxing, not football.

But although, as we have seen, the language of exciting reportage ranges widely in its allusions, these are combined with terms that are highly specialised. In (e), it is the specific context of racing that conditions the use of such expressions as 'the home straight', 'the line', 'the break', and 'the bell'. In (f), there are cricket terms that are equally specialised: for example 'innings', 'leg before' (the ellipsis of *wicket* here shows the writer's complimentary confidence in the reader), 'movement' (referring to the condition of the pitch), 'square-cut'. Similarly with football in (g): 'the League', 'equaliser', 'sending-off', 'penalty area', 'free-kick', 'cross', 'saves', not to mention the implied importance of the time in a match with reference to its total duration: 'an *85th-minute* equaliser'.

It is only to be expected that the jargon of a particular speciality should enter discourse concerned with that speciality, but the important lesson to learn from (e), (f), and (g) is the amount of general-purpose language and figures of rhetoric that occur over and above the specialist language. In other words, a particular purpose has an impact upon the style adopted but by no means necessarily dictates it. Nor are the styles used in any particular field of discourse self-contained: they cross-fertilise with references, both overt and covert, to other fields; above all they reflect the fact that there *is* a general-purpose style that is neutral to any specific purpose.

Taking care

But the features of lively style are by no means always pleasing. We have to be on our guard against using clichés and 'tired' or inappropriate metaphors. In (f), the writer speaks of a cricketer having 'gathered two more boundaries'. This is some sort of metonymy for 'scoring two more fours (or sixes)', but its vehicle is an implausible metaphor, since in the ordinary meanings of the words we cannot easily think of boundaries as things we *gather* (as distinct from 'approaching' or 'crossing').

We should in fact always be alert to defects in the style of others, as well, of course, as thinking carefully about our own, ready to justify any feature we adopt. In passage (b), we read that a product 'was converted into the ketones by treatment with lithium iodide'. This telescopes two processes and puts them out of chronological order, and a simpler report of the experiment might have read:

I/we treated the product with lithium iodide and so converted
it into the ketones.

The version in (b) has *nominalised* this first clause into 'treatment
with lithium iodide' and has made the second clause passive (the
product 'was converted'), omitting mention of the agent 'I/we'.
Scientists and others prefer to write in this way (and may be
editorially instructed to do so) precisely in order to depersonalise
the report. From the scientific viewpoint, it matters less who did
the work than what was done, and the order in (b) (what was
done, and how: 'by treatment . . .') achieves this admirably.

But when such dry reportage is overdone, or the style is transferred to contexts where it is less justified, we may reasonably
object. Certainly, passives and nominalisations do not make prose
easier to understand. Consider the following piece from a hire-
purchase agreement:

> Notwithstanding the termination of the hiring under Clause 6 all
> payments due must be made in respect of the hiring up to date
> of such termination.

In a less legalistic mode of discourse between *us* (the owner) and
you (the hirer), this might have been expressed as:

> Although you can terminate the hiring under Clause 6, you
> must pay all the rental costs up to the date when you actually
> terminate it.

We may sympathise with the hiring firm which has felt obliged
to engage a lawyer to ensure that a wording is adopted that will
stand up in court against a defaulter. But we can sympathise at
least as much with the unfortunate customers who are obliged to
sign an agreement they cannot fully understand. Official en-
couragement is now given in many countries to frame such agree-
ments in language that is as ordinary as possible: in 'plain
English'. In other words, though no one minds how specialists
address other specialists in their own fields, when people speak
across the frontiers between disciplines or between employer and
employed, seller and buyer, government and citizen, they have
the duty to express themselves in a broadly neutral style that their
addressees will have the best chance of understanding.

Nor are stylistic choices to be related only to understanding at the intellectual level: there is *personal* understanding as well. When we speak or write, it is our duty to express ourselves both with a sense of what is appropriate for the purpose and in such a way as to anticipate the difficulties and personal feelings of our addressees. We do not greet a friend's impending marriage in tones of grave gloom:

As you approach this solemn step into matrimony, you have my deepest and most sincere wishes for the future.

But equally, we are not flippant in the presence of death:

It really knocked me when I heard that your old man had snuffed it.

If we have to communicate something technical and obscure, we may reassure our addressee by apology for the tough language — even blaming ourselves for not being able to express things more clearly:

A pilot's intentions can be notified either by what is called *booking-out* (this is where, if I may just explain, he needn't or doesn't want to receive air traffic service) or by a *flight plan* (which would at once entail informing all air traffic service units on the route concerned). I hope I've managed to make these two alternatives clear, but I should have added that the choice is not just a matter of the pilot's preference. For certain journeys a flight plan is mandatory — obligatory, that is; and for others it is highly advisable in any case: flights over the sea, for example, or over mountains and other thinly populated areas.

The initial information here — the distinction between merely *booking-out* and submitting a *flight plan*, and the conditions governing the choice — could have been expressed much more briefly. But the writer has expanded the text with informal warnings about technical terms ('what is called') and implied apology ('I hope I've managed') to give the reader both time and confidence to grasp the communication.

The price of these gains has not, however, been only increased length: it includes what many would object to as the undue intrusion of 'I', the writer. The result is the obverse of the 'scientific' style discussed earlier, where the passive avoids the need for 'I'. It is a good rule that we learn as children (for example, in writing letters) 'to think more of *you* than *I*'; and too much egocentricity in language is as bad as too much impersonal dryness.

Objectivity?

Another valid reason for disliking too much 'I' in speech or writing is that it smacks of subjectivity: a matter of one person's personal view; surely what we should be aiming at is rather an objective presentation? Well, of course, much depends again on the purpose we have on a particular occasion. But in any case, we deceive ourselves if we think that a communication can always be put in totally objective terms.

Not long ago, it was reported that a man was sent to prison for hurting a dog. That account sounds objective enough, though even this cannot fail to imply deliberate cruelty: the verb *hurt* entails an active agent and without interposing some such adverb as 'accidentally' we tend to imply that the act was voluntary: conscious and deliberate. But now let us note the different interpretations that were put on the episode, all doubtless in good faith and in pursuit of objective truth.

In one account of the case, written by someone who obviously thought the sentence harsh, the man was described as 'an elderly gentleman' who was 'reading his Sunday newspaper in the park' when 'a dog jumped upon him and upset him'. In the shock and confusion, the elderly gentleman 'kicked at the animal'.

Here we have a selection of words which reveal the writer's sympathies and which — unless we are careful to note that this is what they are doing — are liable to condition ours. An elderly gentleman cannot easily be thought of as nasty, whereas the words 'old man' are quite often preceded by 'nasty'. But we may readily grant that there are no 'lies' here: most men in advancing years can be described as 'elderly gentlemen', and the writer might well protest that it was a 'fact' — he *was* an elderly gentleman: and he *was* reading his Sunday newspaper; this, too, is a 'fact', though of course it is a fact that is more likely to be noticed if one wants to emphasise the inoffensive, peaceful behaviour of the defendant. A dog disrupts the serenity by jumping upon him and upsetting him, and all he does is not to *kick it* but to *kick at it:* another illustration of the dependence of fact upon viewpoint. From one point of view an idly swinging foot may *kick* something; from another, it may simply *knock* it. From one point of view, if you kick at something, you are making a kicking motion without commitment to the intention of actually kicking; from another, if something is struck by the foot, it is kicked, whatever the intention.

In another account of the same episode, things are put very differently. The dog has become a 'lively puppy', and the elderly gentleman is coolly referred to as 'a man', because it now appears that he did not merely kick *at* the lively puppy: he 'stamped on it' and showed no 'feeling for our dumb friends'. Language can scarcely be more slanted than that! Having made it virtually certain that animal-lovers (or at any rate those animal-lovers who do not read very critically) are already won over to his view, the writer now daringly seeks to widen his appeal with a peroration in which he says how serious a crime is cruelty of any kind, but especially 'cruelty to animals *or children*'.

If an emotive slant can be given to language even when we are striving to be objective, it is easy to understand what can happen in advertising or political rhetoric where objectivity is low among the author's priorities. And we must not forget that the writers of persuasive language do not forget the powerful association of science with the very objectivity they are patently ignoring.

'Scientific experiments have proved that our product makes your clothes whiter.' This is intended to give the impression that 'our product' is the most efficient on the market, and that in fact 'science' has proved it so. But of course this is not actually claimed in the text, and when we study advertisements of this kind carefully, we see that very little indeed is ever 'actually claimed'. The words 'scientific experiments have proved' certainly seem a strong opening, but a moment's reflection is enough to give us doubts. Are they not rather vague? What were the experiments? Who performed them? Under what conditions? Even in a world where 'science' is a magic word, the layman must still venture to ask questions like these. But what in any case are the experiments said to have proved? That 'our product' makes clothes 'whiter'. Makes them whiter than *what*, we must ask. Whiter than when they are washed under absolutely identical conditions using every other relevant product on the market? Or merely whiter than when they are washed in cold water without soap? Or perhaps, indeed, just whiter than they were before they were washed! The advertiser is wisely content to avoid such details, and we too may be content enough, provided that we realise that this is the deliberately vague language of persuasion and that we need not be awed by the gesture of science.

SOME FOLLOW-UP WORK

1 Study some cooking recipes and then (a) write a description of the salient features in their style, and (b) assess the extent to which the style is suited to the purpose.

2 Passages (a), (b), and (c) were described as 'extreme' in their language. The ceremonial English in contemporary royal charters is 'extreme' in a different way. Examine the following (which dates from 1980) and give an account of the linguistic features that strike you as special:

> Elizabeth the Second
> by the Grace of God . . . Queen, head of the Commonwealth,
> Defender of all the Faith:
> TO ALL WHOM THESE PRESENTS SHALL COME, GREETING!
> WHEREAS an humble Petition has been presented to Us . . .
> praying that We should be graciously pleased to grant a
> Charter to King's College London . . .
> NOW THEREFORE KNOW YE that We by virtue of Our
> Prerogative Royal . . . do . . . will and ordain as follows:
>   [19 numbered clauses)
> WITNESS Ourself at Westminster the 28th day of January
> in the twenty-seventh year of our Reign.
> BY WARRANT UNDER THE QUEEN'S SIGN MANUAL

3 Critical commentary on the creative arts often has an unwelcome preciosity. Study the following excerpt on music and explain what you may find objectionable:

> Mostly quiet, more or less tonal, metrically diverse and faintly
> enigmatic, it suggested an exercise in elegant classical
> calligraphy, inscribing as it were its runes in grey ink upon an
> ivory parchment.

4 Assume you have been given the task of rewording the

following public warning so as to make it more speedily understood:

> Lack of adequate ventilation and/or leakage of combustion products into the work space may give rise to carbon monoxide poisoning. In the event affected personnel should be evacuated from the area, the gas supply shut off, the local Region of British Gas plc informed and medical advice sought.

5 Collect the headlines from two or three days' issues of a newspaper. Describe the characteristics of the language; are there significant differences in style between the headlines of news pages and those of the arts section?

6 Marghanita Laski once wrote an article with the title 'Cheap Clothes for Fat Old Women'. From an examination of fashion advertisements in current magazines, write on words that seem to be favoured — and on words that seem to be avoided.

7 a) 'Is there one person among us who does not deplore the cruelty of blood sports?'
This is a 'rhetorical question'. Discuss the role of such items in discourse, explain their effect, and characterise the styles in which the rhetorical question tends to be prominent.

b) Write a frankly partisan argument for or against blood sports (or nationalism or private education or some other topic of your choice). Then, in a contrite fashion, confess the ways in which you have been unfair to 'the other side'.

8 Collect from newspapers or other material:
a) instances of language used with careless woolliness and suggest ways of improving them;
b) instances (for example of advertisements) that seem deliberately vague or misleading, and write an exposure of them.

9 A newspaper proprietor once said that 'interpretation *is* fact, and fact without interpretation is not fact at all'. Explain this view and give arguments both for and against it.

10 'Janet felt well,' 'Janet seemed well.' These differ in that the

first claims to report Janet herself while the second gives only the speaker's impression. Examine some English verbs which differ in similar ways as to the source of authority for what is said.

11 'After his car had crashed into a wall, the driver told police: "I was listening to some taped music and the car went out of control."'
Is he blaming the car? the music? Consider reports of this kind and assess the way responsibility can be disguised.

12 'Elegant variation'. Read the first chapter of any non-fiction book you have to hand, looking for instances of the author's varying ways of referring to the same referent. Discuss the effects achieved.

13 *In*elegant variation. Here are two versions of Ecclesiastes 9.11:

> a) One more thing I have observed here under the sun: speed does not win the race nor strength the battle. Bread does not belong to the wise, nor wealth to the intelligent, nor success to the skilful; time and chance govern all.

> b) Objective consideration of contemporary phenomena compels the conclusion that success or failure in competitive activities exhibits no tendency to be commensurate with innate capacity, but that a considerable element of the unpredictable must invariably be taken into account.

The first is from the *New English Bible* (1970) and the second is by George Orwell ('a parody, but not a very gross one,' he says) from his piece 'Politics and the English Language' (1946, but readily accessible in his *Collected Essays*). What is Orwell parodying? Examine these two versions and explain in detail how they differ. If you wish, you may substitute for the first version a translation of your choice. Compare your analysis with Orwell's own commentary on his version, and follow up his argument by close study of his essay as a whole.

14 Write an account and an evaluation of a play or film or TV programme that you have seen recently, taking particular care to convey your own reaction and to avoid critical

clichés. Alternatively (since we see clichés less easily in our own writing than in other people's), watch such an entertainment with a friend, and when you have both written reviews of about 500 words, exchange them and act the role of stern sub-editor.

Where usage is a problem

Being unable to walk across a room and simultaneously chew gum has been jokingly taken as the mark of supreme incompetence. But when we stop to think about it, even the first part is an extraordinary feat, in which the complex coordination of muscle and balance is only a part. No wonder we have the anecdote of the centipede which, when its attention was drawn to its skill in managing all those legs, was never able to walk properly again because it was now too preoccupied with the sheer mechanics of the action.

Every time we use language — to explain something to a friend, for example — we are performing a far greater feat of coordination, and the story of the centipede's fate can be taken as a warning. If we are made too self-conscious about *how* we use language, we shall not properly fulfil the *purpose* of language: communication.

But the analogy of the centipede must not be pressed too far. There are many differences between walking and talking, and an important one for our present purpose is that, when we walk, no one else need be involved. From this point of view, walking is a *private* activity: so long as our method of locomotion gets us from A to B, we may be content; we do not depend on other people's approval, co-operation, or indeed presence. But talking — the use of language — is *social*; it depends for its success on doing something not merely as we ourselves like to do it, but in such a way as will fit in with what other people like (or expect or understand).

If we used language solely for self-expression, the centipede parable might be more relevant, but this would involve us in only one part of the complex act of coordination. Self-expression is useful, beyond question, but there can be few who would regard it as the most valuable of language functions. We need language for *communication*, and this complicates enormously the degree and kind of necessary coordination.

Moreover, while we do not want to use our language *self*-consciously, there is every reason why we should try to use it *consciously*: every reason why we should strive to express ourselves in full consciousness, not only of what we are saying, but of how we are saying it, and of what effect it is having (or is likely to have) on our addressees. We spend our lives adding to our knowledge of vocabulary and practising our skill in the easy, ready manipulation of whatever complex grammatical patterns are necessary. This always remains in part a fully conscious process, and even the most skilled practitioners in what seems a 'natural', 'easy', or at any rate 'inevitable' form of expression have often torn up several early drafts before presenting readers with the version that is judged so easy and natural. As we shall see in Chapter Sixteen, T S Eliot confessed that, even after 'twenty years . . . Trying to learn to use words', every attempt was 'a wholly new start', leaving him 'still with the intolerable wrestle with words and meanings'. And Robert Graves once insisted that 'every English poet should . . . master the rules of grammar before he attempts to bend or break time'.

Those who favour relying on a haphazard self-expression in the use of English will find little support from practised writers. The fact that we ourselves know perfectly well what we mean is simply not enough. Indeed, it is not enough even if our addressee is only ourselves, as for instance in making notes for future reference. To the 'I' who writes them now, they are clear enough; but what about the 'I' who reads them in a month or a year hence? If self-communion across even a short interval of time can be incomprehensible, we see the need to be all the more careful when what we say or write is addressed to other people.

Every time we express ourselves, we have to coordinate not merely muscular movements in the speech organs or in the fingers poised at a keyboard. We have to relate the *simultaneously* apprehended topic of discourse to the necessarily *linear* linguistic presentation which must communicate it. Moreover, we must do so in such a way that we can be sure our companion or our reader is able to apprehend the topic in the way we ourselves do — which means selecting forms of linguistic expression which will not merely suit the topic but which will suit our audience.

In the 'primary' use of language, we are able to manage this highly complex task fairly well for the most part. This is largely because speaking comes more easily to us than writing (we are more used to it) and because the normal speech situation — face to face — provides liberal opportunity for what communication engineers call 'feedback'; we watch our companion and note his or her expressions of comprehension or doubt, and adjust our delivery accordingly. There is also the fact that, in the ordinary speech situation, we usually know our companions and have in consequence some experience of what they are able to understand — and willing to tolerate. With strangers, we may have difficulty even in speech. We may find it difficult to understand a computer expert who is trying to explain why we are not getting results from our machine; we turn to a colleague to act as 'interpreter'. The same topic, the same problem, but our colleague is in a better position to know how the explanation needs to be expressed, having a better chance of estimating our personal limitations.

Reference was made in the last paragraph to both under-standing and willingness to *tolerate*. We have noted in this book (especially in Chapter Four) that English varies between in-dividuals and groups, and also that it provides us with different ways of saying or writing 'the same thing'. Part of the problem in communication lies in estimating which variant to use so as to be both best understood by our addressees, and most acceptable to them. And of course, a very large part of the advantage offered by acquiring Standard English lies in its guarantee of achieving widespread success in both respects.

With the vast majority of linguistic options, we can be confident that the various choices are familiar to our addressees, fully com-prehensible, and also fully acceptable; our addressees might well use any of these options themselves. All we need worry about is choosing the one that best meets our immediate purpose. We can feel free to say or write:

> I must start work.
> *or*   I must begin work.
>
> She started singing
> *or*   She started to sing.
>
> We went to the theatre on Monday.
> *or*   On Monday we went to the theatre.
>
> What you have to do is work harder.
> *or*   What you have to do is to work harder.

The satellite is now 100 km from earth.
or The satellite is now 100 km from the earth.

John knows his way round Delhi because he lived there.
or John knows his way round Delhi because he has lived there.

This is not to say that these pairs are exactly synonymous; but assuming that the one we choose is the right one for our immediate purpose, we can be confident that it will be both comprehensible and acceptable. Some options that satisfy these conditions are (for example) stylistically very different and would be used in very different contexts; for example, the decision to use either:

The country wants change.
or The country is desirous of change.

Within the fully acceptable options, there are some that are strongly associated with individual habit. Consider, for example, the choice between *outside* (*the building*) and *outside of* (*the building*), between the spellings *judgment* and *judgement*, and between the pronunciations 'ekkonomics' and 'eekonomics'. Neither is superior to the other, and we can be sure that both are acceptable within Standard English, even by people who happen to use the other option themselves.

With another class of options, we can be just as sure that, while both may be comprehensible, one is undoubtedly unacceptable and outside the limits of Standard English. So we reject *alright* and accept *all right*. At the blank in the following, we reject *inferring* and accept *implying*:

He deceived her by . . . . . . that he was going to buy the house.

At the blank in this next sentence, we reject *whom* and accept *who*:

I met a student . . . . . . I thought was from China.

And of course we reject sentences like 'I didn't see nobody.'

Shibboleths

But there is a third set of options where the issue of acceptability is in doubt, where one choice is controversial and well below the

threshold of tolerance for some users of English. The points concerned are small in number, but they loom large in discussions of
usage, and for many people they are truly shibboleths. For example, some of those who pronounce *controversy* with main stress
on the first syllable regard as irritatingly wrong a pronunciation
which stresses the second syllable. Again, many people distinguish between *oral* as meaning 'spoken' and *verbal* as meaning 'in
words — whether spoken or written'. In consequence, they object
strongly to people who use expressions like 'He responded
verbally' with the intended meaning 'He gave a *spoken* reply'. To
the objectors, the expression should mean 'His reply was in
words: he didn't merely nod, grunt, or wave.' A further point
that raises heated discussion is the distinction between *due to* and
owing to, as in:

The accident was due to thick fog.
We were very late owing to the traffic.

Those who make this distinction can get very angry with those
who do not and who may in consequence use *due to* in the second
sentence as well as in the first.

Some of the controversial issues are more concerned with
general patterns than specific items. One of these is the 'split'
infinitive, and many people feel strongly that it is bad English to
say or write 'The Government ought to immediately increase
pensions', or 'She refuses to ever really try'. Another is the belief
that prepositions should not come at the end of a clause or sentence, as in 'He is a difficult person to deal with', or 'That must
be the drawer she took it out of'. A further but probably less common source of controversy is etymology. Among the people who
know that *aggravate* is ultimately related to a Latin verb *aggravare*
which meant 'to make heavier or more serious', there are some
who feel strongly that the common English meaning 'to annoy' is
wrong and that we should use the verb only as in:

Their circumstances were aggravated by poverty.

A still more extreme example is the objection to the modern meaning of *tremendous* ('huge') on the grounds that, etymologically, the
word 'ought' to mean 'that which causes trembling'. We have
even read complaints about the university word (especially in
British use) *postgraduate*. Since achieving a degree makes a student

a *graduate*, so the argument goes, a *postgraduate* 'ought' to mean something like a *former* graduate, possibly even a *dead* graduate!

Scholars and others professionally concerned with teaching and describing languages often deplore such rigidities of attitude; they remind us that languages change and that linguistic pedantry is both snobbish and absurd. Here is Noah Webster on the subject in his *Dissertations on the English Language* (1789):

> Young gentlemen who have gone through a course of academical studies, and received the usual honors of a University, are apt to contract a singular stiffness in their conversation. They read Lowth's Introduction, or some other grammatical treatise, believe what they read, without examining the grounds of the writer's opinions, and attempt to shape their language by his rules. Thus they enter the world with such phrases as *a mean, averse from, if he have, he has gotten,* and others which they deem *correct*; they pride themselves, for some time, in their superior learning and peculiarities; till further information, or the ridicule of the public, brings them to use the language of other people.

It is of interest to note that one of Webster's examples (*averse from*, in conflict with *averse to*) retains something of its shibboleth status to the present time. But it is of equal interest to note his slighting reference to Robert Lowth, Bishop of London. He was one of several people who in the eighteenth century wrote short grammars of English in the prescriptive vein, and these have undoubtedly influenced us (as Webster suggests) to take a rigid view of correctness, irrespective of the usage around us. On the other hand, we cannot blame Lowth and his contemporaries for all of the pet notions we have been discussing. The trailing preposition, for example, is called by Lowth 'an Idiom which our language is strongly inclined to' (illustrating the point as he makes it!), and its descent into disfavour goes back at least to John Dryden who was dead before Lowth was born. Dryden came to feel very strongly that to end a clause with a preposition was 'not elegant'. It was 'a fault' which he proceeded to eradicate from his own writing, and in revising what is probably his finest prose, he frequently 'corrected' it in this respect. So, for example, *the end he aimed at* was changed to *the end at which he aimed; the age I live in* became *the age in which I live; people you speak of* became *people of whom you speak*. Revision sometimes involved more radical rephrasing, and *think himself very hardly dealt with* was changed to *think he had hard measure*.

If distinguished writers can become so unhappily self-conscious about their English, it is easy to understand how people of little education can easily be made to feel inferior when they are accused of incorrect usage. A commercial advertisement promising to help such people (August 1989) claimed that 'thousands of talented intelligent people are held back at work and socially because their command of English does not equal their other abilities'. A picture showed two young women recoiling in horror as a youth says: 'Was you invited to the party tomorrER? Between you and I, John shall be going beside myself.' If you follow the advertised course, the item continues: 'Never again need you fear those embarrassing mistakes.'

Much as we in this book have urged exercising care in the use of English, avoiding slovenliness, and taking pride in expressing oneself at all times, we deplore the engendering of fear and embarrassment and the reduction of communication to stilted prissiness or — worse — to shamed silence. We deplore the focusing upon shibboleths because (a) they are, as we have said, few in number and must be kept in perspective; (b) they show their triviality by changing from time to time (as we see from the examples quoted by Webster); and (c) some are confused extensions from preferred use in formal written style to claimed correctness in all styles.

To illustrate (b), let us revert to the *due to* issue already mentioned. H W Fowler wrote in his *Modern English Usage* of 1926 that sentences like 'Prices have gone up due to increased demand' were 'used by the illiterate' and illustrated an 'impossible' misconstruction. In 1965 when Fowler's book came out in a new edition by Sir Ernest Gowers, the reviser quoted just such an example from a speech by Queen Elizabeth in 1957 which showed that the 'offending usage has indeed become literally part of the Queen's English'.

As for (c), we may illustrate this with the objections made to the tendency to use *who* rather than *whom* in object functions and to the converse tendency to use objective forms of the personal pronouns (*me, him, her, them*) in clause final position, even where they are not functioning as objects. Thus:

Who did you see there?

He is a bit taller than her.
Don't be alarmed: it's only me!

The form of each of these examples strongly suggests casual conversation in quite informal circumstances, and in the view of most educated people, the use here of *who, her,* and *me* is not merely acceptable in this style but is much to be preferred to *whom, she,* and *I* respectively. Those who feel otherwise are seeking to extend into colloquial style forms which are certainly correct and doubtless to be preferred in formal speech and (especially) writing:

The committee will decide whom to appoint.
No one has served the company more loyally than she.
It is I who must now assume responsibility.

Needless to say, irrespective of the qualifications (a), (b), and (c), we are left with the knowledge that some people are offended by transgressions from what they regard as absolute criteria of correctness, and in the interests of harmonious communication we do well to bear such susceptibilities in mind.

But this must be seen as just a part of the wider care over communication that we discussed earlier in this chapter; and there are far more important issues than the overrated shibboleths.

Our duty to our addressee

When we write something, we cannot of course expect to be present when our addressee reads it and thus help with explanatory amendment. This means that we need to make sure it will be read with complete understanding. Fortunately, writing not only enables us to plan our sentences more deliberately than when we speak, but provides us with the opportunity to read them back to ourselves, putting ourselves in the addressee's place, and making any desirable changes accordingly. But putting ourselves in the reader's place requires a real act of imagination. Since *we* know what we mean, it is not easy to imagine that anyone could misunderstand. An official press release once read:

The Government will be providing the public henceforth with far less restricted information on weapon research.

There is nothing wrong with the grammar here of course, but there are two possible interpretations, each unambiguous in the two following parallels:

a) The public is buying far less Danish butter.
b) She now has to buy far less expensive dresses.

The reader of the press release was left not knowing whether the government was going to be providing less information, on the model of (a), or putting less restriction on information, on the model of (b), and so in effect providing *more* information. A writer alert to the (a) and (b) possibilities would have noticed the ambiguity on rereading and would have made some revision.

Such revision often involves radical recasting. Let us assume that you get a letter in the course of a legal wrangle and it stipulates that:

You or your wife should sign the enclosed document and return it to the above address.

You disagree, and you begin to reply:

Neither my wife nor I are willing to sign this document . . .

But you pause: *are*? Should it not be *is*? or *am*? It so happens that there is no satisfactory answer to this particular choice and we are obliged to dodge the issue by recasting, perhaps using a verb form that is without person or number contrast:

Neither my wife nor I can agree to sign . . .
I am not willing to sign this document and neither is my wife
. . .
Both my wife and I are unwilling to sign . . .

The grammatical complexity of a sentence we are constructing can also lead us into a tangle where the only solution is to start again. Someone who had been rearranging a colleague's office left the following note:

I've put most of the books back on the shelves but there are some which I don't know where they should go.

The last three words had then been crossed out and replaced by 'to put them'. Then in parentheses the note ended:

(Sorry! I can't get this right but you know what I mean: some whose correct location I do not know! Wow!)

The final exclamation was presumably an acknowledgement that the revision had led the writer into a more formal and official-sounding style.

Greater grammatical complexity more often results, however, not in the writer but in the reader getting lost. Consider the two following examples which have the same source of difficulty:

> She came to have reasons for living abroad that sounded more congenial to her friends (and especially to those of long standing) and that eventually brought some comfort to her father.

> They developed a concept of loyalty to the state, an idea that created a sense of unity and that was valid in its original historical setting, but that was of course now seriously called in question.

Each example ends with a coordinated *that*-clause, and in each case it is ambiguous. In the first, 'and that eventually . . .' is liable to be read as having *that* as a demonstrative pronoun: 'and *that situation* — her having found better reasons — comforted her father'. So too, in the second, 'but that was of course . . .' is liable to be read as similarly having a demonstrative subject: 'but *that particular historical setting* was now in question'. In fact, we believe that in each case *that* was intended as a relative pronoun, giving a significantly different meaning to both sentences. We need to be aware of these two functions of *that*, and when we are planning a series of relative clauses (which inevitably makes the later ones fairly remote from the antecedent), it is wise to use a *wh*-pronoun instead of *that*:

> She came to have reasons . . . *which* sounded more congenial . . . and *which* eventually brought some comfort to her father.

> . . . an idea *which* created a sense of unity and *which* was valid . . . but *which* was of course now seriously called in question.

Avoiding ambiguity

A further point to remember with relative clauses is that although the precise antecedent is perfectly clear to the speaker or writer, it may not be equally clear to the addressee. Consider the following from a newspaper report:

An American destroyer and a cargo vessel, which had been
heading for Cuba, spent several hours searching the area for the
lost yacht.

Our interest in the lost yacht fades as we switch attention to
wondering why an American destroyer had been heading for
Cuba. Then (let us hope) we pause: *was* the destroyer heading for
Cuba or was it only that cargo vessel? If so, there should have
been a comma after *destroyer* and none after *vessel*.

In that example, difficulty could have been avoided by an
elementary precaution in punctuation, and it must be emphasised
that, when we write and so are obliged to manage without features of spoken language like intonation, we must be careful to
give the reader all the help that is possible from the resources of
punctuation. We may of course agree that it will not matter in
some instances. 'After all I'm a man now' and 'After all this time
I've forgotten' are both straightforward enough without internal
punctuation; but a sentence like the following is susceptible of
several interpretations:

> After all this life in the rough country towns would seem
> ghastly.

(?After all, After all this, After all this life in the rough, After all
this life in the rough country, . . .) Even here, the context might
be sufficiently explicit as to make it possible to argue that no
pointing is necessary, though in general one might say that any
sentence which is liable to hold up a reader — even momentarily
— should be improved if possible. Thus, for instance, the following excerpt from a newspaper does not actually need punctuation
(in fact comma-punctuation would be improper here), but it is certainly difficult to read and the writer's best course would have
been to recast it entirely:

> June output of tin concentrates for a number of companies
> under the management of British interests showed declines over
> the May period.

Again, when we write 'stainless steel sink plugs' we know exactly what we mean, and we know also that we are using a noun
phrase of a perfectly normal and acceptable type. But we must
also anticipate the reader's difficulty and realise that in this case
it would be better to use a structural type that can be more dis-

criminating: 'plugs for stainless steel sinks' or 'sink plugs of stainless steel'. We must always bear in mind the potential problems of both grammar and vocabulary.

But, as we saw in connection with the example about tin concentrates, care with grammar and vocabulary is not solely directed to avoiding ambiguity: we must seek to avoid any momentary interference with communication. Such interference can arise through clumsiness or obscurity, but equally it may arise through the reader's attention being deflected from *what* is being said to *how* it is being said. This often takes place when we thoughtlessly utter a *double entendre* ('There's a bloody stain on your collar') or use collocations which evoke the discomfort or facetiousness of *mixed metaphor* rather than pass unheeded as clichés. For example:

> She decided to chance her arm and it came off.

Either of these idioms would have succeeded in isolation:

> She decided to chance her arm and it succeeded.
> She decided to take a risk and it came off.

Together, however, they clash and divert the addressee into unwanted humour. So also:

> Back trouble is a doctor's biggest headache.
> It would be a great step forward if they were now to sit down and consider where they stand.

Think first!

These examples illustrate the way in which clichés can become so automatic that tired or careless speakers can seem to be totally unaware of what they are saying. A television interviewer was capable of asking:

> Regardless of all that, and taking everything into account, what do you think our policy should now be?

Nor is it only clichés that reveal an internal insensitivity to meaning — and commonsense. On a North American flight, passengers were astounded to hear the pilot announce:

> In a minute or two, you'll see the St Lawrence River directly overhead.

Here the absurdity is obviously caused by an inversion (literally) of relativities: 'We shall be directly overhead', 'The river will be directly below'. But sometimes the error is caused by simply being unfamiliar with a particular word or its meaning. For example, from newspaper articles:

> The shells had hit an aircraft carrier and reeked significant damage.
> Two players were sent off for flaunting the rules.

From a sports report on radio:

> This result is not only unique but very rare indeed.

From a televised discussion:

> And it's no use Monica shaking her head vociferously; she knows it's true!

In Chapter Thirteen, we noted that adverbial elements in a sentence were not constrained in number or in position. This freedom often leads people to place an adverbial so as to leave the sentence ambiguous or misleading:

> They are now refusing to do what they had previously decided to do as a matter of principle.

Is the matter of principle their present decision or their previous refusal?

> At one time, university departments in several countries were given the corpses of people who had been executed for study purposes.

> A memorial service will be held for those who died fighting in the baseball stadium.

We pointed out also in Chapter Thirteen that, with clausal compression, we had to be able to infer the missing parts. Thus in the following, we can understand the first part as 'When Martina was driving to work today':

> Driving to work today, Martina had a marvellous idea for a short story.

It is a common fault to leave listeners or readers to work out for themselves what is missing:

Recalling your review of the Matisse exhibition, you may not know that this will be reprinted in our next issue.

Grammatically, the subject of *recalling* should be *you*, but this would make very poor sense here. More likely, the writer is carelessly compressing something more like:

I recall your review of the Matisse exhibition and so I am writing to let you know . . .

But for the most part, such improperly 'unattached' participles are not so much misleading as absurd:

Using the new management techniques, cattle on most farms are now producing 25 per cent more milk.

A final point from Chapter Thirteen: coordination and apposition. It may not have been noticed that the same words *and* and *or* can be used for both:

My sister and Jonathan are coming for dinner.
My friend and colleague is waiting to see you.
You can have tea or coffee.
This is a vest or singlet.

In the first and the third, we have coordination, and there are two separate referents in each case. In the second and fourth, we have apposition, and there is a single referent in each case but with a different designation. For the familiar reason that, as speaker or writer, we always know what we mean but do not always give our addressees the consideration that is their due, we sometimes leave them thinking we have expressed coordination when in fact our intention has been apposition. The following appeared in a recent serious article on political trends:

Voters are not interested in, or bewildered by, talk of pacts and deals between fringe groups.

This is not merely a superficial ambiguity: it is sheer bad writing. Grammatically there is no ambiguity at all: it *ought* to mean 'Voters are neither interested in nor bewildered by talk of pacts'. In other words, grammatically, *interested* and *bewildered* are coordinated. But this makes such little sense that one must conclude that the writer intended some kind of apposition, in which case the sentence should have read:

Voters are not interested in, or rather, they are bewildered by, talk of pacts . . .

or:

Far from being interested in, voters are bewildered by talk of pacts . . .

or:

Voters are not interested in talk of pacts and deals between fringe groups; rather, they are bewildered by them.

We have come a long way from the inhibited centipede of our opening paragraph, but of course we have by no means covered the myriad of linguistic limbs, muscles, nerves, and delicate antennae that have to be coordinated whenever we speak or write. What we hope we have indeed made clear, however, is that whenever we stumble, trip, or fail to win applause at the finishing line, we have no one to blame but ourselves.

SOME FOLLOW-UP WORK

1 Write two sets of instructions for dealing with a flat tyre by fitting the spare wheel. In the first, assume that your readers are experienced drivers who know the names of tools and the parts of a car. In the second, make no such assumptions: your readers are people who have only recently become qualified to drive.

2 'She is hopefully applying for the vacant post.' This sentence is ambiguous. Write paraphrases which bring out each meaning clearly. Is such ambiguity the reason that makes people disapprove of *hopefully* in some uses?

3 A minister attempting to arbitrate could persuade neither side to accept the other's proposal and was then obliged to seek a compromise which might well displease both. A newspaper report read:

The minister is now trying to find an unsatisfactory compromise.

Explain why this formulation is itself unsatisfactory and attempt something better (but not too much longer).

4 'Edward, the pleasure-loving son of Queen Victoria and a man much courted by high society, was the subject of many risqué stories.' This sounds like a risqué story itself, but in fact the *and* introduces an apposition. Invent some further ambiguities of this sort and show how they could be alternatively and more judiciously expressed.

5 A meeting took place of a discussion group and happily almost everyone turned up; apologies were regretfully received from one member, however. The secretary could not decide between two possible reports for the minute book:

a) Unfortunately, Mrs Williams was the only member who could not attend.

b) Fortunately, Mrs Williams was the only member who could not attend.

Attempt some justification of (a) and (b) in turn; then explain why each is objectionable; and finally write a superior minute (c).

6 In British English, *momentarily* means 'for a moment', in American English it means 'in a moment'. Write three sentences using the adverb so as to illustrate how important the difference in interpretation can be.

C H A P T E R   1 6

Art in words

However much we revere scientists and engineers, however much we admire their products, the noblest and most enduring creations to which humanity can aspire are what we call 'art'. The imagination, observation, and sheer hard work of artists may result in buildings, statues, paintings, symphonies: but there are those whose material is *words*, those whose product is literature.

When we hear the word 'literature', we may think of drama, fiction, and verse. But this is a very narrow and generic view: seriously distorted, moreover, both in what is seems to include and in what it seems to exclude. Many works of history, philosophy, social satire, political theory, and scientific observation are works of literature. Most plays and works of prose fiction, in our view, are not; nor, probably, is most verse, when one considers the vast numbers of hackneyed rhymes and cliché phrases in birthday cards and the like. For our part, we prefer to take a more pragmatic and language-based view. A work of literature is one which distils creative imagination into excellence of linguistic expression. Originality it usually has, but this is not essential: 'What oft was thought, but ne'er so well expressed', as Pope put it, may well be literature. The vital feature is expression, the use of language, irrespective of the purpose or indeed the moral character of the writer, irrespective of the form — verse or prose — which he or she chooses for the work. Irrespective of the reader's or hearer's purpose, too. Milton did not write *Areopagitica* as 'literature', nor did his original readers study it as such. The Bible has served the devotional purposes of millions for many centuries, but it is also a great work of literature: none, perhaps, greater. Purpose, genre, form are not criterial: creativity and expression are; and these may be admirably satisfied in a five-act play or a one-minute bar-room joke.

Nonetheless, there is indeed a good deal of professionalism in the craft of literature, and it is not surprising that what by common consent constitutes our best literature is mostly produced by those who single-mindedly practise that craft: our novelists, dramatists, and poets. And as the rest of us strive, in our ordinary day-to-day use of English, to find the best words and the best sentences for what we want to express, it is some comfort to know that those novelists, dramatists, and poets, who seem to manage English so excellently, readily confess to the same difficulty. Here, for example, is Dylan Thomas, struggling

> . . . to twist the shapes of thoughts
> Into the stony idiom of the brain,
> To shade and knit anew the patch of words
> Left by the dead who, in their moonless acre,
> Need no word's warmth.

'From love's first fever to her plague'

Elsewhere, too, he writes of the yearning to articulate, the long bitter discipline to give his passion its full expression:

> Were that enough, enough to ease the pain,
> Feeling regret when this is wasted
> That made me happy in the sun,
> How much was happy while it lasted,
> Were vaguenesses enough and the sweet lies plenty,
> The hollow words could bear all suffering
> And cure me of ills.

'Out of the sighs'

Talk of vaguenesses, sweet lies, hollow words, with the implicit assertion that they are *not* enough, reminds us sharply of the *Four Quartets* and of Eliot's austere arraignment of degenerate expression in 'East Coker':

> So here I am, in the middle way, having had twenty years . . .
> Trying to learn to use words, and every attempt
> Is a wholly new start, and a different kind of failure
> Because one has only learnt to get the better of words
> For the thing one no longer has to say, or the way in which
> One is no longer disposed to say it. And so each venture
> Is a new beginning, a raid on the inarticulate
> With shabby equipment always deteriorating

> In the general mess of imprecision of feeling,
> Undisciplined squads of emotion.

Earlier in the same poem, he shows his dissatisfaction with 'periphrastic study in a worn-out poetical fashion', which leaves him 'still with the intolerable wrestle with words and meanings'.

With this intolerable wrestle, we have the area in which the interests of the writer, the critic, the linguist, the grammarian converge. It is an area of special interest in an age like ours which, on the whole, rejects 'poetic diction' and accepts the view that the spring supplying literary language must be 'ordinary language': broadly, the 'neutral' style of Standard English discussed in Chapter Fourteen.

Ordinary language

In his essay 'The Music of Poetry', Eliot reminds us that 'Every revolution in poetry is apt to be, and sometimes to announce itself to be a return to common speech. That is the revolution which Wordsworth announced in his prefaces and he was right; but the same revolution had been carried out a century before by Oldham, Waller, Denham and Dryden, and the same revolution was due again something over a century later,' because, as Eliot goes on to say, poetic idiom tends regularly to become traditional, while language itself, equally regularly, tends to change.

It is noteworthy that in succeeding generations the urge has been felt to make a search in this direction, to find the received language of literature inadequate for the expression of the keenest sensibilities, and to feel that only a re-engagement with something rather gropingly called 'ordinary language' can equip the literary artist for what he wants to express. To Dryden and Wordsworth we may add, for instance, Shelley who in his Preface to The Cenci agrees that 'in order to move men to true sympathy we must use the familiar language of men'. One might also add Gerard Manley Hopkins, whose concern was for poetry to base itself upon 'current language' (Letters to Robert Bridges, p. 89), and W B Yeats, who singled out 'the lack of natural momentum in the syntax' as the mark of inferior and 'pretty' poetry: and by this — as Donald Davie supposes — he must refer to the necessity for contact with living speech (Articulate Energy, p. 95).

The urge itself to turn from traditional language is surely a sound reflection of general linguistic experience. It is not only poets who find that 'one has only learnt to get the better of words/ For the thing one no longer has to say'. In Dryden's time, in another field, it was this problem that exercised Thomas Sprat in the interests of achieving a written prose style which should break with a tradition of persuasive rhetorical tropes and figures, and be an adequate vehicle for objective description in experimental science. For both Dryden and Sprat, as for Eliot and Einstein, inappropriate modes of expression have to be replaced for the sake of contemporary needs, and the primary source to turn to is the unwritten language of daily discourse which — whether it is adequately expressing them or not — is certainly in full engagement with these contemporary needs. From this viewpoint one may say, as Eliot in fact does, that 'the task is to catch up with the changes in colloquial speech, which are fundamentally changes in thought and sensibility' ('The Music of Poetry').

The extent to which spoken language is, from an expressive viewpoint, so to speak 'ahead' of the corresponding sphere of written language, and the means by which it achieves a lead, are matters still in need of thorough investigation, but what little experimental evidence we already have would seem to confirm the impression that such a lead exists. But this is not by any means to say that spoken language, merely as such, is wholly effectual: still less that it is to be bodily transferred on to paper to constitute an ideal literary medium, whether for scientific or poetic purposes. Coleridge, Shelley, and Sir Walter Alexander Raleigh are among those who have uttered warnings about carrying 'the ordinary language' approach too far. While conceding that people must be addressed 'in their accustomed tongue', Raleigh goes on:

> The public, like the delicate Greek Narcissus, is sleepily
> enamoured of itself; and the name of its only other perfect lover
> is Echo.

In consequence:

> He who has a message to deliver must wrestle with his fellows
> before he shall be permitted to ply them with uncomfortable or
> unfamiliar truths.

The advent of a mass audience, coupled with the advent of a naturalistic style, may dangerously invite a reduction of language to a prime factor of banality:

> We talk to our fellows in the phrases we learn from them,
> which come to mean less and less as they grow worn with use.
> Then we exaggerate and distort, heaping epithet upon epithet in
> the endeavour to get a little warmth out of the smouldering pile.
>
> *Style*, pp. 66f, 80, 87

The art of informality

We have seen something of the truth of Raleigh's remarks in
Chapter Fourteen, and it must be obvious that it is not in Eliot's
mind to imitate such features when he speaks (in his essay on
'The Social Function of Poetry') of regaining contact with the 'language as it is actually spoken around him'. Sweeney's language
is not the ideal:

> That's all the facts when you come to brass tacks:
> Birth, and copulation, and death.
> I've been born, and once is enough.
> You don't remember, but I remember.
> Once is enough.
>   . . .
> I tell you again it don't apply
> Death or life or life or death
> Death is life and life is death
> I gotta use words when I talk to you
> But if you understand or if you don't
> That's nothing to me and nothing to you
> We all gotta do what we gotta do
> We're gona sit here and drink this booze . . .

One might, however, just add in parenthesis that the poet finds
it no less a wrestle to compose language like this: it is no easy
task to create on paper an image of even the most 'ordinary' or
'actual language'. A threefold distinction has to be made between
kinds of 'usage': *actual usage, believed usage,* and *preceptive usage.*
The forms that people in fact use are often different from what
they believe they use, and these in turn may be different from
what they think they *should* use. It is 'believed usage' that a
writer usually puts on paper to represent natural English. Or else
he abstracts from speech, or from *some* speech, features which
seem particularly striking and which he takes to be the essence

of speech. Perhaps it may be disjointed fragmentary syntax like Mr Jingle's in Dickens; or the recurrent speech 'fillers' like 'well' that Swift satirises; the exaggerated and overworked epithets in Thackeray's *Book of Snobs*; or — used more seriously — the hypocritical and repetitious syntax of Mr Casby in *Little Dorrit*. Or it may be the clipped, staccato, tongue-tied language of the narrator in that early 'campus' novel, *The Catcher in the Rye* (1951), where J D Salinger looks back to classics like *Huckleberry Finn* and *David Copperfield* but in a style as deliberately remote from traditional accounts of boyhood as Thomas's 'Fern Hill', and indeed explicitly distinguished in the opening paragraph from 'all that David Copperfield kind of crap'. Or it may be the ironic semiotics-tinged discourse between academics that we meet in the much later campus novel of David Lodge (*Nice Work*, 1988):

> 'Any good?' she inquired, nodding at his book.
> 'Not bad. Quite good on the de-centring of the subject, actually. You remember that marvellous bit in Lacan? . . .'
> Robyn frowned. 'What do you think that *means*, exactly? I mean, is "truth" being used ironically?'
> 'Oh, I think so, yes. It's implied by the word "alibi", surely? There is no "truth", in the absolute sense, no transcendental signifier. Truth is just a rhetorical illusion, a tissue of metonymies and metaphors, as Nietzsche said. It all goes back to Nietzsche, really, as this chap points out.' Charles tapped the book on his lap.

In short, whether for satirical or for serious purposes, the imaging of actual speech on paper *is* imaging and not a transcript of the real thing. It involves the working out of conventions, a deliberate weighing of words, at least as much as any other kind of writing, and the relationships of such conventions to those of ordinary speech are, incidentally, much in need of serious study.

In any event, Sweeney's language is not what Eliot is referring to when he speaks of the poet's catching up 'with the changes in colloquial speech, which are fundamentally changes in thought and sensibility'. Rather, it is the converse: it is a dramatisation of the 'shabby equipment' with which the inarticulate pathetically make do. This is what justifies the raid. And the 'intolerable wrestle' is poignantly made Sweeney's own problem: 'I gotta use words when I talk to you' — the more poignant because so banal, so inadequate for expressing 'thought and sensibility'. The wrestle is something which confronts not merely the poet, the thinker, the scientist.

Eliot's interests in the functioning of language and the problems of communication are in fact far more deliberately therapeutic than Wordworth's. He is far more concerned than most of us about the defects in ordinary speech, what he calls (in his essay 'Poetry and Drama') 'its fumbling for words, its constant recourse to approximation, its disorder, and its unfinished sentences', and he explicitly draws attention to these features as sharply distinguishing speech from either prose or poetry. 'No poetry', he in fact says in 'The Music of Poetry', 'is ever exactly the same speech that the poet talks and hears,' but poetry has to have a direct linguistic relationship to ordinary speech; the poet 'must, like the sculptor, be faithful to the material in which he works'. Let us look at what he means by being 'faithful'.

Conquest and submission

In 'East Coker', he speaks of conquering 'By strength and submission' and later on, with a different metaphor, 'We must be still and still moving / Into another intensity / For a further union, a deeper communion'. In 'Little Gidding', he is again concerned with speech, and these concerns impel him 'To purify the dialect of the tribe / And urge the mind to aftersight and foresight'. These themes recur again and again in his essays. In 'The Social Function of Poetry', for example, he says that a poet's foremost 'duty is to his *language*, first to preserve, and second to extend and improve'. Elsewhere (in 'The Music of Poetry'), he writes: 'I believe that any language . . . imposes its laws and restrictions and permits its own licence, dictates its own speech rhythms and sound patterns. And a language is always changing; its development in vocabulary, in syntax, pronunciation and intonation — even in the long run, its deterioration — must be accepted by the poet and made the best of.' Here we see the 'submission' and the being 'still' of 'East Coker'; but he goes on: '[The poet] in turn has the privilege of contributing to the development and maintaining the quality, the capacity of the language to express a wide range, and subtle gradation of feeling and emotion; his task is both to respond to change and make it conscious and to battle

ART IN WORDS 247

against degradation below the standards which he has learned from the past.'

The poet's position is thus closely analogous to that of the scientist. 'Last year's words belong to last year's language,' but, in rejecting the outworn periphrasis of an earlier age, the poet can afford no more than the scientist to fall back on the 'habitual phrases' of a contemporary sleepy Echo. As Joshua Whatmough put it in that rather eccentric book on *Poetic, Scientific and Other Forms of Discourse* (1956), the poet and the scientist are equally creative in their use of language, prompted by analogous urges. Both kinds of language 'are precise, each in its own way, the one in its probabilities of choices (*le mot juste*), the other in logical and mathematical forms'. 'The creative imagination of a Shakespeare or a Milton, of an Einstein or a Newton: both demand the total resources of form and meaning of a language.' 'In both kinds of discourse, scientific and poetic, there is a goodness of "fit".'

To relate Eliot's purification image to Whatmough's engineering metaphor, 'goodness of "fit"', and to bring both into the terms of linguistics, we need only say that both poet and scientist must undergo the discipline of basing their expression on the vocabulary, grammar and transmission system used naturally in speech and *as* used naturally in speech, if they are to perform the social function of communication. Moveover, in proceeding from this point to ply us, as Raleigh says, 'with uncomfortable and unpalatable truths', such new expressions as are necessary must conform to the graphic, phonological, grammatical, and lexical conventions obtaining in the language. Poetic — like scientific — language must be creative, but creative in terms of the language's own 'laws and restrictions', as Eliot says.

Thus our language permits many consonant clusters, as in *triumphs, squibs,* or *judged,* but there are restrictions which make it very unlikely that industrial chemists will call their next synthetic product *zdabf* or *ftrime-goshk.* Eliot's *aftersight* (with a quite different meaning from the familiar *hindsight*) is not, according to ordinary dictionaries, from our actual word-hoard. But it accords with his theory of submission to the restrictions of ordinary language, as one can see from its parallelism to the coordinated *foresight* ('urge the mind to aftersight and foresight'), and also in fact from our being unsure whether or not it is already part of our vocabulary until we have looked for it in the dictionaries. The word conforms with the conventions of the everyday English around us in a way that a projected synonym such as *sightafter* or *vision-post* would not.

What is true of word-formation in this example, or of the slightly more linguistically complex 'at smokefall' in 'Burnt Norton' or Thomas's 'windfall light', is true also of syntactical structures, where the poet can exploit the language's own licence but again with adherence to its own restrictions. We have seen earlier in this book that words are related in sentences both by grammar and collocation, that both grammatical analogy and semantic analogy operate when we use language. To take a simple example, in the utterance 'He's an odd sort of man', there is decidedly more restriction upon occupation of the place filled by *sort* than there is upon the place of *odd*, and more upon the place of *odd* than there is upon the place filled by *man*. Moreover, both semantic and grammatical analogy must control the replacement of *odd* and *sort*: the replacements will not merely have to be adjective and noun respectively but will tend to be like *odd* and *sort* semantically as well: *strange* and *type*, for instance.

Now, when in his poem 'Fern Hill' Dylan Thomas uses an expression like *all the sun long*, he is tampering with the paradigmatic system of a phrase which might be set out for ordinary usage as comprising the following terms: 'all the day long', 'all the night long', 'all the week long', and perhaps a few others. The paradigm *day/night/week* involves both grammar (a noun) and meaning (a unit of time). By partial compliance with this set, replacing *day, night, week* by a form which is grammatically consistent (another noun, *sun*), Thomas obliges us to consider it as semantically consistent as well, making a new member of the paradigm with *sun* functioning as a unit of time (the notion that is being explored in the poem), *as well as* continuing to carry the semantic value that it has independently of this context: a new member which is a sub-class of one of the existing terms, 'all the day long', because not all days are sunny, and it is the sunniness of his memories of the days that Thomas wishes to convey. Later in the poem, by a further extension of the paradigm, we have 'all the moon long', which is in a similar sub-class relationship to the 'all the night long' of everyday language.

There are many instances of this device in Thomas's poems, some of them with ironic effect, some poignant, some amusing.

They admirably illustrate Thomas's striving to infuse with new life the 'vaguenesses' and the 'hollow words' that he refers to in 'Out of the sighs', and they illustrate also the 'submission' to ordinary speech which accompanies and conditions — as Eliot sees it — the paradoxical struggle to move beyond ordinary language.

New versus old

But how far, we may wonder by this time, does poetry move from 'ordinary language'? For Eliot, after all, poetry 'is essentially a disturbance of the conventional language', and it disturbs the conventional consciousness 'by its syntax more than by its sentiments' (F O Matthiessen, *The Achievement of T.S. Eliot*, p. 86). And the Hopkins letter already quoted says that the ideal poetic language is 'current language heightened, to any degree heightened and unlike itself, but not an obsolete one'. It would thus appear that, if poetry can depart from ordinary language in the direction of creativeness based on the structure of ordinary language, it cannot depart from it in the direction of the past.

Yet one may have doubts here too. Whence comes, for instance, the widespread popular belief that the proper language of poetry has an archaic flavour? How does it happen that Hopkins' assertion seems so flatly to contradict Gray's, that 'The language of the age is never the language of poetry'? By what odd chance is it that this seems to be so thoroughly accepted by a general public to whom its author's *Elegy* remains the only poem they know well and the one which epitomises for them poetic expression at its best? Surely it is the mating of current speech and the poetic tradition from generation to generation that provides poetry with a good deal of that range of licence that Eliot discusses. Does not this range result from the co-existence with the *actually* current of a *potentially* current wealth of linguistic patterns and forms, readily associable in the receiving mind with the discourse of sensibility?

It is this potential currency which enables even Eliot to express himself through *a carvèd dolphin* in 'A Game of Chess', though it is doubtful if a dissyllabic *carvèd* is current outside what one might provisionally call the language of the poet; which enables him in 'The Fire Sermon' to postpose an adjective as in 'the young man carbuncular', to use a highly restricted word-order like 'him shall heavenly arms enfold' in 'The Hippopotamus' or 'Issues from the hand of time the simple soul' in 'Animula'. And if it is objected that Eliot expects his reader to react to the echo from elsewhere — another age, another poem — is not this just another way of saying that the poet takes his language not only from that around him, together with what he can add to it by his own creativeness, but also — delicately and selectively — from the accumulated Golden Treasury of the past? Michael Hamburger's lines 'Creation's monster, metaphysical man / Across the garden moves his soft machine'; C Day Lewis's 'Yet fools are the old who won't be taught'; and Edmund Blunden's 'Sweet this morning incense, kind / This flood of sun': all these embody linguistic, syntactic arrangements which are not current in everyday speech but which are manifestly current in the language of poetry.

A poet at work

Nor should such Golden Treasury vocabulary and syntactic inversions be written off as language familiar to and appreciated only by those of high-brow literary tastes. They are in the birthday-card verse as well, and they are as much in the most popular songs ('So deep is the night, alone am I . . .') as they are in the most highly-wrought work of serious poets. Even a poem strenuously seeking to sound contemporary chords, and to represent contemporary issues, unhesitatingly embraces traditional language and poetic phrasing. Consider for example two stanzas from a 1989 poem by Oliver Reynolds, contrasting the coexistence of wealth and poverty in Chelsea, an area of London redolent of affluence:

> A man sits in a blossom-flecked Daimler
> and reads the FT, stroking his wattles.
> All the pinks! It's spring in car-phone country
> and every bird's buttonholing the sky
> with the latest prices. Worms are up, up!
> A key turns, setting pistons whispering
> on a sheen of irreproachable oil.
> High above the city, a plane draws out
> a slow burr of sound like a glass-cutter
> scoring a window. One tap and you're through.
>   . . .

Phylacteries guarding what's most precious,
burglar-alarms line the mews. His home's wheeled,
his life portable. What's the going rate
for this des. res. in SW10:
a shopping-trolley crammed with all mod. cons.
(newspapers, blankets, carpet remnants, rope,
sticks, old shoes, a Japanese umbrella . . .)?
Parked by a new flat's security gates,
eyes veering and orbiting, he mutters
to no one in a stricken falsetto.

Amid the savagely ironical colloquialisms (like 'all mod. cons.'),
we have the poetic tones of 'high above the city', 'a slow burr of
sound', and the compound modifier 'blossom-flecked'. This has
a delicate precision in the context of a London spring, where fall-
ing cherry petals magically carpet footpaths and lawns in white
and pink. But here the noun modified, the object carpeted, is a
mundane symbol of material wealth, a luxury car. And in it sits
a man who is not marvelling at the pink blossom but studying
the pink paper on which the *Financial Times* is printed; it is here
referred to in its colloquial designation among business people,
'the FT', for this is 'car-phone country'.

The contrast between the financier's position and that of the
tramp is made all the more absolute by the pair of wheeled
vehicles — the rich man's Daimler and the tramp's old super-
market trolley, loaded with his pitiful belongings. But both the
stanzas quoted are preoccupied by the protection of wealth: the
ending of the first suggests that the noise of an aircraft reminds
the businessman of a burglar cutting through a window. The
second, where the focus is going to be on the destitute tramp,
opens with the supreme irony conveyed by the striking and (for
most people) rare word *phylacteries*. We may not know that this
is derived from a Greek word meaning 'security, safeguard', but
our willingness to accept it as a metaphorical reference to the
security boxes warningly placed on the outside of houses needs
to be based on knowing at least the word's current literal meaning: a little leather box containing scriptural passages and worn
by Jewish men at morning prayer.

Discussion of this word brings out what is possibly the most
outstanding feature of language at its literary best, its evocative
ambiguity and its compact density. Does the muttered falsetto at

the end form a link with the implicit prayers of *phylacteries*? The connection between birds and worms in the first stanza is clear enough, but the connection of worms with rising prices is evocatively left to our imagination. 'All the pinks!' simultaneously alludes to the blossom and to the number of FTs to be seen in this 'car-phone country', enabling their reader to radio 'button-holing' messages to colleagues elsewhere. But the phrase also suggests a political musing over possible threats from socialist ('pink') influence.

Let us glance at one further example of compression and multiple allusion. In Herman Melville's *Battle Pieces* (1866), we see young soldiers in the American Civil War facing their first engagement untried, innocent, ignorant of war. At once they 'Perish, enlightened by the vollied glare'; simultaneously lit up in the blaze of firing and enlightened (but too late) on the horrors of the battle-field.

Art in prose

Although we insisted earlier that literary art was by no means synonymous with poetry, we have found ourselves nonetheless — as so frequently in discussions of this kind — talking as though poetry was the obvious genre to turn to in seeking to illustrate the best literary use of language. This is partly because it probably is; and partly because, in any event, poems in their characteristic brevity (poems of epic length are rare today) make them a more convenient means of illustration. It is certainly not that cunningly chosen words and well-wrought sentences are rare in prose, or ever have been. Few writers can have succeeded in making syntax more suggestive, even mimetic, than the voluble (if now rarely heard) Carlyle: 'So wags and wavers this unrestful world, day after day, month after month. The streets of Paris, and all cities, roll daily their oscillatory flood' (*The French Revolution*, V. ix). He makes the syntax oscillate with the flood. Not surprisingly, perhaps, *flood* is an important word for Carlyle; notice it in this passage where he is writing of Coleridge:

> To sit as a passive bucket and be pumped into, whether you consent or not, can in the long-run be exhilarating to no creature; how eloquent soever the flood of utterance that is

descending. But if it be withal a confused unintelligible flood of
utterance, threatening to submerge all known landmarks of
thought and drown the world and you! — I have heard
Coleridge talk, with eager musical energy, two stricken hours,
his face radiant and moist, and communicate no meaning
whatsoever to any individual of his hearers, — certain of whom,
I for one, still kept eagerly listening in hope; the most had long
before given up, and formed (if the room were large enough)
secondary humming groups of their own.

John Sterling, viii

It requires no pedestrian *explication de texte* to see here the tie
between 'a passive bucket' and the grammatical passive 'be
pumped into', but there are other features to note. For example,
the sentence which describes the unintelligible flood becomes itself a flood in which the writer is so to speak drowned, and he
does not finish it.

We have lived through a century that has responded to great
prose, uniquely remarkable, of course, in the case of James Joyce.
To Joyce's we may add the prose of D H Lawrence, Virginia
Woolf, Kingsley Amis, Philip Roth, V S Naipaul, Alison Lurie —
naming names almost randomly from among those chiefly associated with fiction alone. But there is also the prose of historians
such as Winston Churchill and critics such as Christopher Ricks.
Consider the opening sentences of Noel Annan's biography of
Leslie Stephen (1984):

> When Andrea Mantegna chose to paint St Jerome, a favourite
> subject of early Renaissance artists, he did not picture him, as
> others did, aged but vigorous, calmly contemplating folios of
> theology as he sat in his study, his little dog beside him, or in
> the open air, guarded by his lion. He chose instead to paint
> St Jerome in the wilderness. In the foreground looms a massive
> rocky mountain which provides a cell, but in the distance one
> can see the sunny smiling landscape laced with twisted roads
> along which a hermit would plod to end his days in penitence
> among these crags. Before his cell the saint sits wrapped in
> melancholy. His eyes are cast down so that he looks at what lies
> at his feet, the symbol of worldly pride and power — his
> cardinal's hat. All that appears to sustain him are his books, two
> of which await him on a stone which serves as a table while he
> grasps a third. The saint is at the end of his days.

> Some such picture is conjured up when people think today of
> Leslie Stephen . . .

Whether or not 'some such picture' is indeed 'conjured up'
when we think today of Leslie Stephen, we can enjoy the shock
of surprise that the biography of a man described accurately in
the book's subtitle as 'the godless Victorian' should begin with a
paragraph on one of the godliest of men, St Jerome. But the images of that paragraph enable Annan to refer in the second to
Stephen as a 'pioneer Alpinist' whose 'imagination ranged' over
a 'lonely wilderness'. More broadly, the evocation of Jerome, who
renounced paganism, embraced Christianity, and set to work on
what was to become the Vulgate Bible, is in telling counterpoint
to a man who renounced Christianity, embraced agnosticism, and
virtually created the *Dictionary of National Biography*, described by
the Earl of Rosebery as 'the monumental literary work' of the Victorian era.

So much for the general rhetorical strategy, the context planned
for this opening paragraph. What about the internal texture of the
paragraph itself? Note the cunning perversity of the first sentence,
not merely ignoring Leslie Stephen but going into graphic detail
about the way Mantegna did *not* paint *Jerome*! It is however that
kind of negative sentence which sets our expectations, semantically and grammatically, for the positive correlate. Compare the
well-known words of J F Kennedy: 'Ask not what your country
can do for you; ask what you can do for your country.' Annan's
positive correlate cannot convey such conclusive satisfaction, but
it is studiously short and thus helps to impress on us 'the
wilderness' which, as we have seen, is to be replicated in the next
paragraph as an image in relation to Stephen.

After this short sentence we have, as we might expect, a
description of that wilderness, and we note that the inversion of
normal element order to AVS enables the writer to place rhetorical
focus upon a lengthy noun phrase, 'a massive rocky mountain
which provides a cell'. But before we are told more about the cell,
we have to look beyond it to a landscape of crags and winding
roads — again providing Annan with a forward link in his third
paragraph to Stephen the Alpinist, 'a walker to whom 40 miles in
a day was a stroll'.

After this tantalising diversion, we return to the cell which is
foregrounded as the scene-setting adverbial for the next sentence

— another short one with its climax in *melancholy*. Let us observe the force of *cast down* in the next sentence: the grammatical subject is 'his eyes', but semantically this phrasal verb works also with 'what lies at his feet': the cardinal's 'symbol of worldly pride and power' seems also to have been 'cast down'. This is formally endorsed by what follows ('All that appears to sustain him are his books'), and we note that both the reduction and the climax on *books* are achieved by a paraphrase of what we called in Chapter Thirteen the '*wh*-cleft' construction: what remains are his books. Which brings us within comfortable reach of Leslie Stephen, though the curtain rises on him only after a further short and this time sombre sentence: 'The saint is at the end of his days.'

Writing like this is the product not only of hard work and careful craftsmanship but of a talent that is thinly distributed among humanity. But if in our well-founded modesty we cannot produce linguistic art of this quality, it is within the reach of everyone to *enjoy* it. One of the great contributions of education (and no small part of our aim in this book) is to develop the critical faculty that can reject the slovenly and impoverished use of English — our own along with that of others — and savour with pleasure the delicately chiselled phrases, the imaginatively chosen words that make speech and writing a glory to be treasured.

SOME FOLLOW-UP WORK

1 Examine what can be achieved by the following phrases and explain in each case their connection with everyday English:

> once below a time
> once upon a dream
> dressed to die
> a grief ago

2 The following quatrain by Horace (*Odes*, I. 36) is accompanied by two English translations, the first by John Conington, the second by C K Ogden:

> Omnes in Damalin putres
> deponent oculos nec Damalis nouo
>   diuelletur adultero
> lasciuis hederis ambitiosior.

> Every melting eye will rest
> On Damalis' lovely face: but none may part
>   Damalis from our new-found guest;
> She clings, and clings, like ivy, round his heart.
>
> Though all on beauteous Damalis
>   Repose their putrid optics twain,
> Never will that ambitchious miss
> Unclasp her last adulterous swain;
>   Like ivy clinging to the oak
>   Lasciviously, she's nailed her bloke.

Compare these translations, noting the difference in tone and examining the linguistic means by which the differences are achieved.

3 Critically evaluate the views on literary art presented in the second paragraph of this chapter and show — with examples — the extent to which you agree or disagree.

4 Scrutinise the dialogue in a recent novel you admire (or in a play by, for example Tom Stoppard or Harold Pinter), and consider the success with which the properties of 'real' conversation have been captured and the extent to which they have been idealised.

5 Choose a favourite poem written within the past twenty years and examine the extent to which the author has exploited (a) ordinary language of today and (b) language with a traditionally archaic 'poetic' flavour.

6 a) Write out three jokes that have recently amused you and examine the ways in which their humour depends upon verbal art.

b) Explicate the ways in which the following exchange is linguistically clever:

A: Keep alert.
B: I'd rather keep aloof — it's cheaper to feed.

7 a) We saw in Chapter Fourteen that sports writers often strive to make their reports lively. One commenting on a golfer recently wrote that he was a player who could 'unleash a torrent of birdies'. Another stated: 'His father

buys, sells and breeds horses, so he was literally born in the saddle.' Consider the enlivening role of metaphor and why mixed metaphor can be so objectionable yet apparently go unnoticed by the author.

b) The preception of 'mixed' metaphors suggests that to be effective a literal meaning must be fully appreciated as a condition of our accepting a metaphorical one. Consider in this connection: 'The crime was a carbon copy of one committed the previous month.' 'The two philosophers went at it hammer and tongs.' 'The President probably agrees in his heart of hearts.' 'She is now hoist with her own petard.'

8 Miles Kington wrote an anecdote (*Independent*, January 1989) about a doctor who was called as an expert witness to testify to the medical impossibilities recorded in a popular novel:

> 'Her heart skipped a beat', for instance, or 'the sight of him set her blood racing' . . . If your heart misses a beat, you're usually dead. If your blood races . . . then you're also doomed . . . 'Jemima received a letter which made her blood run cold.' That should have killed her as well, or at least revealed that she was not really a mammal.

Adducing similar examples fit only for mockery, write a satirical article in the Kington vein (?vein).

For further study

Excellent treatments of linguistics are to be found in
  Language and Linguistics, by J Lyons (Cambridge University
    Press, 1981); and
  Modern linguistics, by N Smith and D Wilson (Penguin, 1979)

For a study of language in relation to the mind, see
  Psychology and Language, by H H and E V Clark (Harcourt
    Brace Jovanovich, 1977)

The complexities of meaning relationships are examined in
  Semantics, by G Leech (Penguin, 2nd edition, 1981); and
  Linguistic Meaning, by K Allan (Routledge and Kegan Paul,
    1986)

A full treatment of English grammar, accompanied by an account
of word-formation, intonation, punctuation, and textual structure,
is provided in
  A Comprehensive Grammar of the English Language, by R Quirk,
    S Greenbaum, G Leech, and J Svartvik (Longman, 1985)

There is an attractive study of many aspects of style in
  Stylistics, by G W Turner (Penguin, 1973)

On the history of English from Anglo-Saxon times, together with
an account of foreign influences upon the language, see
  A History of the English Language, by A C Baugh and
    T Cable (Routledge and Kegan Paul, 1978)

INDEX

Acknowledgements

We are grateful to the following for permission to reproduce copyright material: Chambers Publishers for 'Character' entry in *Chambers English Dictionary* (1988), © W & R Chambers Ltd; Wm Collins Sons & Co Ltd, London & Glasgow for 'Character' entry in *Collins Concise Dictionary* (New edn. 1988); Collins E.L.T. for 'Character' entry in *Collins Cobuild English Language Dictionary*. Copyright © 1987 William Collins Sons & Co Ltd; Faber & Faber Ltd/Harcourt Brace Jovanovich Inc for extracts from poems 'East Coker' in *Four Quartets*. Copyright 1943 by T.S. Eliot, renewed 1971 by Esme Valerie Eliot, & 'Fragment of an Agon' by T.S. Eliot from *Collected Poems 1909–1962*. Copyright 1963, 1964 by T.S. Eliot; Harper & Row Inc for 'Character' entry in *Funk & Wagnalls Standard College Dictionary*. Copyright © 1977 by Harper & Row Publishers Inc; Houghton Mifflin Company for 'Character' entry in *The American Heritage Dictionary, Second College Edition*. Copyright © 1985 by Houghton Mifflin Company; Houghton Mifflin Company/Reader's Digest Association Ltd for 'Character' entry *The American Heritage Illustrated Encyclopedic Dictionary*. Copyright © 1987 by Houghton Mifflin Company (reprinted in *Reader's Digest Great Illustrated Dictionary* 1984); Longman Group UK Ltd for 'Character' entries in *Longman Dictionary of the English Language* (1984) & *Longman Dictionary of Contemporary English* (New edn. 1987); Merriam-Webster Inc for 'Character' entries in *Webster's Third New International Dictionary*. © 1986 by Merriam-Webster Inc. & *Webster's Ninth New Collegiate Dictionary*. © 1989 by Merriam-Webster Inc. publisher of the Merriam-Webster ® dictionaries; Oxford University Press for 'Character' entries in *Oxford English Dictionary*, (2nd edn. 1989), *The Oxford Concise Dictionary of Current English* (7th edn. 1982) & *Oxford Advanced Learner's Dictionary of Current English* (4th edn. 1989); Random House Inc for 'Character' entry in *Random House College Dictionary* (Revised edn. 1988). Copyright © Random House Inc 1988; the Author, Oliver Reynolds for his poem 'Oliver and Tone have moved to Chelsea' which first appeared in the *Times. Literary Supplement* Sept. 1–7 1989; Simon & Schuster Inc for 'Character' entry in *Webster's New World Dictionary* (2nd College Edn 1970). Copyright © Simon & Schuster Inc 1984.